Violence Against Latina Immigrants

Violence Against Latina Immigrants

Citizenship, Inequality, and Community

Roberta Villalón

NEW YORK UNIVERSITY PRESS
New York and London

NEW YORK UNIVERSITY PRESS
New York and London
www.nyupress.org

Library of Congress Cataloging-in-Publication Data
Villalón, Roberta.
Violence against Latina immigrants :
citizenship, inequality, and community / Roberta Villalón.
p. cm.
Includes bibliographical references and index.
ISBN-13: 978–0–8147–8823–3 (cl : alk. paper)
ISBN-10: 0–8147–8823–8 (cl : alk. paper)
ISBN-13: 978–0–8147–8824–0 (pb : alk. paper)
ISBN-10: 0–8147–8824–6 (pb : alk. paper)
[etc.]
1. Women immigrants—Violence against—United States.
2. Latin Americans—Violence against—United States. 3. Women immigrants—
United States—Social conditions. 4. Latin Americans—United States—Social
conditions. 5. United States—Emigration and immigration—Social aspects.
I. Title.
HV6250.4.W65V5214   2010
362.83—dc22   2009053608

New York University Press books are printed on acid-free paper,
and their binding materials are chosen for strength and durability.
We strive to use environmentally responsible suppliers and materials
to the greatest extent possible in publishing our books.

Manufactured in the United States of America
c   10 9 8 7 6 5 4 3 2 1
p   10 9 8 7 6 5 4 3 2 1

For all survivors of violence

and

For Beatriz and Isabella

Contents

Acknowledgme

I would like to express my gratitude to all th
that have made the creation of this book po:
I am indebted to the immigrant survivors of v.
advocates who were willing to share their stor
me; without them, this book would serve no pui

I am also thankful for my mentor, Peter Ward
allowed me to pursue my studies at the Universe
this institution, I was fortunate to work with a g
fessors among whom I would especially like to tl
who inspired and guided this research; Gideor
shared many hours of invaluable conversation o
Young, who never hesitated to push me forward;
Roberts, and Henry Dietz, who accompanied m
a graduate student in Latin American studies un
Ph.D. in sociology. I was able to develop my rese;
ity of the Department of Sociology Fellowship a
rial Fellowship for the *Latin American Research i*
of Texas at Austin. I also found collegial and in;
professor at my new home, Saint John's Universit
where Dawn Esposito, Ino Rossi, and Natalie B;
encouraging, and where I was twice awarded a gr
Support of Research Program. The work by my e
her assistant, Aiden Amos, at New York Univers
ful comments from anonymous reviewers have als(
the development of this project.

My family and friends were vital as well—*por si(*

1

Introduction

Theoretical and
Methodological Approach

Angela, Claudia, Julia, Luisa, Laura, Martha, Rosa, Manuela, Ana, Susana, Clara, Silvana, Rosario, Mónica, Samuel, Yolanda, Patricia, Ramona, and Leticia were all immigrants. With or without immigration documents, they had all left their native lands to help their families survive. In love, and in pain, they had all endured intimate partner violence in the United States. Courageously and fearfully, they had all tried to break free from their abusive relationships and sought help. Some found their way out. Others did not. In this book, I explore the disparate fates of Latina battered immigrants in their search for nonviolence, autonomy, and citizenship by uncovering and defying entrenched discriminatory principles and practices still at work in this country from a feminist of color perspective.[1]

Latina, black, postcolonial, and critical race feminisms have been particularly acute in their contribution to the struggle to end violence against women. As the battered women's movement developed, and violence against women was redefined first as a social problem (as opposed to an acceptable private matter)[2] and later as a human rights violation, feminists of color underscored the need to shift from universalizing to differentiated accounts.[3] While it is true that all women can be victimized on a gender basis (as "white" liberal and radical feminists initially claimed in order to legitimize the need to end violence against women and make it a policy priority), intersecting racial, ethnic, and socioeconomic backgrounds, immigration status, and sexual, religious, and political orientations also come into play in terms of the kinds of violence perpetrated, and the resources available to overcome abusive conditions.[4]

For instance, immigrant women's vulnerability is based not only on their gender but also on nationality, race, ethnicity, language, religion, documented or undocumented immigration status, threatened legal status, situational isolation from family and community, cross-national frames of cultural and legal reference (including ideologies, laws, and practices in regard to gender equality and sexuality), and socioeconomic status.[5] Latina, black, postcolonial, and critical race feminisms have focused on the specific constraints that limit minority battered women, with the aim of elaborating strategies, programs, policies, and laws that better reflect their experiences and improve their particular situations—as opposed to those of the "universal" battered woman, which in fact were modeled after white, middle- or upper-class heterosexual housewives.[6] Similarly, feminists of color have stressed the need to provincialize mainstream and Western accounts of violence against women by taking into account the specific cultural and social contexts of the community where the women live or used to live, contrary to understanding oppression from a hegemonic standpoint,[7] which perpetuates "new forms of colonialism" and is "out of touch with the realities experienced at the grass-roots level."[8] With the goal of meeting the particular needs of the most disadvantaged, feminists of color have adopted a methodology committed to building knowledge *from below*, that is, in collaboration with the people about whom the research is being developed, because "without them, the myriad individual and collective histories that simultaneously run parallel to official accounts of historic events and are their sequel, almost inevitably get submerged"[9] and become invisible.[10]

In this spirit, I developed activist research[11] at a local nonprofit organization in Texas to learn about the experiences of Latina battered immigrants in their quest for U.S. citizenship through the Violence Against Women Act (VAWA) and the Victims of Trafficking and Violence Protection Act (VTVPA). Advocates, activists, and scholars alike have considered these laws as successful achievements for women's and immigrants' rights movements.[12] In principle, VAWA and VTVPA legitimize battered immigrants in their particular victimization and provide them with services conducive to breaking free from abusive relationships and becoming legally and economically autonomous U.S. citizens. However, through my research I found that formal and informal barriers that filter immigrants either as worthy to become legitimate citizens of the United States or as illegitimate subjects remain in place. Intersecting gender, sexual, racial, ethnic, and class inequalities not only permeate the current legislation but also tend to be reproduced by nonprofit workers. This results in the exclusion of the most underprivileged immigrants (those Latina immigrants who are women of color, extremely poor, with few years of formal education, undocumented, in relationships with residents or other undocumented immigrants, originally from Mexico, homosexual, and/or unable to fit within "normal" standards of civil behavior) regardless of their histories of abuse.

My analysis of how and why the most disadvantaged battered Latina immigrants are left unprotected and my suggestions on how to turn this around are based on activist research at a legal nonprofit organization that I will call the Organization for Refugees of America/Organización para Refugiados de América (ORA). ORA proved to be an excellent example of how extreme cases contribute to the understanding of the construction of difference and normalcy, marginality and dominance,[13] because of the type of services it offered, its location, the population it served, its organizational history, and its staff's profile. From 2000 to 2008, ORA was the only organization in central Texas that provided free legal services to underserved immigrants, identified as individuals with earnings below 125 percent of the officially defined poverty line (i.e., annual earnings lower than $17,500 for a household of two in 2008);[14] at the same time, it was the only organization providing these services that was not affiliated with a religious group. Four of its five legal programs were devoted to immigrant survivors of different kinds of abuse (domestic abuse; sexual abuse; extortion; false imprisonment; human trafficking; and political, racial, ethnic, religious, gender, or ideological persecution). Additionally, ORA's location in Texas, a border state with one of the largest numbers of documented and undocumented immigrants in the United States,[15] and with a high proportion of incidents of family violence in terms of its population,[16] made the organization a good selection for a case study, particularly during the hostile environment after September 11, 2001. An overwhelming majority of ORA's clients were from Mexico and Central America, but the organization served immigrants from all over the world. ORA, with its ethnically diverse staff, presented itself as an inclusive organization that provided services to all immigrants, regardless of their ethnic, religious, or political background, in their language of origin. In this way, ORA allowed me to explore the workings of culturally sensitive organizations, which have been both celebrated as safe havens for immigrants[17] and questioned as colonial and patriarchal by many feminist researchers.[18] Its history also made it a good choice for a case study: ORA developed from a politically radical, volunteer-based grassroots legal group into a politically moderate employee-based nonprofit legal organization. While this kind of institutionalization process is common,[19] the in-depth study of ORA provides clues to overcome its exclusionary effects.[20]

I worked for two years as a part-time volunteer intern in the ORA's battered immigrant assistance program, which provided legal services free of charge to low-income immigrants who qualified as applicants for citizenship under VAWA and VTVPA. As such, I worked with ORA staff in providing services to immigrants, including screening interviews on the phone and in person, collection and translation of immigration and abuse histories, translation from Spanish to English of affidavits and supporting documentation related to the cases, preparation of immigration forms and citizenship applications, and other on-demand tasks. My direct participation in these activities allowed me to gather data about the ways in which immigrants presented themselves; talked and wrote about their experiences of migration and violence; expressed their demands and concerns about going through the application for citizenship; showed their feelings, fears, frustrations, and hopes; made sense of their situations; and reacted to the formal and informal requirements of the application process. Furthermore, my participation also allowed me to observe the legal assistants, attorneys, and other ORA staff in their interactions with the immigrants (or "clients," as they were called in the organization), such as how ORA staff expressed themselves, the verbal and body language they used with the clients and with their coworkers, their reactions to the histories of abuse, and their attitudes toward law enforcement officers and immigration authorities. I also participated in meetings related to immigration and women's issues to which ORA staff were invited on a regular basis (such as meetings on legal advocacy and violence against women), which made it possible for me to collect primary data on how legal and social workers organize their activities and modify their services on the basis of changes in legislation and one another's work experiences (e.g., in their discussions about successful or complex cases, or their conversations about lobbying activities). After my workday, I recorded my field observations in journal form, including not only immigrants' and staff members' stories but also my own role, feelings, and thoughts.[21]

I complemented my participant observation by performing personal interviews with the attorneys, legal assistants, and other ORA staff. Through these interviews, I gathered primary data on how nonprofit workers comprehended (made sense of, rationalized, felt about) and embodied (performed, implemented, applied) immigration and citizenship norms, rules, and regulations. I also addressed how they viewed themselves in their double role as subjects of law vis-à-vis the state and as officers of law in front of the immigrant applicants. What were their thoughts, perceptions, justifications, doubts, and feelings about their tasks and skills, their commitments toward the state and grantors, their responsibilities toward the local community, the immigrants, and their clients? How did they see themselves in their interactions with others? What would they like to change about their jobs and about gender violence and immigration laws? Although I had these issues in mind when I conducted my interviews, I did not follow a rigid form but instead adopted a more informal frame of dialogue with the interviewees, which let me "emphasize the informant's world of meaning and utilize the informant's categories of understanding"[22] rather than my own. In this way, both the participant observation and the unstructured interviews allowed me to reduce the hierarchical filters of data gathering (I say reduce because filters and interpretation dynamics are always at play during research or any other human interaction), as I intended not to purposely frame the subjects' thoughts, views, feelings, and experiences as they emerge and develop.[23]

Archival research and secondary sources contextualized my primary data collection. I conducted archival research and analysis of the text of laws, bills, and acts related to gender violence, and of immigration procedures and regulations. I researched websites of organizations working for or against these issues in order to understand how related knowledge is built and shared. I looked into these organizations' brochures, informative manuals, advocacy tool kits, publications, and other materials, which in general were part of their outreach strategies to inform people about gender violence legislation and the struggles for and against it. Such archival data helped me explore the formal framework (i.e., legal parameters, profiles, requirements, uses of language, references, tactics, and strategies) within which the state and nonprofits interacted with battered immigrants. Naturally, my research has been inspired by the state of the art of the literature about intimate partner violence against Latinas, which for the most part tended to be written from social work and health care perspectives with the end goal of improving the services offered to this particular group of survivors. Examples of this kind of research are the recent studies by Hazen and Soriano,[24] and Brabeck and Guzmán.[25] Specific patterns of intimate partner violence among or toward Latina women who were U.S.-born, immigrants, or seasonal migrant workers were gathered through interviews and surveys and statistically analyzed by Hazen and Soriano, who found "high rates of victimization"[26] for sexual, psychological, and physical aggression, and thus underscored "the need for culturally appropriate screening for intimate partner violence in health care and other settings that serve Latina women."[27] Brabeck and Guzmán focused their research on Mexican-origin women to find differences and similarities between this group and other immigrant groups. They studied both the formal and the informal ways in which these women seek help to survive abuse and suggested strategies to better serve this population. On the one hand, they found that the vast majority of survivors had accessed "more than one formal help source"[28] (such as shelters, police, counseling, and legal and medical services) and had a positive yet constructively critical perspective on them—these findings countered "the popular stereotype of 'backward, submissive' battered Latinas and immigrant women."[29] On the other hand, they found that "a slightly higher percentage"[30] of the survivors in their study had accessed informal sources of help over formal sources, and they did so with greater frequency. Most Mexican-origin survivors had reached out to, in order of importance, immediate family members, friends, the abuser's family, religious officials, and coworkers; these findings showed that in this regard Mexican-origin survivors acted similarly to survivors from other countries. Battered Mexican-origin immigrants also made use of similar personal strategies to survive abuse (like avoidance, defensive, spiritual/psychological, social/familial, and escape strategies), but they found that many of these were "unhelpful" and thus "less effective in terms of surviving abuse than accessing informal and formal sources of help."[31]

While such studies (gradually growing in number but still scarce) have been helpful in addressing the particular needs of diverse survivors, their exclusive focus on service provision has left broader questions unattended. The work by anthropologists Salcido and Adelman is, to my knowledge, one of the few exceptions in the academic literature devoted to Latina survivors of intimate partner violence, since it brings "a domestic violence perspective to immigration policy and an immigration perspective to domestic violence research."[32] By sharing the stories of four undocumented Mexican survivors, these authors defy dualistic understandings of migration as a documented/undocumented process, and medical interpretations of intimate partner violence as a pathological and traumatizing experience that must be successfully overcome. They show that battered immigrants may have become undocumented as a result of their battering and that they may have chosen to stay in the violent relationship as a survival strategy. Salcido and Adelman remind policy makers, researchers, and advocates of the contradictory and unequal character of immigration and domestic violence policies and call for a reconceptualization of intervention strategies for undocumented battered immigrants.

My work contributes to the understanding of violence against immigrant women by linking gender violence with citizenship and social inequality. These links have been analyzed before, but to my knowledge not in regard to Latina survivors in the United States and not in as much ethnographic depth as my activist research revealed. My work is in dialogue with the literature that has explored the triad of gender violence, citizenship, and inequality,[33] among which I have been very much inspired by Crenshaw's research on violence against women of color; the intersection of race, class, and other "patterns of subordination";[34] and the possibilities of advancing the rights of women of color by fostering coalitions between groups with intersecting oppressions that have tended to have diverging, essentialist agendas. I have also built on Abraham's research about marital violence in South Asian immigrant communities in the United States as it exposes "systemic ways by which American cultural, economic and political institutions contribute to the violence against ethnic minority women, especially immigrant women, both legal and illegal"[35] and emphasizes the role that community organizations and immigrants played in challenging the overlapping oppressions facing South Asian women. Rudrappa's ethnography of an Indo-American center and a shelter for battered South Asian women has provided me with a fundamental counterpoint to Abraham's positive take on ethnic organizations. While these organizations are perceived as "safe havens"[36] for the maintenance of ethnic identity and autonomy beyond the influence of the state or any other external institutions, Rudrappa claims that, in fact, they reproduce existing structures of gender, racial, and class inequalities. Ethnic enclaves are not necessarily sites of social dissent and political challenge; on the contrary, they can foster dominant and oppressive practices and discourses that feed the hierarchical citizenship order of the United States. Similarly, Ong's ethnographic analysis of Cambodian refugees in California looks into the particular ways in which racial, ethnic, class, and gender systems of inequality currently are embodied and re-created in local-level (well-intended) grassroots organizations in the United States. She notes that, on the one hand, Asian American and Hispanic feminist agencies have sought to "counteract images stigmatizing poor female immigrants as welfare mothers or passive wives and empower them by providing an alternative structure of access that would help overcome male oppression at home."[37] On the other hand, "whatever the good intentions of individual social workers, the internal logic of compassionate domination produces this double submission—majority women dominating minority women, who dominate minority men . . . with the effect of feminizing ethnic men and masculinizing ethnic women."[38] Menon and Bhasin's research on the process of India's bloody partition of 1947 and its legacies, in which 1 million people perished and more than 10 million were displaced, has offered me another pivotal example of the contradictory workings of well-intended community organizations across borders. With the aim of contesting official historical accounts (which silenced the experiences of women and other oppressed groups), these authors include powerful narratives of women survivors of partition and look into women's organizations, female activists, and social workers, who devoted themselves to "rehabilitate women"[39] who had survived partition's extreme sexual violence and gendered brutality. While these organizations and workers frankly hoped that their assistance would ease these women's transition into well-being, the authors found that "they functioned very much within patriarchal structures, often displayed rather patriarchal attitudes and were influenced by urban middle-class conceptions of socially accepted roles for women and men."[40] Accordingly, their intervention attempted to liberate women by helping them become economically independent, develop a sense of self-worth, and learn accepted social codes "through a repetition of restrictions on sexuality and mobility"[41] inherited from colonial structures of power and preexistent hierarchical systems of domination.

The work of all these authors points in the same direction—toward the complexity and embeddedness of gender oppression—and has led me to develop research that pays attention to the interplay of structural, institutional, and relational mechanisms of creating and reproducing difference and inequality. Gender violence per se, I have learned, always tends to be more than that; gender violence tends to be an expression of dominance in its intersection with sexual, racial, ethnic, and class oppression, as well as the construction of nationhood and citizenship. The respective works by Haney López,[42] Omi and Winant,[43] Feagin,[44] Bonilla-Silva,[45] Hing,[46] and Johnson[47] on the racialized and thus exclusionary structure of the immigration system in the United States, together with research by Glenn on the gendered and racialized character of citizenship and labor policies and practices in the United States;[48] Ngai's historical analysis of the exploitative use of undocumented immigrants in this country as they were conceived as "illegal aliens" and thereupon grouped as "a caste, unambiguously situated outside the boundaries of formal membership and social legitimacy";[49] Luibhéid's study of the preservation of a heteronormative patriarchal order through U.S. immigration controls of sexuality at the border;[50] Calvo's critical analysis of the pervasive legacies of the doctrines of coverture and chastisement in spouse-based immigration laws;[51] and Chapkis's close reading of the ambivalences in the treatment of victims of sexual trafficking by VTVPA when it was first enacted[52]—all have informed my critical perspective on the construction of citizenship and nationhood in this country. In thinking about the latter, I have drawn on Foucault's ideas about sovereignty, which is reflected in the "mechanisms of disciplinary coercion"[53] by which the state is able to maintain and re-create social order. Power "is not that which makes the difference between those who exclusively possess and retain it, and those who do not have and submit to it. Power must be analyzed as something which circulates, or rather as something which only functions in the form of a chain."[54] Because the key in the reproduction and exercise of power and domination is not in the center but in the "myriad of bodies which are constituted as peripheral subjects"[55] and in the diverse mechanisms and techniques of power, which have been accompanied by ideological productions to determine social disciplinary structures, my focusing on how battered Latina immigrants and advocates in the community negotiate these forces seems crucial to collaborate in the effort to dismantle complex systems and practices of inequality and ultimately challenge oppression from the bottom up.

Because it shapes the activist research process from beginning to end, feminists of color have made an effort to stress the importance of acknowledging and incorporating one's standpoint to one's projects. As articulated by Anzaldúa, "The personal and cultural narratives are not disinterested, objective questionings of identity politics, but impassioned and conflicted engagements in resistance."[56] One's involvement in a particular struggle is never arbitrary or irrelevant; my commitment to the struggle to end violence against immigrant women and discrimination across the board is threefold. It emerges from my own history as a random survivor of state violence against my family during the Argentine military regime of the 1970s, during which women suspected of political activism were specifically targeted and tortured by state military forces,[57] my experience as a victim of intimate partner violence in a context where specific laws or services were not available,[58] and, last but not least, my current status as a Latina immigrant in the United States. These three interconnected motivations (interconnected because none would have happened without the other) kept me moving forward with this project, which in turn was an "invitation to transformation"[59] and a reaffirmation of "the continuing need for fundamental social change."[60]

By adopting a "reflective practice," as theorized by feminist ethnographer Naples, I was able to incorporate my standpoint and also remain "sensitive to the perspectives of others" and critically aware of the "power dynamics" at play in the community where the research was situated.[61] For instance, even though my background gave me the opportunity to quickly gain access to and build trust with the immigrants and the non-profit workers, my involvement at ORA posed some problems regarding my double role as researcher and worker. While I was performing ORA's job by respecting the organization's rules and interests, I also had a critical understanding of the activities and processes that were taking place during my working days. To cope with tensions resulting from my double role, I maintained a transparent attitude with the members of the agency and the clients and regularly wrote about my observations, thoughts, and feelings in a journal. I also paid close attention to how my personal characteristics shaped "ethnographic encounters"[62] "to reveal the inequalities and processes of domination that shape the 'field.'"[63] I wondered, how did my occupation, nationality, immigration status, race, ethnicity, gender, sexual orientation, socioeconomic status, and age permeate my relationship with both battered immigrants and ORA staff? On the one hand, the immigrants tended to be comfortable with me because of my position as a volunteer and researcher, my sympathy as a woman survivor of intimate partner violence, my young age, our shared status as Latina immigrants in the United States (which took precedence over my light skin color or seeming whiteness), and my open attitude about sexual preferences. Class differences were mostly manifested in two aspects: immigration status and education. My documented immigration status as a researcher and my ability to speak and write Spanish and English fluently differentiated me from the immigrants seeking services at ORA, who did not seem uncomfortable with this gap as long as I was assisting them through their citizenship application process before U.S. Citizenship and Immigration Services (USCIS). However, I often was the one who became upset because of the imbalances resulting from their underprivileged positionality as opposed to ORA staff's or mine. On the other hand, ORA staff tended to be comfortable around me and grateful for my volunteer work. They perceived me as similar to them in terms of class background, gender, openness in regard to sexual preferences, and age and different from them in terms of my nationality and occupation. Some of them took me as a foreign focal reference with whom they could either clarify or discuss cultural differences; others maintained some distance as they recalled my double role as a volunteer and researcher and occasionally thought of me as threatening their authority at the workplace.

My position as an "outsider within"[64] at ORA yielded both advantages (such as the possibility of immersing myself in the organization while keeping a critical angle) and disadvantages (such as the possibility of becoming too involved and consequently jeopardizing my critical ability, or finding resistance from the staff against my attempted suggestions to address what I believed were problematic working practices). In retrospect, I faced four main challenges in conducting the research. The first challenge was the transition from having an enthusiastic and idealist perspective about gender violence–based immigration legislation as well as the organization to being frustrated with the laws and ORA staff as I discovered their biased character. I dealt with these changing feelings by incorporating them into my field notes, thinking about them critically, and, when appropriate, talking about them with ORA staff in order "to become aware of, and diminish the ways in which, domination and repression are reproduced in the course of research and in the products of [my] work."[65] Finding a way to handle my feelings (and "emotions are always present in personal interactions in ethnographic work")[66] was vital to the research process because they affected my work as a volunteer, my relationship with ORA staff, my access to the organization, and my analysis. The second challenge was deciding which data could be included: even if I had obtained informed consent from the participating research subjects, I considered some of the information they provided too private or compromising to be quoted in my writing. If these data were crucial to the analysis, I referred to them indirectly without exposing the subjects unnecessarily. Two examples of this dilemma were the inclusion of very sensitive details about the violence that immigrants had experienced, and of private comments that ORA staff made to me in confidence. My own ethics helped me to draw this fine line, which reflected my subjectivity and priorities as an activist researcher.[67] The third challenge was barriers to activist research: while my role as a volunteer intern made my research participatory as I was providing services to the immigrant community, the extent of my activism was limited by ORA's reactions to some (or most) of my proposals to modify what I considered to be problematic work practices. For example, my suggestions and efforts to provide child care options, expand counseling opportunities, and enrich outreach presentations were initially welcomed but then later ignored or rejected. These contradictory reactions were frustrating and disturbing as I realized that my interest in addressing ORA's services with the aim of moderating unequal practices did not coincide with the goals of ORA staff and made me wonder if I was being too idealistic or demanding. These pitfalls were counterbalanced by my involvement with the broader community of immigrants' advocates, specifically, by sharing the findings of my research in national meetings and online networks devoted to Latina battered immigrants. The fourth challenge was overcoming the temptation to expand my research: as I went forward with my fieldwork, I often saw potential ways to expand the scope of analysis and activism, both of which I had to contain to complete the project at hand. To keep focused, I took note of these thoughts for future teaching, research, and activist endeavors. Despite these four challenges, there was not a moment when I doubted the richness of qualitative research methods and the potential benefits of activist research. These tensions and reflections fed my research, which I hope will further our understanding of "what it is" and better our actions toward "what can be."

In the following chapters, I weave the experiences of battered immigrants Angela, Claudia, Julia, Luisa, Laura, Martha, Rosa, Manuela, Ana, Susana, Clara, Silvana, Rosario, Mónica, Samuel, Yolanda, Patricia, Ramona, and Leticia and of founding, former, and current ORA staff, Sophia, Valerie, Cathy, Maggie, Jenna, Courtney, Lucy, Marina, Carlos, John, and me with theoretical debates about gender violence, citizenship, and inequality. Given that my research was in essence ethnographic and respected methodological principles of feminists of color who stressed the relevance of portraying as faithfully as possible the community where the research is being developed, I included the stories of *all* the immigrants with whom I worked at ORA *at length*, regardless of their country of origin, immigration status, or gender. Eighteen of the nineteen immigrants were originally from Latin America (sixteen from Mexico, one from Venezuela, and one from Colombia), and one was from Nigeria. Seventeen immigrants had entered the United States undocumented; only two had documents, which eventually expired. Eighteen immigrants were women, and one was a man. All of them were heterosexual. Sixteen were married to their current abusers, and three were in common-law unions. Eleven abusers were U.S. citizens, six were legal permanent residents, one was an undocumented immigrant, and one was unknown (the victim did not know her abuser's immigration status). Only four of the nineteen were interracial couples (the Colombian and three Mexican immigrants were in relationships with white/Anglo citizens). Six of the Mexican women immigrants were married to Mexican American citizens, five were married to Mexican legal permanent residents, one was married to an undocumented Mexican immigrant, and one was married to either a resident or an undocumented Mexican immigrant. The Nigerian immigrant was married to a legal permanent resident from Cameroon, but racially and ethnically she identified herself with him; the Venezuelan immigrant was married to an African American citizen (she identified with him racially because of her African roots, but differentiated ethnically because of her Venezuelan origin). All the immigrants were poor, seventeen had few years of formal education, and only two were fluent in English. In regard to the nonprofit workers included in the research, I included those with whom I interacted at the organization and also those with whom I was able to establish access despite the fact that they had left ORA; there were a few who had been influential in the development of the organization in the past but who, unfortunately, I was not able to contact at the time of my research.

My hope is for the actual stories of survivors and advocates to constitute the core of this book. Similar to Menon and Bhasin's work, "the stories might supplement each other, or sometimes serve as counterpoints, but each is distinct and dwells on those experiences that related most directly to the themes which emerged with sharp clarity from the accounts":[68] the harsh complexities of the lives of Latina battered immigrants in the United States; the intersecting gender, sexual, racial, ethnic, and class inequalities embedded in the formality of the gender violence laws and reproduced in the informal interactions at the nonprofit organizational level; the nuanced ways in which immigrants and advocates negotiate structural forces; and the possibilities of challenging systems and practices of inequality that shape the very composition of U.S. society. Finally, an important note: while I base my analysis in the experiences of these nineteen immigrant survivors in their interactions with advocates at ORA, I do not intend to portray this as a universal account of battered immigrants and advocates in the United States, but as "part of an unfolding history."[69] Adapting Garfield's methodological claim, "I recognize that the experiences of any small and select group cannot capture the complexities and varied lifestyles that are of concern to all [immigrant] women [and advocates]. But I do believe that their particular experiences contribute . . . important chapters to the volumes of stories that make up the whole of what it means to be"[70] a battered immigrant and a nonprofit advocate of immigrant survivors of violence in the United States.

In chapter 2, I present a *model case* of violence against immigrant women and the legal remedies currently available under VAWA and VTVPA. By sharing the story of Angela at length, I begin to show the complexities beneath abusive relationships, migratory journeys, living in poverty as an undocumented immigrant, working under exploitative systems and practices, and finding refuge within laws and nonprofit services in place in the United States. Angela's story, an example of a woman who was able to succeed in her quest for autonomy, nonviolence, and citizenship through the existing legislation with the help of a well-intended community organization like ORA, is a testament to the concrete gains of the battered women's and immigrants' movements. However, not all the battered immigrants that I met at ORA were as "fortunate" as Angela. The next two chapters uncover problematic aspects of VAWA and VTVPA and nonprofit organizations like ORA by looking into the stories of immigrants who, instead of finding protection, ran into exclusionary formal and informal obstacles in their search for personal, legal, and economic independence.

In chapter 3, I focus on what I will refer to as the *formal barriers* embedded in VAWA and VTVPA. Despite their achievements, these laws reproduce patterns of gender, sexual, racial, ethnic, and class discrimination that are embedded in the immigration law system of the United States. The stories of Claudia, Julia, and Luisa illustrate the patriarchal and heteronormative character of immigration laws inherited by VAWA and VTVPA. The stories of Laura, Martha, Rosa, Manuela, and Ana reflect historical racial and ethnic discriminatory parameters, which continue to prioritize U.S. citizens over immigrants and their experiences of abuse. Finally, the story of Susana exemplifies the historical classism of the immigration system as it pervades VAWA and VTVPA and bars the neediest survivors from access to citizenship. All in all, this chapter shows the intersection of gender, sexual, racial, ethnic, and class oppressions within the law itself from a critical race feminist perspective.

In chapter 4, I investigate the *informal barriers* that emerge at the nonprofit organization level. Besides the formal barriers within the legal texts, informal obstacles surface in the interaction between immigrants and nonprofit workers. The stories of survivors Clara, Silvana, Rosario, Mónica, Samuel, Yolanda, Patricia, Ramona, and Leticia reveal the preferences that nonprofit advocates at ORA had in regard to their "clientele." Immigrants who behaved in particular ways tended to be better served by nonprofit workers; immigrants who did not fit these patterns of civil behavior tended to be excluded from the process despite their eligibility under VAWA and VTVPA. The analysis of the relational aspects in the process of inclusion of immigrants into U.S. society contributes to the understanding of how disciplines of citizenship and principles of nationhood are reproduced beyond the direct intervention of state officials even by nonprofit advocates who are working to advance the lives of underprivileged immigrants.

In chapter 5, I focus on how formal and informal barriers can be reproduced or challenged by looking at the agency of battered immigrants and nonprofit workers and suggesting ways to dismantle systems of inequality. Here I bring back the stories of the immigrants presented earlier and include nonprofit workers' views on these issues. I offer an explanation of what I will call *nuanced agency* and include notions from social movement theory in order to consider the possibilities for change. Humbly, I suggest ideological and practical alternative actions for change with the caveat that I would rather elaborate these in tandem with the workers in the organization that plans to put them into effect. To end the book, I provide concluding thoughts and articulate the theoretical and empirical contributions that my activist research provides to the knowledge about and struggle against violence against Latina immigrants.

⫽ 2 ⫽

Violence against
Latina Immigrants
and Immigration Law

While it is true that anyone can become a victim or a perpetrator of intimate partner violence, gender, sexual identity, race, ethnicity, class, and immigration status influence the way in which violence is inflicted and endured, as well as the resources available to escape and overcome the abusive relationship. The case of Angela poignantly shows the complexities of violence against Latina immigrants, revealing the rationale beneath the legal provisions and community services for battered immigrants through the Violence Against Women Act (VAWA) and the Victims of Trafficking and Violence Protection Act (VTVPA).

Violence against Latina Immigrants: Angela's Case

Sitting down on the edge of the chair and clutching her hands, Angela waited for my questions. Trying to put her at ease, I explained what the intake appointment was about and clarified that we could take it as slow as necessary. She took a deep breath and moved back into the chair. We began: name, address, place and date of birth (her own and those of her husband and her sons). Hesitant to share details about her entry to the United States and her employer's identity, Angela was relieved when I repeated that everything she told me was confidential; undocumented immigrants, particularly those who have been repeatedly threatened by their batterer, live in fear of being deported and thus are reluctant to trust others, from teachers to doctors, from policemen to nonprofit workers. As I began to inquire about her abusive relationship, Angela's pain and sadness swamped her nervousness. By the end of the appointment, I knew that she could be assisted by ORA, but until the lawyer approved her case, I could not say much to her. When I returned from the copy room, Angela was looking at a poster that was hanging on the wall of the office where we had been meeting. She commented, "I didn't know. I never thought that it was that . . . that it was this . . . violence, domestic violence. But, I guess that was it." I sat next to her and said, "I know what you mean. It is always very hard to think about one's experience as such." Then I told her that the organization that had designed the poster about domestic violence against immigrant women that Angela was referring to offered various services free of charge. Thankful, she left.

At our appointment the following week, Angela could not believe that it was true, that she could become a documented immigrant; that she could help her sons become residents of this country; that something "good could actually happen." For a long time she had believed that she "had ruined it all," but this news once again gave her "hope." Battered immigrants, like any survivors of intimate partner violence, are convinced that they are to blame for the abuse; at the same time, their feelings of despondency are intensified because they are unaware of or most probably have been given a distorted version of their rights as undocumented foreigners. But once they find out about having real opportunities to break free from their abusive relationships and rectify their immigration status, most survivors change their perception of possibility: some women break from their past of abuse and dependency; other women reinstate the terms of their intimate relationships from a more leveraged position (only the ones who are still deeply immersed in the abuse continue their lives as they were). Angela followed the first path. Once she realized the nature of her relationship and her rights, she did not look back for a second and relentlessly took all the necessary steps to achieve the end goal: autonomy, nonviolence, and legality for her and her family. She wrote her sworn statement, a detailed history of the abuse, a pivotal part of VAWA self-petitions, about which we had several conversations with the aim of clarifying and expanding parts of it—the goal, ORA's brochure explains, is to show immigration officers that the applicant is indeed a survivor of violence, and her story, in her "*own words*" makes "all the difference" in her case. An indispensable piece of the citizenship application process that battered immigrants put together with their advocates, its composition is daunting and painful yet helpful (in regard to the VAWA application itself, as well as the healing process that survivors go through as they think of their relationship as a case of intimate partner violence). In closing, Angela wrote:

I tried to include as many things as I could in this affidavit about my past, but unfortunately there were so many bad things that happened, that my chest aches from remembering. I only wanted to have a family for my sons. I wanted my sons to have the support of a man. I wanted to be respected. I had fallen in love with Richie and I was blind to his mistreatment. I thought it was my entire fault.[1]

Originally from one of the Mexican states with the highest rates of undocumented migration to the United States,[2] Angela was in her thirties when she left. Her two sons stayed with her parents in Mexico while she tried to find work in Texas to support her family. Like most other Mexican immigrants, Angela's decision was based on the economic conditions of their country vis-à-vis the United States: "Mexico, the country that sends the most [undocumented] immigrants to the United States, contrasts sharply in wage differences, and the disparities in earnings remain the main impetus for cross-border migration . . . half of the 104 million residents in Mexico live in poverty, and one-fifth in extreme poverty (defined as living on less than $1 a day)."[3] Like most undocumented immigrants from Mexico, Angela "had few problems finding jobs in the United States,"[4] and her efforts paid off as she was soon able to send money back to her family even though her income was below the official U.S. poverty line (an annual income of less than $16,000 at the time of her application),[5] since her occupation was "restricted to the most menial types of low wage labor with few opportunities for upward mobility."[6] It was while searching for work that she met Richie, an enticing, "cowboy"-looking man who, "smiling," told her that she could certainly work for the cleaning company whose trucks he drove. Blushing, she recalled, "The first time I saw Richie, I fell in love with him." Shaking her head, she told me that he was also attracted to her. Only a few days later, "He asked me if I wanted to go out with him," but Angela refused because she did not feel comfortable dating someone so soon after arriving in the United States. Richie persisted, and after several months of seeing each other at work, Angela began to go out with him. At first, she recalled: "Richie was a gentleman; he was very polite and nice to me. He would invite me to have lunch with him. While we were working, if it was hot, he would bring me water and sodas to drink. He used to open the car door for me, bring me flowers and leave me love notes. He seemed to be very interested in me. He wanted to know if I was married, if I had kids."

These questions were of great importance to Angela; Richie's reaction to "the truth" would determine the future of her commitment to him. A single mother of two boys who were both the result of rapes, Angela felt "happy and relieved" because Richie was "very understanding and didn't judge" her. His willingness to accept her sons was also reassuring for her parents, who learned about the relationship over the phone when Angela told them that she was probably going to move in with Richie. Angela's brother, who lived in Texas as well, did not trust Richie right away "because he didn't know too much about him . . . and thought that Richie smoked marijuana and drank." But Angela's conviction that Richie "didn't do those things, and that his red eyes were because he was overworking and didn't get enough sleep" eventually convinced her brother, who ended up supporting her decision to be with Richie and even offered them his family's residence when they needed a place to stay. Angela and Richie were very happy together. As she said in our interview, "Those were good times." Smiling, Angela recalled, "He used to bring me breakfast in bed. We used to go out dancing. He used to cook dinner for us." Richie began to confide in Angela, who faithfully helped him go through legal quarrels related to his younger son and his mother's drug addictions, two problems that would frighten Angela a year later when police officers knocked on their door with a search warrant and an order to arrest Richie.

With calm restored upon Richie's avoidance of imprisonment, they continued with their demanding work routine, cleaning bars after closing time and taking care of a nursery during the day. Months of savings allowed Angela to buy a ticket to Mexico while Richie stayed in charge of everything in Texas. Immigrants' desire to reunite with their families tends to outweigh the risk and cost of crossing the border undocumented again and again; Angela and the other immigrants I met at ORA confirmed this. But Angela's awaited trip ended sooner than planned when she learned that Richie had been arrested. Angela responded to Richie's cry for help. She "was feeling very bad about all this trouble. . . . Richie used to feel very sad and cry. His son's mother was in New York and had never showed up to help them." Back in Texas, Angela began to work right away and remained loyal to Richie.

Once given a work release, which allowed him to leave the prison to work during the day and return at night, Richie asked Angela to marry him because she had been "so supportive and understanding." Angela asked him to wait; she was "confused about all the troubles." But "he had everything arranged to get married the following day; he had the witnesses and all the papers ready. I couldn't resist, and I agreed to get married. I was in love with Richie, but at the same time it felt very fast." Embarrassed, she remembered:

I was so nervous before the marriage that I lost my ID. We had to go to get a new temporary ID for us to be able to get married. Once we had my new temporary ID, I misplaced it. It took us a while to find it. We were all getting more nervous, but we finally found the ID and went to court to get married. Then, while Richie and I were getting married, I was so nervous that I began to laugh. I really couldn't control what happened, and the judge started to get angry.

Angela and Richie had to postpone the celebration until the weekend because he had to go back to jail; however, they "were very happy about having gotten married. . . . I couldn't believe that I had found somebody that loved me and that, more importantly, accepted my sons and promised to love them as if they were his." Angela's past sexual attacks and experience as a poor single mother who had negotiated the "legitimacy of normative expectations of men"[7] led her to disregard Richie's troubles (and her own nervousness) in hopes of having "a normal family," a loving husband, and a father figure for her sons. Like the women in Roy and Burton's study of low-income single mothers' efforts at paternal recruitment, Angela wished to find a man "who could fulfill some of the most basic expectations of fatherhood"[8] and maintain some level of involvement with her children, in order to possibly emerge as a role model[9] for both her "own" and her "children's well-being."[10] Angela also had redefined her intimate relationship in regard to her "maternal advocacy" and tried to minimize the risks to her children during recruitment,[11] but, "consumed with finding legitimacy and stability with a father and a partner,"[12] Angela entered a relationship that turned out to be abusive.

Only four months after their marriage, Angela found out that Richie had been cheating on her. "Very disappointed," she "couldn't stop crying." Richie was angry with her because she asked him about seeing other women:

He told me that he didn't care anymore, that I was a stupid woman, and that if I didn't believe what he was saying, he would end our relationship right then and there. He went to our bedroom, grabbed the marriage act, tore it into pieces, and threw it in the toilet and garbage bin in the bathroom, where I was crying. I thought I was going to die; I felt so bad and deceived. It was horrible, I felt like watching a sand castle being destroyed all of a sudden. I thought it was all my fault, I believed that I was a failure. The following day, Richie continued with the fight. He was threatening me that he was going to leave me, and

I told him to go ahead and do it. He got angry at my reaction, so he screamed and cursed at me. Then he threw the laundry basket and the garbage bin at me, which physically hurt me. They didn't leave bruises when they hit me, but they wounded my heart. I felt so bad; I thought I was going to die.

Like most victims of intimate partner violence, Angela was silenced in shame—she did not tell anybody about what had happened.

This incident was just the beginning of what can be considered a paradigmatic case of intimate partner violence against immigrant women; an eight-year-long cycle of abuse of power and control that, besides the typical abusive tactics, included specific means to attack the survivor's foreign background (her legal and economic vulnerability, culture, language, distance from her family and community of origin, and lack of knowledge of the laws of this country).[13] There were the nights that Richie would drink while they were at work, cleaning the nightclubs, and then would leave Angela and their coworker, her friend Patricia, stranded in the middle of road. There were the days that Richie would humiliate Angela as she tried to "tell him not to drink anymore because it was changing his personality." There were the moments that Richie would beg for forgiveness and ask for Angela's help, like the time he had a serious illness and "was afraid that he was going to die." There were incidents involving jealousy, drugs, money problems, cheating, beatings, verbal humiliation, threats of deportation, and isolation—all inextricably followed by apologies and promises of change and eternal love, which were usually taken seriously by Angela, whose sympathy and hope would be shattered again and again, as typically occurs with immigrant survivors.

Practically secluded because Richie did not want her to communicate with her family or to tell anybody where they were living, Angela confronted him about his addictions. Richie slapped her in the face and threatened to call immigration officials on her. "Sad and afraid," Angela did not say anything back to Richie. But after he got fired from his job and was living off the earnings from Angela's extra hours of work, she confronted him again. She did not believe his excuses and stressed his irresponsibility. Angry once his lies resulted in losing the truck she had been paying for, Angela "felt very weak. He was not trying or willing to change even though we had talked about it."

"Things got even worse," she said. As she thought of leaving him, Richie got in touch with her boss and manipulated him into firing her.

Once Angela was out of work, Richie forced her to stay in the apartment, forbidding her to go out to look for a job. Angela recalled somberly, "I felt awful, like an animal in jail. We didn't have anything to eat, we didn't have a phone, nothing; it was so embarrassing." One day, Richie went back to the house and got mad at Angela because she did not have dinner ready for him. When she told him that they did not have or could not afford to buy any more food, he accused her of being "useless, good for nothing." He hit her. As he threw her clothes in her face, he ordered her to leave the apartment. When she tried to leave, he grabbed her by the arms and would not let her go. Bruised, Angela waited until Richie left the apartment the following day to run away to a nearby hotel to use its phone. Her friend Patricia knew about Richie's temper, and when she tried to pick Angela up, Richie had come back and would not let her in. Feeling "ashamed," Angela "couldn't believe that was happening." One day later, Richie threw all of Angela's clothes outside the apartment. This time, Patricia was able to take Angela away.

Battered immigrant women's isolation and their immersion in and shame over the violent relationship often impede them from reaching out, but once they do, the support of friends and kin (be it emotional, informational, or material) is vital for their efforts to get free. For example, Abraham's research on marital violence among South Asian immigrants in the United States shows the negative impact that the community's emphasis on the privacy and sanctity of the family has on battered immigrants' efforts to break free of their abusive relationships, particularly when friends or family members refuse "to intervene in ways that would send the abuser the message that his abuse would not be condoned. Abused women fear that, rather than getting support from friends, they will be blamed for their abusers' behavior."[14] Organizations to end intimate partner violence have recognized the critical role that family, friends, and coworkers (followed by police officers, health professionals, teachers, and church officials) have in legitimizing the survivors' experiences. With this in mind, organizations have made significant outreach efforts to educate people in their respective communities about the abuse problem and the available solutions by providing informational and training sessions, as well as print and online resources in various languages. For instance, organizations have offered guidelines on what to do if "someone you know— your mother, sister, friend, coworker or neighbor—is a victim of domestic violence. Your support and encouragement can be of tremendous value to a friend involved in an abusive relationship. You can ease the isolation and loss of control your friend may feel by listening, providing information on domestic violence, and helping to explore options."[15] In Angela's case, Patricia was essential: she provided emotional support, shelter, and also a job reference at a nursing home. Angela took the job, but unfortunately, it turned into a grim experience. After a month of living and working there, she had not been paid. Her boss did not allow Angela to use her own name or to use the phone. As Johnson articulates:

> With the fear of deportation shaping all social and economic interactions, many undocumented immigrants, not surprisingly, accept what employers offer, no questions asked, and work long hours for low wages and few benefits. Understanding that undocumented immigrants enjoy little in the way of actual legal protections and deeply fear deportation, many employers cannot resist the temptation to exploit them. The making of demands by undocumented immigrants on employers means loss of a job. Laws other than the immigration laws also contribute to the exploitation of undocumented immigrants.[16]

Undocumented immigrants' race, ethnicity, national origin, gender, sexual orientation, and socioeconomic status are all added into discriminatory practices and systems. The general vulnerability of undocumented immigrants is further intensified if they are battered by their intimate partner, as in the case of Angela, who tried to break free from her multiple traps, but to no avail. She recalled:

> It was horrifying; I was very scared and sad. I didn't know what to do. I had to call my parents and sons and I had to send them money. I was terrified; I was very scared of that woman. One day I confronted her and said to her that if she was not going to pay me, that I needed her to bring me back to my house. I told her that I had some money saved in my house, so if she brought me there, I could get the money and send it to my family in Mexico. She agreed to take me home that night.

While her boss waited in the car, Richie attacked Angela. "He slapped me in the face. He told me that I was a bitch because I had left him. I didn't know what to do; my two options were both terrifying, but I thought that staying with Richie was going to be easier than going back to that nursing home where I was being kept as a criminal." Because Angela was "his wife," Richie persuaded Angela's boss to leave. Then he threatened Angela by saying he would call immigration officials "so they would take care of taking the trash out of the United States." She stayed with him, "trapped and terrified."

Richie's addictions and aggressions did not cease. Again, Angela found out that he was seeing another woman—this time, one who spoke in English, as she overheard their romantic phone conversation. Richie "used to do that all the time, he used to talk in English, curse at me in English so I would feel even worse because I couldn't understand everything he was saying" (another common feature of intimate partner violence against immigrants). A day after a fight regarding his infidelity, Richie was particularly violent against Angela. While they were on their way to clean a nightclub in the suburbs, Richie would not stop cursing at Angela, who later recounted:

> I started crying but stayed quiet, so he got even madder. Once we were in the club, he continued to curse at me and he threw chairs and stools at me. One of the stools hit me in the feet, another in the back. There was no one else in the club; it was just the two of us. What Richie was doing to me hurt me a lot, and I worried that he would get even more violent. I started to run. I ran away from the club and asked a person in the road to give me a ride back to my apartment. Once I got there, I called my friend. I was crying and feeling so many emotions at once. I asked her to please let me stay in her house because I was having trouble with Richie. She accepted, so I went to her house.

But soon, Richie found Angela. Swearing his love, Richie begged for forgiveness (as most abusers do after being "too" violent and perceiving the frustration and possible departure of their victims).[17] Then, Angela tested his commitment to change:

> I didn't know if I should believe in him. So, I asked him if he would go to Mexico with me. I told him that we could start anew, work down there, and be with my family. I told him that in Mexico we could be together as a family. Richie accepted my offer, so I thought that if he wanted to do that for me, he was being honest about changing for good and starting all over again. I thought that we could do it. I only

cared for my family; I loved him and wished to start anew in Mexico. I thought that we could work well down there and still help my family. I believed that we loved each other and that we could do better. I had expectations. I was hopeful.

While staying at her parents' house, they found jobs—Angela in a hardware store, Richie in a butcher shop. But Mexico did not change Richie (a disappointment for Angela, but an expected result for intimate partner violence and addictions specialists). Soon, he began to make friends, whom Angela described as "drunks." Careless, Richie would curse at Angela in English in front of her parents; if she served dinner to her sons and parents before she served him, he would get particularly angry. Tired of Richie's behavior, Angela's mother asked her if he had been like that in the United States. "No," lied Angela. But her mother asked Richie to leave. He disregarded her request, "as if it were a joke." The night that Richie stuck a piece of chewing gum in Angela's hair in front of her family was "the worst moment." Tearful, Angela relived the experience:

> I felt awful. I felt something was going up and down my stomach, my face was red and then white, I felt so embarrassed. All my family remained silent. I stepped out of the house and he followed me. Richie told me that I was a bitch. He told me that I didn't care about him anymore. I told him that wasn't true, that I loved my family and him, and that I wanted him to feel he was part of it. He kept screaming and cursing at me, and left. I went inside the house. Later, we found that he had written "bitch and *puta*" on the metal house door and entrance. He had scratched the words in English and in Spanish into the metal, maybe with a key. After that incident, he would pass by the house and scream curses against us. It was a terrible feeling; I was sad, embarrassed, and frightened. My family was concerned, because Richie would come by and throw rocks at the door.

One day, Richie came by the house to apologize. But in a matter of minutes, he began to argue and curse at Angela again. He grabbed her by the neck. Her son saw what Richie was doing and began to cry, and when her brother-in-law heard the boy crying, he told Richie to leave right away. Angela explained: "I was sad and scared. Richie's actions hurt my feelings and my heart so much that I would forget the physical pain. We were all scared of him, and I hated to think that my family could get hurt. I was going to do whatever it took to protect my family." With his next apologies, Richie proposed to Angela that they move out of her parents' house. Thinking that was the better move to prevent harm to her family, Angela accepted his offer. Her parents wanted Richie out of Angela's life—"I love him" was Angela's response to her mother's call to stay—a typical reaction for survivors of intimate partner violence while they are trapped in the web of abuse, power, and control that has been built over time.

Despite Richie's promises, he did not change. He continued to go out late and come back drunk, to curse at Angela, to tell her that she was "good for nothing." He would accuse her of not cooking for him, even if she was working both a day job and a night job, and he would get angry at her because she earned more money than he did. After she brought her children to live in their house, he got even angrier with her. He would say, "Why are you bringing those bastards to live with us?" While she recognized that Richie "didn't love them," Angela recalls, "I would tell him that my sons were going to live with us because they were my sons, and that they were going to be wherever I was. It was horrible, but I was not going to give up being with my sons any longer." Once they moved in (and to Angela's regret), her sons witnessed and became involved in several violent episodes, such as a fight in which Richie accused Angela of lending money to her sister and having sex with her sister's husband. Hearing the screams, curses, and punches, her seven-year-old boy came into the room to try to stop the chaos, but upon seeing Richie's violent reaction toward her son, Angela broke free and managed to take the children away to her parents' house.

After waiting for some hours, she returned to the house to see if Richie had calmed down, but he was still furious. When she came in, he threw a ceramic sugar bowl and a glass at her (the bowl hit her on the ear and left a bruise, and later her ear was swollen; the glass left a bruise on her back and fell to the floor and broke). Then Richie threw all the furniture—table, chairs, any item he found in the house—to the floor. After that, he pushed Angela onto the bed and hit her in the face. While she was crying, he jumped on top of her, but at that moment, Angela's parents came to the house and knocked on the door. Richie pretended nothing was wrong and told them to leave. Angela "wanted to yell out for help," but she was "afraid of what Richie would do" if she did that. Angela's parents went to the police to accuse him of battering her. But the police told them that Angela was the one who had to go to the police and file a report. Instead, her parents filed a report against Richie, accusing him of possessing marijuana. The police detained Richie. Based on his promise of leaving her family alone, Angela helped him to get out of jail. Richie left town, going south to take care of a ranch.

After a while, Angela started to visit Richie at the ranch. She "wished for things to go well," so she wanted to "try again to see if he had changed." The first visits were fine, and Angela was proud of having had faith. But one night, while they were in Richie's bedroom:

> We began to argue because he was saying bad things about my kids. He didn't love them. He had a rifle in his bedroom, and he took it out while I was still lying on his bed. He shot it inside the room, toward the other wall. The bullet bounced off of the brick wall but didn't hit me. I was terrified. I tried to leave, but Richie hit me in the back and pulled me onto the bed. Then he raped me. I was very scared. I never told anybody what had happened that night. I only wished I could have a normal family like anybody else. But Richie was very jealous of my love for my sons. I would explain to him that it was a different type of love, but he didn't understand me.

After that incident, Angela did not go back to the ranch again. She only heard about Richie a couple of months later: he had moved farther south. Angela decided to go back to Texas; her work there would be of much more help to her family. Her sons stayed with her parents again—Angela was heartbroken, but she thought it was the best for them all. As she had predicted, Angela found work as soon as she returned to the United States and was able to send money back to her family immediately.

After several quiet months, Richie resurfaced. Unannounced, he dropped by Angela's apartment and, crying, asked her to forgive him. He told her that he was terminally ill and that Angela "was the only person in the world who he wanted to be with." He begged for forgiveness. Shocked, compassionate, flattered, and hopeful, Angela "ended up accepting his apologies and believing that he had changed." Her insistence, typical of a survivor of repeated sexual and intimate partner violence, may seem puzzling, particularly after the last incident in Mexico. One may wonder, "Why did not she leave him already? How come did she believe in him again?"[18] These questions are a double-edged sword. On the one hand, they may feed outsiders' will to understand the survivor's complex and traumatic attachment to her abuser and, consequently, to stand by her. On the other hand, they may reinforce ideals of independence, detachment, awareness, self-worth, and possibility that hardly ever match the realities of battered immigrant women because of psychological, sociological, and cultural reasons and, consequently, obliterate the survivor's sense of legitimacy.[19] Being a survivor of intimate partner violence myself, as well as both Latina and aware of the background of immigrants like Angela (for whom "the pursuit of safety may not embody the [traditionally] recommended form" of separating from or reporting the abuser to state authorities because these "may intensify or engender new forms of battering and illegality"),[20] I knew how easy it was to further oppress the victims with one's disapproving attitude, and so I attempted to set these kinds of prejudices and assumptions aside. Indeed, as argued by Rudrappa, "A woman's capacity to survive violence depends on a community of sympathetic listeners."[21] Time and again, I observed the difference it made if ORA staff were either supportive or frustrated with their "clients," as I will further analyze in chapter 4.

Angela herself, like many other survivors, was frustrated about her relationship and her own persistence; thus, when her decision to give Richie another chance seemed to work out, she was not only pleased but reassured, thinking that her own criteria were legitimate. Richie invited her to meet his family in the Northeast, a gesture that Angela interpreted as an indication of trust, love, and union. Their family visit was prolonged, and they settled in Maryland, where one of Richie's brothers was living. Richie began to work at a hardware store, while Angela took care of one of his nephews. But what took Angela by surprise was Richie's offer to help her legalize her immigration status and bring her family to the United States (an amnesty was in place at the time). They took a trip to Washington, D.C., to pick up the forms at the immigration offices. After taking several days to complete the papers back in Maryland, Richie asked his brother to do them a favor and take the paperwork over to the immigration office on his way to work before the deadline. Later, Angela "began to cry" when she found out that the papers were never filed; she was in disbelief (of the situation, of Richie, of his family, and, last but not least, of herself). Richie defended his brother's decision not to send in the papers—his family thought Angela "was only taking advantage of Richie." His family's sabotage, typical of abusers' relatives, who frequently are distrustful of the motives of immigrant spouses, further victimized Angela, who "felt very bad." She did not want to stay there any longer, but Richie forced her to remain with him. They argued. He pulled on her arms violently, and when Angela attempted to call the police, "he took the phone away and hit" her in the face with it. Angela showed me the scar over her right eyebrow. Feeling "sad," Angela endured his family's threats until she convinced Richie to let her go.

Once back in Texas, Angela began to work right away. She recalled, "I was relieved because I was able to send money back to my family in Mexico." A month later, Richie reappeared, and as a testament to his repentance and love, he offered to file the immigration papers for her again (another typical control and power tactic of citizen and resident abusive spouses of immigrants). An attorney explained the process to them: Angela would have to go back to Mexico, and they would have to pay several fees to complete the application. "But," Angela recalls the logic, "if I went back to Mexico, I was not going to be able to earn enough money to maintain my family and pay for the paperwork. We ended up forgetting about the whole thing." When immigrants have the opportunity to legalize their status, the costs and complexity of the process are the main reasons they remain undocumented (the main reason they are undocumented to begin with is a result of the lack of legal opportunity to become documented, i.e., the lack of work visas for the kinds of jobs that "undocumented Mexican workers are critical to . . . agriculture, hotels and restaurants, construction, and the domestic-service industry").[22] As I discuss in the next two chapters, both formal and informal barriers stand in the way of battered immigrants' will to legalize their immigration status.

Angela's discontent faded the day she began to bring her family to the United States. First, her youngest son and her father crossed the border into Texas. "I was really happy to have them here with me," she said. But her joy triggered Richie's jealousy. Richie, who continued with his addictions, economic abuse, and violent behavior, felt threatened by Angela's love for her family. She remembered:

> One day, Pablo had a stomachache, so I was rubbing his belly to make him feel better. Richie got mad and threw a table and a chair to the floor. He screamed at me, saying that I was a pig, and that I was a dirty pig because I was touching "that bastard" in that way. I told him to shut up and not to talk in that way in front of my son. He didn't listen to me and continued cursing and screaming, so I called 911 for the first time. I called but didn't say anything; I just left the phone off the hook. When the police came to the house, my son was scared and confused, and crying told me, "No mommy, please." I didn't report Richie. . . . Afterward, he apologized and said that he loved me.

A year filled with incidents and apologies, pain and hope, passed by. Angela's older son and her mother's arrival to Texas outweighed her sadness; but not for long. Weeks after their move, Richie struggled with Angela when she tried to stop him on his way out to take yet another appliance to the pawn shop:

> He hit me in the face. Then he threw me to the floor and I fell against an armchair. My lip was opened and bleeding. I also hit my chest on the floor. The following day, the manager of the apartments came to my door and asked me what had happened. I had bruises on my arms, but I was wearing a long-sleeved shirt. I told her that I had fallen down, but the neighbors had told her about hearing a fight. My family also asked me, but I told them that I had fallen down. I didn't want to tell my family because Richie used to threaten me with reporting them to immigration.

Richie would often tell Angela that he was "very pleased" that she was "never going to be an American." He would scream at her, "You are never going to be able to do anything good for your family. . . . You are always going to be trash." Richie used to call Angela's bosses to manipulate them into firing her because she was "illegal." He did the same against her brother. Mexican Americans, such as Richie and part of his family, may be taken over by "internalized racism"[23] because they have "learned to despise all things Mexican" as a result of the "lynchings, land theft, and virulent racism" following the Mexican-American War, which ended in 1848, and the "en masse" deportations of "people of Mexican origin—citizens and noncitizens alike" during years of economic depression.[24] Immersed (and discriminated against) in the highly racialized and hierarchical U.S. society, Mexican-origin people and other Latina/os have come to believe that "white is better,"[25] as long as "whites have often ranked and categorized [non-European immigrants] along the light-to-dark, and close/not close to European-American culture, continua. Often the lighter a group is, and the more Anglicized it seems to whites, the better it will be treated and viewed."[26] Mexican-origin people "were initially categorized at or near the black end of the white-to-black continuum" and have been treated as "mixed-blood," that is, "not white," by whites.[27] Simultaneously, "tensions between Mexican Americans and Mexican immigrants are rooted in class . . . differences. . . . and reflect competition for the scarce resource of social status."[28] Because of internalized histories of oppression along racial, ethnic, and class lines as members of non-European racial/ethnic groups in the United States, Latina/os "may be conditioned to believe that other Latinos, particularly recent immigrants, are unfairly taking advantage of U.S. social services,"[29] or of those immigrants who have officially become part of this country. Richie's family's interference with Angela's citizenship application and Richie's manipulation of his acquired citizenship status to overpower and humiliate Angela illustrate how this detrimental phenomenon frequently works in tandem with gender and sexual oppression.

A month after the last violent incident, Richie and Angela had to move to another apartment complex because of the disturbances their fights had caused. The aggression against Angela and her family continued: slammed doors, lockouts, destroyed phones, thrown objects, punches, threats, and furious jealousy. Angela recalled with frustration, "He would smell all my clothes, including my underwear. He would accuse me at all times that I was having sex with other men. I was getting tired of putting up with Richie." One night, he came back to the apartment while drunk. Angela was taking a shower when he came into the bathroom and ripped down the shower curtain. He said, "Why are you showering? Are you getting ready to go out with some other man?" Then he pushed Angela against the wall; she slipped and fell. "Bitch," he screamed, as he threw the phone in her face and then smashed it against the floor. Angela ran away to call the police. Meanwhile, Richie threw a rock at the windshield of Angela's car and broke it. By the time the police came, Richie was gone. Angela was "terrified," and this time, she did file a report.

Richie did not return to the apartment for a while, but he frequently called both Angela and her brother to threaten them with deportation. After three weeks, Richie came back to the house with the excuse of packing up his belongings; he would not leave, however, and ended up staying. The drinking, cursing, and beating continued, but it was not until Angela found out that Richie tried to persuade her children to drink along with him and his friends that she demanded his "respect." But, according to Angela:

> Richie didn't care. Whenever we would ride with him on the truck, he would drive like crazy and say that it was better if we all died. . . . All of his actions were driving me crazy. Whenever he would argue with me, he would hit me. He hit me in the stomach; he bit my arms, fingers, and ears. He would throw objects at me; he would throw me

in the bathtub, and tear the shower curtains apart, while accusing me of having had sex with other men. He had a sick jealousy. He wouldn't let me dress without accusing me of being a whore. He would check my body and my breasts.

After one of the many fights they witnessed, Angela's sons broke down and implored her to leave Richie; if she did not, they would move in with their grandparents. Angela asked her sons to be patient because she needed time "to leave him . . . carefully so nobody would get hurt." She knew that she had to, but she "didn't know how" to break free from Richie. Arguably, her sons' intervention proved to be a turning point in her history of violence: as much as she had tried to end the relationship before, it was only with her sons' plea that she became conscious of the harm she had endured and, more important for her, of the harm she had made her own children witness and suffer. She was then determined to leave, and to do so cautiously.

Two months later, one last incident brought an end to eight hurtful years. One morning, while Angela was getting ready to go to work, Richie was stubbornly forcing her to stay in the house. He wanted to use the van, so he told her that if she so much wanted to go to work, she would have "to go on foot." Angela insisted on taking the van (she was the one going to work, and the van was hers). As she was about to start the engine,

Richie got into the van through the back door and pulled my hair from behind. Then, he hit my hands and fingers very hard. After, he tried to strangle me with a chain I was wearing while he was pulling my hair. He punched me in the face . . . he hit me in the stomach. I tried to scream for help; I saw that there were neighbors around watching, so I asked them to call the police. While he was pulling me by my hair, I managed to hit him in the face, and then he left.

I ran toward the apartment and asked the people there to call the police, but nobody moved, they stayed standing still, watching. The neighbors were all his friends, so they didn't do anything to help me. I got to the apartment and when I was going to close the door, he stopped me. I ran to the phone to call the police, but he managed to unplug the phone. I ran into the bathroom and closed the door, but he followed me, opened the door, and hit me again in the face. Then, he threw me to the bathtub. While I was lying there, he continued to curse at me. Then, he grabbed me by my hair and threw me back into the tub. Then, he left and took the van. I got up and went to call the police. When the police arrived, Richie had already left.

After that incident, Richie did not come back. There was a warrant out for his arrest, but the police had not found him yet. The police provided her with the phone number of a local organization where she could seek legal help. Resolved to "change and provide a better future" for her family, Angela called the Organization for Refugees of America/ Organización para Refugiados de América to find out more information, and since then, she has relentlessly made every effort to *salir adelante* (to move on and move forward).[30] Angela qualified for protection under the Violence Against Women Act, and ORA accepted her case. After four months of preparation, her three-inch-thick application to become a resident under VAWA was sent to the U.S. Citizenship and Immigration Services (USCIS). Another four months later, Angela's self-petition was granted, deportation procedures were deferred for her and her sons, and after their interview with the immigration officer in charge at USCIS, they received their legal permanent residencies. On the ride back from USCIS, Angela told me that she was "happy" but mostly "relieved." Then she said, "Sometimes, one is like in a pause; it takes something from the outside world to make you react."

Immigration Law: VAWA and VTVPA

There are two ways to become a citizen of the United States: by birth (on this country's soil or to U.S. citizens abroad) or by naturalization. Sixty-five percent of the immigrants who initiate their path to become naturalized U.S. citizens do so through family ties with citizens or residents who must actively sponsor their application process before USCIS.[31] Forty-seven percent of these applications are made by immediate relatives of citizens (26 percent are spouses, 11 percent are parents, and 10 percent are children); of the other 18 percent, 8 percent are spouses or children of residents.[32] Richie, who was a U.S. citizen, could have sponsored Angela's naturalization on the basis of their marriage. However, he used his power to keep Angela dependent on him. Richie's behavior was typical of abusive citizen or resident spouses who tend to use their privileged position to control their immigrant partners, particularly those who are undocumented (and, therefore, in fear of deportation, lacking job stability, earning low incomes, and without health or other benefits). First, they promise to sponsor their application, but then they either fail to present the paperwork on their behalf to USCIS (like Richie did the first time), or they begin the application process but later stop it by refusing to pay or collaborate in paying the related fees (as Richie did the second time), by retrieving the paperwork, or by not showing up for citizenship interviews at USCIS, all of which succeed in limiting the immigrants' chances to become residents.

Since the 1970s, activists struggled to reduce the power that the citizen or resident spouse has over the immigrant partner. Then, in 1994, with the enactment of VAWA, legal options were created to help immigrant survivors of intimate partner violence such as Angela.[33] VAWA's chapter on battered immigrants acknowledges their particular vulnerability and allows documented and undocumented immigrant spouses of residents or citizens to apply for residency and become citizens without the sponsorship of their abusive spouses. To do so, an immigrant survivor must prove that she, or he,[34] (1) was married to a U.S. citizen or a legal permanent resident,[35] (2) was married in good faith, (3) resided together as wife and husband, (4) was subject to domestic violence and/or extreme cruelty (including emotional, mental, and sexual abuse) during the marriage in the United States, and (5) is a person of good moral character (which means that she or he does not have a criminal background). Once the VAWA self-petition is approved by USCIS, the battered immigrant is granted deferred action (meaning that immigration authorities acknowledge that the self-petitioner is in the United States and will not try to deport her because of her faulty immigration status) and is allowed to apply for an employment authorization (renewable yearly) while she waits for her legal permanent residency application to be processed and approved. If the battered immigrant was married to an undocumented immigrant, or was separated but not divorced from a previous spouse while engaged in the abusive relationship, she can apply for a U visa through the Victims of Trafficking and Violence Protection Act. This visa offers temporary legal status for up to four years, meaning action on deportation procedures is deferred, and authorization to work in the United States for one year with the option to renew the permit twice. After three years of continuous and lawful presence in this country, U visa holders may be able to apply for legal permanent residency.[36]

Activists, advocates, and researchers alike have considered VAWA and VTVPA to be pivotal in the struggle to end violence against immigrant women, and thus in the actual chances they have to become citizens of the United States. The numbers of VAWA self-petitions and U visa applications have tended to increase since they became available in 1994 and 2000, respectively,[37] despite the fact that the application process before USCIS is lengthy (it can take from eight months to more than eight years to change immigration status), expensive (application fees and costs of supporting documentation may add up to $2,000, not including lawyers' fees), and complicated (so much so that immigrants are strongly encouraged to seek assistance from social workers and representation by certified legal assistants or attorneys in their application process). The continuous efforts of advocates and activists have contributed to making the process more accessible for battered immigrants: VAWA and VTVPA were amended to shorten the adjustment waiting periods; battered immigrants have been persuaded to go through the application process despite its length; fee waivers have been included in the provisions of the laws; nonprofit organizations and pro bono attorneys have increasingly provided free services to low-income battered immigrants; and tool kits, training materials, and networks have been developed to assist immigrants and advocates. Angela's case is a paradigmatic illustration of the benefits brought by gender violence legislation, the efforts by women's and immigrants' rights activists, and the work by advocates at nonprofit organizations like ORA.

However, the provisions for battered immigrants in VAWA and VTVPA cannot be simply read as a success.[38] Even if VAWA and VTVPA intended to protect all survivors of gender violence, regardless of their nationality, immigration status, race, ethnicity, class, or religious, political, and sexual orientation,[39] in my activist research I found that discriminatory parameters formally and informally permeate the evaluation of the battered immigrants' eligibility for legal protections and their chances to become U.S. citizens. VAWA and VTVPA have not escaped the historically biased character of the immigration system in the United States,[40] or the inequalities of U.S. society, both of which continue to privilege male, heterosexual, white, Protestant, middle- to upper-class individuals.[41] As one of the many mechanisms that the state employs to create citizens, immigration laws and regulations have been intimately connected with the making of nation-states.[42] First, immigration laws and regulations are a major component of the gates that the state creates to reaffirm its sovereignty (since they regulate which individuals are welcomed to form part of its population). When battered immigrants claim to be granted lawful status (be it temporary relief, employment authorization, legal permanent residency, or citizenship) on the basis of their unlawful victimization under VAWA and VTVPA, the authority of the state is reinforced. Ultimately, it is the state that may accept or decline the immigrants' petitions, thus including immigrants as legitimate subjects or excluding them as illegitimate outsiders. As the classic work of Weber points out, a sovereign state seeks to be the ultimate institution controlling the legal, bureaucratic, and punishment devices over a determined territory and population; the state's control over national membership (citizenship) reinforces its sovereignty.[43]

Second, immigration laws and regulations shape the state's nationhood (by setting citizenship ideals along racial, ethnic, gender, sexual, and class lines). VAWA and VTVPA, as I will elaborate on in the next chapter, do not escape this logic; the provisions for battered immigrants in these laws prioritize certain survivors over others on the basis of their national origin, race, ethnicity, gender, sexual orientation, or class background. Simultaneously, immigrant advocates reproduce these parameters in their work practices as they prioritize certain survivors over others. As theorized by Foucault, the state relies not only on formal laws but also on "mechanisms of disciplinary coercion" to maintain its sovereign power and sustaining ideologies.[44] The state intends to create citizens who will abide by law by means of disciplinary mechanisms, such as setting expectations of desirable social behaviors and punishing subjects who do not follow the norms, and by means of technologies of government that are "the policies, programs, codes, and practices (unbounded by the concept of culture) that attempt to instill in citizen-subjects particular values (self-reliance, freedom, individualism, calculation, or flexibility) in a variety of domains."[45] Disciplined citizens are then aware of what is considered permissible and forbidden, or desirable and undesirable, behavior in society and behave according to such social norms. In this process of normalization, individuals (unwittingly or not) sustain state sovereignty and legitimize the rule of law and behavioral ideals dictated by the state. The state's decisions to reward or punish citizens' behavior and to include or exclude immigrants as members of society strengthen its sovereign authority and reinforce dominant ideals of social order and citizenship behavior along gender, sexual, racial, ethnic, and class lines.

Third, immigration laws and regulations (or the lack thereof) control the state's productivity (since they determine the number of foreign laborers who can legally join its workforce). Historically, the state has enforced immigration laws "in ways that provide employers with a ready supply of low-wage labor";[46] when these workers are no longer needed, the "revolving door of disposable labor"[47] has been locked. A battered immigrant's quest for lawful status under VAWA and VTVPA includes the petition for an employment authorization, which allows the immigrant to work legally in the United States and can be renewed on a yearly basis. While the petitioner may wait for her legal permanent residency, citizenship, or U visa for several years, the employment authorization takes only a couple of months to be processed. As soon as they obtain their work permit, battered immigrants regularize their work status, are relieved of their fear of deportation while working, and find that their chances of finding jobs with health and other social benefits open up somewhat. By granting employment authorization in such an orderly fashion, the state first and foremost legitimizes the labor power of battered immigrants on the basis of their traumatic past. Thus, the state reinforces its liberal Anglo-American citizenship ideals (and theories), which pose an "ineluctable connection established between freedom, the naturalism of market exchange, and individual rights."[48] Becoming a lawful member of the United States begins, then, with the possibility of participating legally in the labor market, which also means the duty of collaborating with the taxation system (another instance of economic membership).[49] Years later, and only if the application process is successful, the immigrant may be granted status as a permanent resident; finally, and only if additional paperwork is filed and paid for, the resident may be granted citizenship status, the only type of status that offers political rights (i.e., the rights to vote and to run for political office). This sequence of rights and duties reflects liberal and neoliberal conceptions of citizenship in economic terms, which insist on "the civic duty of individuals to reduce their burden on society and to build up their human capital."[50]

Historically, immigration policies have worked as a safety valve of political, economic, social, and cultural struggles, reflecting various degrees of discriminatory sentiments against foreigners. While pro-immigration folks stress the multifaceted value of immigration and vote for policies devoted to improve immigrants' life chances, anti-immigration folks associate immigration with disruption and deviance and push for border control measures and the like. All in all, immigration laws and regulations have been critical tools for the inclusion and exclusion of persons, and, respectively, for the struggle against or re-creation of inequality. The study of Latina battered immigrants' quest for citizenship under VAWA and VTVPA reveals the intricacies of this exclusive/inclusive process. The paradigmatic case of Angela is testament to the extent to which a justifiably celebrated effort to include those who were once considered marginal continues to exclude many others: oddly enough, Angela was privileged. Her history of abuse and migration, illustrative of the experiences of most battered immigrants, together with her attitude and abilities, not such common traits, made her a model applicant in the eyes of USCIS and a preferred "client" at ORA; her VAWA self-petition was completed and approved in record time (four and four months, respectively). However, many other immigrant survivors of intimate violence have not been as fortunate.

In chapter 3, I present the cases of Claudia, Julia, Luisa, Laura, Martha, Rosa, Manuela, Ana, and Susana to illustrate the biases embedded in the formalities of these laws by determining who the battered immigrants are that might become citizens, and consequently, how VAWA and VTVPA contribute to the preservation of the gated access and hierarchical structure of American society. In chapter 4, I will share the cases of other unfortunate survivors to reveal the informal obstacles that stand in the way of battered immigrants' quest for citizenship.

3

Formal Barriers to Citizenship

The all-inclusive spirit of the Violence Against Women Act and the Victims of Trafficking and Violence Protection Act is tainted by gender, sexual, racial, ethnic, and class discriminatory parameters that end up excluding many battered immigrants, regardless of their history of abuse. The cases of Claudia, Julia, Luisa, Laura, Martha,[1] Rosa, Manuela, Ana, and Susana, in contrast to Angela's, illustrate how VAWA and VTVPA work within long-standing formal legal structures that prioritize men over women, married over nonmarried, heterosexual over nonheterosexual, American over foreign, and working, middle, or upper class over poor. This chapter uncovers the intricacies beneath the selection of battered immigrants as subjects worthy to become U.S. citizens as the state hopes to sustain its sovereignty, nationhood, and productivity along a hierarchical, disciplinary social order through immigration laws.

Gender and Sexual Discrimination

Inconsistent with the origin and spirit of these laws, the gender violence–based immigration provisions in VAWA and VTVPA are permeated with gender and sexual discriminatory legacies. The marital status and sexual orientation of the abused determine the options available to them. Whereas married, heterosexual survivors of gender violence are fully protected, nonmarried, separated but not divorced, and nonheterosexual survivors are partially protected as long as they find more obstacles than opportunities along the way. This gradation was visible in the cases of all the immigrants who approached Organization for Refugees of America/Organización para Refugiados de América (and those who did not; in my two years of work at ORA, I never learned of a nonheterosexual immigrant survivor of a crime seeking services even if such an individual could have found relief through a U visa). Among those immigrants who sought services, Angela, Claudia, Julia, and Luisa provide good illustrations of the embedded gender and sexual discrimination. While all of them were survivors of extreme physical, sexual, and psychological violence perpetrated by their respective abusers in the United States, their and their husbands' marital status led these battered immigrants to diverging routes to citizenship. Whereas Angela enjoyed full protection (as I presented in the previous chapter), Claudia, Julia, and Luisa had different luck.

Claudia

Claudia, originally from Mexico, had migrated to the United States in search of work opportunities to help her family survive extremely poor living conditions and health problems. The mother of seven children—three living in Mexico (one with brain paralysis), three in the United States, and one who had recently passed away—Claudia had come to her appointment at ORA with her youngest boy. While Maggie, the legal assistant in charge of the intake, explained to Claudia that the appointment consisted of a long questionnaire designed to determine if she would be eligible for some sort of legal remedy, I smiled at the young boy and showed him a couple of toys that Maggie kept in her office. Maggie began with the "easy questions": name, address, nationality. Soon, however, she asked more compromising questions that interrupted the flow of the intake: "When was the last time that you entered the United States? Where? How?" Claudia looked puzzled, and Maggie told her that it did not matter if she did not have documents when she entered and stressed that all the information was confidential. Claudia smiled uncomfortably, paused, and nervously answered. Then, Maggie asked if she had had any contact with an immigration officer, and Claudia replied that she had not. Maggie reacted to this answer with an enthusiastic "Excellent!" because if a battered immigrant had had contact with immigration officers and charges were brought against her, the citizenship petition could be denied by U.S. Citizenship and Immigration Services.

Maggie continued to follow the questions on the intake form, which led her to specifics about Claudia's abuse: "Was the abuse physical, emotional, sexual? Are you married to the abuser? Have you lived together with the abuser? Do you have documentation to prove that you were living together? Is the abuser a citizen, a resident, or undocumented? Is the abuser divorced? How many times have you and the abuser been married before?" While Maggie jotted down the answers and nodded, Claudia told us that she had been a victim of domestic violence since she was very young, and that one of her daughters had also been victimized when she was only four years old. Then, Maggie continued with a list of twenty detailed questions about the abuse that Claudia had been through with her current partner. With her head down, Claudia gave plenty of positive answers: "yes," she had been punched, cursed, and screamed at; "yes," her hair had been pulled; "yes," she had been threatened with death; "yes," she had been prevented from working; "yes," she had been told that she was going to be reported to immigration authorities and deported; "yes," she had been threatened with being separated from her own children; "yes," she had been cut with a sharp object; and "yes," she had been prevented from having or spending any money. Maggie pointed to the box of tissues on her desk, but Claudia did not need them. Claudia's son silently listened to the questions and answers.

Maggie continued with the questionnaire and, smiling, said, "There are only two more pages to go." Claudia took a breath and continued to give her answers: "no," she had never been arrested; "no," she had never been to counseling or lived in a shelter for abused women; and "no," she had never filed a police report. Maggie paused and, without making eye contact with Claudia, her son, or me, looked into her desk drawer and pulled out a yellow sheet. Smiling, she told Claudia that if her partner ever threatened to take her children away, she should call 911. "The police?" Claudia asked. Maggie nodded and explained that it was perfectly fine to call the police: "The police are not supposed to or allowed to ask immigration questions. They are here to help you, so if you are having trouble, you should call them." Claudia's face revealed uncertainty; she claimed that she feared deportation and did not trust the police. Maggie insisted, and while she recognized that it may be difficult to think about the police without fear, the local police had been very helpful with immigrant victims of domestic violence. Without trying to convince Claudia any further, Maggie pointed to another phone number on the yellow sheet and explained, "If you feel unsafe, you can always go to a shelter for battered women. Our city's shelter is very good, and it also offers counseling services for children and adults." Claudia showed interest and said that she really wanted psychological help—"for my daughter, she has been very sensitive to the violence, you know."

Then, Maggie said, "Unfortunately, ORA cannot help you at that moment because you are not eligible for VAWA. But next time something happens, make sure to call the police. Once you get a police report about your partner's abuse, do get in touch with us because then ORA might be able to help you" (with the report, Claudia could be eligible for a U visa). Perceiving that the end of the appointment was nearing, Claudia quickly asked if ORA could help her get a Texas ID. Maggie told her that as an undocumented immigrant she could not get a U.S. ID, but that she could go to the Mexican consulate to apply for some form of Mexican ID. Disappointed, Claudia replied that she had already been there and could not get any help. "That's odd," said Maggie, who then asked Claudia if she had any further questions. To conclude, Maggie said, "I am proud of you. You have taken the most difficult step," which was to separate from her abuser. Claudia thanked her and left the office holding her son with one hand and the yellow sheet with the other.

As Claudia walked away, Maggie saw my expression of astonishment and told me that she also felt bad about Claudia's situation. This was one of the first intake appointments in which I sat in, and I was not only upset but also confused. In those initial weeks as an intern at ORA, I learned about some of the intricacies of the laws. Claudia was not eligible for VAWA because she was not married to the abuser, and even if they had lived together for six months, they had not considered each other husband and wife—a requisite of common-law marriages in Texas. Maggie knew this from the very beginning of the lengthy intake, but she had continued with the process because she thought Claudia could be eligible for a U visa. Disappointed, Maggie told me, "Unfortunately, immigrants are afraid of the police. I doubt that Claudia will ever report the abuse. . . . *Pobrecita* [poor thing]."

Julia

Like Angela and Claudia, Julia was originally from Mexico, and escaping extreme poverty, she had migrated to the United States looking for an opportunity to bring her family out of minimum survival conditions. Once in Texas, she met and married Paco, a legal permanent resident, originally from Mexico. Soon after their wedding, Paco began to be physically, sexually, and psychologically violent against Julia. He used almost all the abusive techniques mentioned in the intake questionnaire, including threats of deportation, manipulation of immigration papers (he had initiated paperwork to change her status in 1995 but never followed up), and prohibition of learning English. Julia had seven children with Paco and also a miscarriage related to his mistreatment. Paco had left her three years before the date of our appointment and had been living with another woman for almost as long. "I can't believe he was capable of doing all these things to the mother of his own children, and now, that he hasn't seen them for more than seven months, and that he doesn't send them money or anything. . . . Fine, don't see me, but the kids? They are yours!" Their children began to have problems at school after Paco left, and the oldest sons dropped out because they were left with no money, and the entire family needed to eat. Julia explained, "I didn't want them to drop out, but they chose to do so; they wanted to help." Julia's children were very loving and supportive of their mother and did not want to have their father around, particularly the oldest, who had witnessed Paco trying to run over Julia with a truck. Whenever Julia mentioned something about their father, her children would say, "Don't talk to me about him anymore, he never loved us." Julia made $300 per month by picking up temporary work cleaning houses with another woman; with this income and that of her oldest sons, they barely managed to get by. Julia's tranquillity during the intake seemed to be grounded in a very deep sadness. "I am alone, lonely—I don't know what to do," she told me. I gave her information about shelters for battered women that offered counseling and other services, such as lessons in English as a second language, for free. Enthusiastically, Julia asked for more information.

Later that week, I met with Kathy, the lawyer assigned to Julia, to review the case: "Julia seems to be eligible to apply for VAWA, but we cannot proceed with the case until we know her exact civil status: Is she still married? Is she divorced? Did she have divorce papers?" Her husband could have filed for divorce without her knowledge, and if Julia had been divorced for more than two years, she would not be eligible for VAWA. Jenna, the legal assistant in charge of Julia's case, showed me the administrative steps one had to take to check a person's civil status; I was to explain these to Julia, who would have to get the information on her own. When I met with Julia again, I explained to her that in order for ORA to take her case to apply for VAWA, she had to check if she was or was not divorced. Scared, Julia told me, "I don't know. . . . He threatened me to file for divorce many times, but I don't know if he had done it or not." As I explained the steps she needed to take to find out about her civil status, she told me that it was going to be very difficult for her to get to the indicated office. I showed her the available public transportation options, but she continued to say how difficult it would be for her. She was upset and confused. I offered to accompany her, but she was not convinced, so I told her that she could also request the information by mail, which would be significantly slower than in-person requests (it would take two and a half months longer to get results). "That's better," Julia said. She was relieved with that option, since her working hours and the distance she would have to travel to the office would mean the loss of a work day for her. When we were about to complete the mail-in application, Julia stopped me, saying, "Oh, no. . . . No, I can't. I don't have money to spare." Julia left hoping that at our next appointment I would bring her good news: that ORA would help her pay the nine-dollar application fee.

After the appointment, I talked with Maggie and Jenna about Julia's impediment. They told me that ORA could pay the fee as long as she promised to pay it back. I offered to go to the state office to request Julia's divorce papers on my own. "Oh! That's so nice of you!" said Jenna. "If you want to do it, go ahead, but we never do those things for the clients. . . . You can do it by mail, you know?" explained Maggie. But I could not stop thinking that waiting for only two weeks rather than waiting for two to three months would make a big difference in Julia's situation, so I went to the Texas Bureau of Vital Statistics, requested a check on Julia's civil status, and paid the fee. Finding the office was not easy: I went into three different buildings looking for it, and it was only in the third one that I found somebody who could give me precise directions. Once I found the crowded office, I looked around for instructions and forms, which were available only in English. I completed the form and waited in line for an hour. The staff spoke only English and were cordial but demanding. Julia would have had trouble filing her petition on her own, and I was glad that I had decided to do it for her. ORA would get the results in two weeks, and then Julia would know whether her chance to become a citizen was realistic or not.

Two weeks later, ORA received Julia's civil status; fortunately, she was not divorced. ORA officially took Julia as a client and began to prepare her VAWA self-petition. Julia was ecstatic and hopeful for things to work out—"*si Dios quiere*" ("if it is God's will"). She began to go to individual and group counseling sessions at the local shelter for battered women and wanted her children to go as well because they had been very upset with all the incidents. Two years later, Julia's VAWA self-petition was approved, her removal conditions were suspended, and her employment authorization was granted. While Julia continues to wait for her legal permanent residency, she can renew her work permit yearly (she will have to wait from five to eight years because Paco was a resident and she is Mexican; I explain more about this later, in the section titled "Racial and Ethnic Discrimination").

Luisa

Luisa was a survivor of physical, economic, and psychological domestic violence perpetrated by her partner, Richard, a U.S. citizen, who was incarcerated after the last violent episode. Luisa approached ORA in search of legal help in regard to her immigration status because the police had informed her of her rights to apply for a U visa, which would allow her to live and work in the United States legally on the basis of the abuse she had endured. In our first meeting, the intake appointment, I followed the steps to gather as much information as possible so the attorney could review the case and decide whether Luisa could become a client of the organization. The appointment was unusually long, lasting almost three hours. The first set of questions regarding biographical information was daunting for Luisa: the dates and places of her marriage, the birth of her children, and her entry to the United States, as well as complete addresses were difficult to remember. Regarding her marital status, Luisa told me, ashamed, that she had not married Richard because she was "*casada, bien casada*" ("married, really married") back in Mexico. Then she explained to me that even though she was still married, she had lost touch with her husband after migrating to the United States years ago. Luisa got involved with Richard because she had considered herself separated, and they had lived together for several years. Luisa had four children, all of whom had different fathers. Her children were still living in Mexico.

Regarding her history of migration, it took me more than an hour just to clarify when she had arrived in and left the United States. She told me that she had come in 1991 and that she had never returned to Mexico, but as I checked the birth dates and birthplaces of her children, three of them were born in Mexico in the mid-1990s. I thought she had gotten confused between 1991 and 2001, but she insisted, "No, miss, 1991. . . . But, no, it was 1991 . . . 1991, I'm telling you!" It was only after many explanations that she realized that we were currently in the 2000s and not the 1990s. Luisa laughed, embarrassed, when she realized it.

As we began to talk about her current and past addresses, she could not recall exact information and was certain that she did not possess any leases, since her rentals had been arranged informally, including her current one. After Richard was incarcerated, Luisa moved out and rented a room from a woman who did not even give her the key to the apartment—"I have to leave the apartment at the same time the other woman does, and then I have to wait outside until she comes back from work late at night," Luisa explained. After hearing about her current living situation, I gave her information about shelters for battered women. Luisa showed interest and asked, "Can you help me? I don't have a phone in the apartment." I let her use the phone at ORA (the closest public phone that she could use was miles away from her residency). When the person at the shelter picked up the phone and replied in English, Luisa handed me the receiver, saying, "I don't know what they are saying, miss. Please. . . ." As soon as I began talking about Luisa, the shelter employee apologized, "We don't have any vacancy at the moment." Then Luisa called another shelter, where some workers spoke Spanish. After ten minutes or so of questions, the shelter employee told her that the shelter could not accept her because her children were not residing with her, and the shelter was "exclusively for mothers with children." Finally, she called a third shelter, which was farther away from the city where Luisa lived. Nobody spoke Spanish, so Luisa asked me to talk with the employee in English. The shelter had space available, so the employee began to arrange Luisa's move with me. I offered to give Luisa a ride that same afternoon, but she reminded me, "I don't know when I will be able to get in the apartment, late at night probably. . . . I can't go there without my things, and they are all in there, in the apartment." As we spoke, one of the ORA staff came to the office and told us that we had a message from one of the shelters saying that it could make an exception and take Luisa in (this was the shelter that accepted only mothers with children—after all, Luisa was a mother whose children were back in Mexico). Excited, Luisa said that she preferred this option because the shelter was in town, and she could use public transportation to go to work. Then, I canceled the arrangements with the other shelter, thanked the employee and apologized for the cancellation. We called the shelter for mothers and arranged for Luisa to move in there the following morning. I would pick Luisa up by car the next day because she could not bring all her belongings in the bus on her own.

After these preparations, I explained to Luisa the next steps at ORA (her file would be reviewed by the attorney and then, in our next meeting, I would be able to let her know what her options were). Next, I helped her look at the bus map and schedule to see if she could take a bus from ORA to her place of residence. It was very hard for her to understand me, so I walked her almost as far as the bus stop. She thanked me and continued to walk with a doubtful and fearful demeanor. "'Bye, Luisa," I called after her, "see you tomorrow morning. Take care!" Upon my return to ORA, Kathy, the lawyer, and Maggie and Jenna, the two legal assistants, expressed their surprise at the length of my meeting with Luisa. "Oh, Roberta, you are too nice," said Kathy, while Maggie and Jenna nodded.

The following morning I went to pick up Luisa but did not find her. I was worried, thinking that something may have happened to her, or that maybe I had gotten a wrong address from her. I went to ORA and, after an hour or so of trying, reached her friend by telephone. Her friend reassured me, "I'm sure that Luisa is working. . . . Yes, I'll tell her about the shelter and the next appointment. No problem, miss. Thank you." I called the shelter, explained what had happened, and was told, "Don't you worry. We will do our best to get in touch with her."

Before the next appointment, Luisa called to let me know that she was not going to be able to make it because "a work opportunity that she could not miss had come up." We rescheduled our meeting, and when I asked if she had gotten in touch with the shelter, she told me that she had, but "I have to call them again to see how I will bring my things over—I can't bring my bag, the table, my bookcase, and the other things on the bus, as I told you." As much as I understood how important her belongings were for Luisa, I thought that she was not convinced of the benefits of moving to the shelter—perhaps she feared the loss of proximity to the one friend who had provided her with emotional, informational, and material support; perhaps she felt that living in a shelter would deprive her of her autonomy (as opposed to what shelter advocates aim for, which is to provide a safe haven for survivors and help them regain their sense of self and independence).[2] Not possessing the keys to the apartment where she was living was not as disturbing for her as I had originally thought.

At our rescheduled appointment, I was excited to tell Luisa that ORA had approved her case—she qualified to apply for a U visa. After I explained the steps to follow (particularly the requirement of collaborating with the police in the investigation of the crime committed against her), and the benefits of applying for this visa (i.e., deferred action on deportation procedures and employment authorization), I asked, "So, Luisa, do you want to go ahead with this?" "Well, I don't know, miss. What do you think? Should I?" I explained everything one more time, and then Luisa agreed to do it.

The supervisor of Luisa's case, Courtney, was ORA's expert on U visas. She had told me to "go easy on the case because until we got the certification from the police, we should not waste resources on it." I tried to advance on other matters related to the case as much as possible in order to have everything ready for when the certification arrived. Luisa missed many appointments (because of temporary work opportunities and even threats from her abuser's relatives), so the pace was very slow in comparison with other cases I had worked on. Whenever we met, Luisa brought questions about her immigration application status—it was difficult for her to understand that despite all the paperwork being done, there was no news about her case—and expressed her fear of her abuser and his family's threats, particularly about being deported: "I'm so scared, miss; what can I do? I thought all of these would help, but you tell me there's nothing yet." Luisa's confusion and concerns were legitimate, especially at a time when raids of undocumented workers were increasing and debates about restricting immigration flooded the media. Although my explanations were not necessarily pleasing, at least she knew who to call and what not to say or do if she were apprehended by immigration officers.

I followed up on Luisa's case with Courtney at least once a month because I could not believe how long the police were taking to give her certification (in particular because Richard was indeed incarcerated on charges of domestic violence against Luisa). Courtney, who was not surprised at the length of the wait, explained, "I wait an average of four months to receive responses from the police." After seven and a half months had passed since the intake appointment, I received an e-mail from Courtney that read, "The police denied Luisa's certification. They claim she did not cooperate in the investigation (they called Luisa but she did not return their phone call)." When I asked Courtney if there was anything Luisa could do about the decision, she explained that she could call the police and explain that Luisa never got their message because she had moved several times. Luisa followed our instructions, and in her conversation with the police, she reiterated that she was willing to collaborate in the investigation of her abuser's crime against her.

After several weeks, I tried to get in touch with Courtney to check on Luisa's case, but I did not hear back from her. Three months later (i.e., eleven months after the intake appointment with Luisa), I was finally able to get an update from Courtney: the police had refused once again to certify Luisa, and consequently, ORA was not able to proceed with her U visa petition. Courtney disagreed with the police's double denial of Luisa's certification; frustrated, she told me that it was "plain bullshit." When I asked her if we could further complain, she replied hastily, "I cannot take care of her case at the moment. I'm busy with other U visa applicants." As I left her office, Courtney said, "*Pobrecita*" (poor thing) and clarified that she would get in touch with Luisa (Luisa could complete a victim's compensation petition). After receiving the news from Courtney, Luisa never came back to ORA.

Legacies of Coverture: Patriarchy and Heteronormativity

The cases of Angela, Claudia, Julia, and Luisa illustrate how, in mirroring the family-based immigration system, VAWA and the clauses in VTVPA for battered immigrants married to undocumented immigrants are still influenced by the legacies of the English common-law doctrine of coverture, under which "women ceased to legally exist upon marriage."[3] This doctrine gave the husband "total power and control over" his wife and allowed him to chastise her to "force obedience" to his demands.[4] Coverture and the derivative doctrine of chastisement legitimized not only men's domination and violence against women but also heteronormativity (the oppressive institutionalization of heterosexuality in society). Early spouse-based immigration laws in the United States incorporated the principles of coverture by providing male citizens and resident aliens "the right to control the immigration status of their alien wives";[5] that is, immigrant women were able to access immigration benefits if, and only if, their citizen or resident husband petitioned for them. Subsequent changes in immigration laws in 1952 and 1965 tried to address the gender disparity derived from the coverture doctrine by using neutral language, but they did not fully eliminate its assumptions and "the potential for spouse abuse underlying those policies and practices"[6] or modify the assumption of marriage being only a heterosexual union. Indeed, the 1952 act targeted homosexual immigrants, who were considered to be a threat to the security and integrity of the United States and were thus excluded and deported "on the grounds of psychopathic personality."[7] Moreover, the Immigration Marriage Fraud Amendments that soon followed the Immigration Reform and Control Act of 1986 "substantially strengthened the notion of spousal domination"[8] with the inclusion of a two-year conditional status on alien spouses, after which they became deportable unless a joint petition was filed by both spouses and the marriage was deemed legitimate by an immigration office during an interview where both spouses had to be present.[9] At the same time that these amendments "recodified marriage as a heteropatriarchal institution that was central to immigration and the nation, lesbian, gay, and other kinds of relationships remained invalidated."[10] The Immigration Act of 1990 maintained the family-based immigration system and the role of heterosexual spouse–based immigration but, in an effort to overcome the legacies of coverture, included a provision in defense of battered spouses allowing them to request a waiver to change their status from conditional to permanent residency without the cooperation of the abusive spouse. These waivers were arbitrarily assigned, and the Violence Against Women Act of 1994 addressed these difficulties on behalf of immigrant battered women. Despite the various achievements of VAWA, "coverture in spouse-based immigration has not met its demise,"[11] insofar as citizen and resident abusive spouses, who continue to be predominantly male, still have control over their immigrant spouses, who continue to be predominantly female.

The options for battered immigrants in VTVPA follow a similar pattern: the accomplishments of this act in regard to the protection of noncitizen victims of crimes committed in the United States are counterbalanced by the ways in which victims are differentiated as deserving or nondeserving of protection. For instance, battered immigrants are requested to collaborate in the investigation of the crime committed against them, but if the police believe that the immigrant was not helpful and therefore do not certify her as cooperative, her chances to apply for a U visa perish. This is problematic for several reasons. First, conclusive evidence (and the same evidence that has been used to exempt VAWA applicants from pressing charges against their abusers) shows that survivors of violence, particularly those who have children and/or are still traumatized, prefer not to accuse their aggressors, the main motivation being to avoid the risk of retaliation. Indeed, these risks are higher for U visa than for VAWA applicants because the abuser (and sometimes his family as well) is undocumented and may be deported as a result of the investigation. Second, battered immigrants' trust in the authorities is already limited because they associate authorities with incarceration and deportation (many have been convinced by their abusers that all police officers are anti-immigrant, have learned about police officers working in tandem with immigration officers, or have had previous negative encounters with police officers in their country of origin or the United States). Third, battered immigrants' capacity to follow the prescribed steps to get certification by the police frequently is limited by their unstable living conditions (because they tend to move frequently, live in residences without phone access, and have temporary employment, attempts by authorities to make contact with immigrants to request and obtain cooperation tend to be unsuccessful). These survivors' circumstances contribute to a perceived dichotomy between helpful and unhelpful victims that "run[s] the risk of reinforcing barriers to help [victims of human rights abuses] rather than removing them."[12]

The legacies of coverture were palpable in my day-to-day experience at ORA, as exemplified by the cases of Angela, Claudia, Julia, and Luisa and the fact that in my two years at the organization, I never heard of a case of a nonheterosexual immigrant survivor. Angela was a battered immigrant originally from Mexico with two sons, married to a U.S. citizen who soon became abusive. Her marital status allowed her to qualify under VAWA, and her path to citizenship was short and certain. Claudia was also a battered immigrant from Mexico. The mother of seven children, Claudia had been a victim of domestic violence since she was very young and had been abused by her current partner, a U.S. citizen. However, the fact that Claudia was not married to her abusive partner and had not engaged with her partner in a common-law union made her ineligible for VAWA. She could try to apply for a U visa if she called the police on her abuser and collaborated with the authorities in the investigation of the crime. Julia was another battered immigrant originally from Mexico, a mother of seven who had been abused physically, sexually, and psychologically. But, unlike Angela or Claudia, Julia was married to a legal permanent resident, who had left her three years before the date of the appointment and had been living with another woman for almost as long. Initially, Julia seemed to be eligible to apply for VAWA, but ORA had to know her exact civil status: if her husband had filed for divorce without her knowledge more than two years before the estimated application date, she could not apply for VAWA. Like Angela, Claudia, and Julia, Luisa had migrated from Mexico to escape extreme poverty. Her abuser was a U.S. citizen with whom she had cohabitated for a couple of years, and who was incarcerated at the moment as a result of the last violent episode. Luisa was not married to her abuser because she had not legally divorced her husband, who still resided in Mexico. Because of her marital status, Luisa could not apply for VAWA but rather needed to petition for a U visa.

Despite these women's histories of abuse and their willingness to become citizens in the United States independently from their abusers, the legacies of coverture embedded in the immigration laws shaped their future. Angela's match with VAWA and ORA's formal (and informal) expectations allowed her to move forward and move on quickly and certainly; she obtained her and her sons' legal permanent residency in only eight months. Upon ORA's suggestion to call the police and collaborate with the authorities in the investigation of her abusive partner, Claudia expressed fear and mistrust based on negative experiences of friends, relatives, and other immigrants in her community when dealing with the police, who either had contacted immigration officers to initiate deportation procedures or had prioritized the testimonies of English speakers over non–English speakers. Claudia never returned to ORA, which probably meant that she did not apply for a U visa. Julia, on the contrary, was able to become a legal permanent resident once ORA resolved the enigma about her marital status: her husband, fortunately for Julia, had not filed for divorce, so she was able to seize the opportunity opened by VAWA. Luisa, unlike Claudia, decided to collaborate with the police, with whom she had been in touch when her abusive partner was incarcerated, and petitioned for a U visa. Luisa took the necessary steps suggested by ORA, but the police refused to certify her as a U visa applicant by claiming that she had not been cooperative enough because she had not returned their phone calls. Luisa had not been able to do so because she had moved to various temporary residences, without phone lines, due to her financial instability and the continuous threats from her abuser's family members. Even though ORA complained to the police and requested a revision of their denial, the police once again refused to certify Luisa. ORA decided not to follow up on her case because of resource limitations, and so Luisa's opportunity to initiate her path to citizenship was closed. While the cases of Angela, Claudia, Julia, and Luisa represent the legacies of formal gender discrimination, they also illustrate other formal and informal selectivity issues that I will explore later in the book.

Nonheterosexual immigrant survivors (be they gay, lesbian, bisexual, transgender, or queer [LGBTQ]) face a further multifaceted jeopardy. While they are subjected to similar abuses as other battered immigrants, their sexual orientation intensifies their oppression in legal, social, and cultural terms as they live in a heteronormative society. I paraphrase Kanuha's classic study of lesbians of color to reflect the intersecting challenges that face LGBTQ immigrants of color:

> Because they are battered, they struggle to maintain a sense of their psychical, emotional, and spiritual selves in the midst of daily terrorization. Because they are [LGTBU], they are a stigmatized, invisible group often silenced by powerful influences of homophobia . . . because they are [people] of color, they have survived a centuries-old legacy that oppresses them based solely on the color of their skin.[13]

And, because they are immigrants, they fear deportation or the end of their temporary immigration status, work in unstable conditions, earn low incomes, lack health benefits, may partially understand or speak English, and find themselves in a foreign culture. LGBTQ battered immigrants are thus affected simultaneously by "xenophobia, ethnocentrism,"[14] classism, "sexism, racism, violence, [and] homophobia."[15] Legally, while LGBTQ individuals are accepted as immigrants, since their exclusion was removed in the Immigration Act of 1990, their relationships continue to be unacknowledged as a basis for gaining legal permanent residency to the present day (even if same-sex marriages have been legalized in some states, they remain illegal federally and, thus, in the eyes of USCIS).[16] Therefore, LGBTQ immigrant survivors of intimate partner violence do not qualify for the same benefits as heterosexual battered immigrants; LGBTQ survivors are not eligible to apply for citizenship through VAWA.[17] LGBTQ battered immigrants can make use of VTVPA and apply for a U visa if they have suffered "substantial physical or emotional injury" as a result of being subjected to crimes like rape, sexual assault, abusive sexual contact, and sexual exploitation (but not domestic violence) committed against them in the United States (only if the crime is reported and law enforcement certifies the victim's collaboration in the investigation).[18] However, besides the quantity and procedural impediments of U visas that I discussed earlier, the sociocultural barriers to complete such a process are higher for LGBTQ individuals than for heterosexual battered immigrants, since they probably will encounter sexism and homophobia, in addition to the already challenging process. As of January 2009, ORA had never processed a U visa for a LGBTQ battered immigrant.[19] All in all, as Luibhéid put it, "Immigration control has been equally integral to the reproduction of patriarchal heterosexuality as the nation's official sexual and gender order."[20]

Racial and Ethnic Discrimination

Together with their ironic legacies of gender and sexual discrimination, and despite their celebratory spirit of diversity, VAWA and VTVPA are permeated with racial and ethnic discriminatory legacies. The national origin and immigration status of the abuser determine the options available for battered spouses through VAWA and VTVPA. These hierarchies were reflected in the cases of all the immigrants who approached ORA. For example, Angela, Laura, Martha, Rosa, Manuela, and Ana were all survivors of extreme physical, sexual, and psychological violence perpetrated by their respective husbands in the United States. However, their abusers' nationality and immigration status led each of these battered immigrants to significantly different paths to become citizens. Angela found the shortest and safest route because her abusive husband was a U.S. citizen; Laura, Martha, Rosa, and Manuela found less certain (and, when available, longer) routes because their husbands were legal permanent residents; and Ana found the least certain and longest route because her abuser was an undocumented immigrant.

Laura

Laura was born in Mexico, where she met Carlos when she was eleven years old. They got married after eight years of dating. Laura and Carlos were living in very poor conditions, so one month after their marriage, Carlos migrated to the United States in order to provide for them. Eight months later, he returned with some savings. Their living conditions improved, but very little. Soon after, Laura got pregnant. "I was very happy," she recalled, "but Carlos was not very excited." When Laura was three and a half months pregnant, Carlos hit her with his belt. As Laura remembered, "We had to run to the hospital because I was in too much pain. We got there right in time; the doctor said that my baby and I could have died." In shock, Carlos asked Laura to forgive him and promised never to beat her again. Laura stayed with him.

Their first son was born, but Carlos "was not affectionate with the baby or with me." Laura was hurt and confused, wondering, "Why didn't he let me use any kind of birth control? Why did he want me to have more children if he didn't care about us?" Soon, Laura got pregnant again, and the birth of their second child did not ease Carlos's indifference. Carlos used to travel back and forth to the United States to earn a living, but he sent back very little money. Laura explained, "We had three more children. But Carlos never changed his apathy toward them. Eventually, I began to doubt about his feelings. He used to spend more time away than at home, and I found out that he was cheating on me." When Laura confronted him, he violently refused to tell her the truth. Later on, he apologized and promised not to do it again.

Carlos had obtained his legal permanent residency and decided that Laura could move with him to the United States permanently. At first, they brought only their youngest daughter, but seven months later, they were able to bring the rest of their children with them. Laura got pregnant again, and their seventh child was born in the United States. "I thought that our lives here were going to be better, but Carlos continued to mistreat us," Laura recalled. Carlos psychologically abused Laura, and verbally and physically abused all their children. He had taken up drinking and spent a lot of time partying with his friends. "I felt alone, isolated, and very sad. But I never thought of leaving Carlos."

Four years later, Laura got pregnant again. Things between her and Carlos did not change. She recalled: "Carlos was not excited and did not take care of our newborn or me. He would not pick our older children up from school, attend parents' meetings, or play or go out with them. He would always say that I was worthless. He never thought that raising our children and taking care of our home had any value. I did not know what to do about it; I only wished things would change for the better."

She got pregnant again two years later. "This time," she explained, "Carlos was angry. He told me that he did not want another baby from me and that he was not going to be able to maintain them all. He told me that if I wanted to have that baby, I would have to go out to work to pay for the costs." He began to be particularly pejorative toward her; "he would yell at and humiliate me at all times." Laura was feeling "very bad and depressed, and when I went to the clinic to check on my baby, the doctors found that my baby had died in my womb." Carlos picked Laura up from the clinic because he received the emergency phone call, but on their way home he "did not show any emotions. I thought that he was happy that I had lost the baby." After two weeks, Laura did not have the natural abortion the doctors had told her would occur. She wanted to go to the clinic again, but Carlos did not allow her because it was going to be "too expensive." Instead, he wanted her to go back to Mexico to take care of her health because the cost would be cheaper. Laura recounted:

> I did not want to leave my children or the United States. I was in so much pain, and I was scared not to be able to return. But Carlos forced me to take the trip to Mexico. I stayed there for four months recuperating from the surgical procedure. I stayed in touch with my children, but I wanted to come back, I missed them so much! Also, I knew that Carlos was spending the nights out of our home and was not taking care of the children at all.

Upon her return to Texas, Laura could tell that Carlos had changed. His mistreatment and neglect continued as usual, but "I perceived that there was something else going on." Three days after her return, Carlos left. "He never told me where or why. I thought that he would eventually go back to our home, but he did not. I was very depressed. I wanted to kill myself. I didn't have a job, or money, and I didn't know how I was going to maintain all of my children." After Carlos's departure, the older sons dropped out of school, and the rest of the children began performing badly at school. They were all suffering the consequences of abuse, neglect, and abandonment.

One day, Carlos called Laura and confessed that he was going to have a child with his mistress, which was the reason he had left them. "I thought that I was going crazy," Laura recalled. "I could not believe that he had chosen his mistress over our family and me. I had a nervous breakdown, and one of my sons called an ambulance." Laura recuperated, but she fell into a severe depression. All her children were very upset and begged her "to be well and not to leave them alone." Sometimes, Carlos would call Laura and tell her that he would come visit their children. "I would dress them up and they would wait anxiously for him. He would never show up. It was very disheartening, particularly for the younger ones."

Months later, Carlos told Laura that he regretted his deeds and wanted to start all over again. He made plans to move to another state. Laura and the children met him, and they all went away together. "Carlos dropped us in a house where other men were living and promised to come back in a couple of hours. He did not return. Later, I realized that he had taken us there to distance us from him." After several days, Laura "took courage" and brought all her children back home. They were all very disturbed and grew less and less tolerant of Carlos's abuse.

Two years after this incident, Carlos reappeared. He met Laura and convinced her to give him a ride back to his house because he had been drinking too much. "I resisted but finally agreed to drive him. When we arrived at his home, Carlos locked the doors of the truck and raped me." Laura contracted a sexually transmitted disease from this attack. After this episode, Laura never saw Carlos again. She got in touch with ORA, as suggested by one of the doctors who treated her. Laura was accepted as a client at ORA (Carlos had never filed for divorce and was still a legal permanent resident) and went through the process secretly to surprise her children—"I have not told them that I have been coming here to *arreglar los papeles* [fix the papers, that is, regularize their immigration status]." Teary, Laura told us about the vision she had: "Imagine, to give them such a surprise. . . . That is what they want, to *arreglar los papeles*!" USCIS approved Laura's VAWA self-petition eighteen months later: Laura's and her children's removal conditions were waived, and they received renewable work permits. They are now waiting an estimated five to eight years to obtain their legal permanent residencies.

Martha

Martha, who originally was from Nigeria, had come to the United States with a temporary visa as part of an international exchange program. Martha met Tom, a legal permanent resident originally from Cameroon, soon after her arrival. As she recalled, "He was very nice and attentive. I was very happy that I met him because he was the only person I knew that I could talk to in my own language." When they began dating, "he would take me out to the movies and to have dinner. He would take care of me, buy food for my apartment, fill up the fridge, and treat me very nicely. I was having a good time with him; I was happy. The only problem was that Tom was very jealous." After six months, Tom and Martha decided to get married. "I am a Christian," she explained, "and I was not comfortable with the fact that we had been dating and having sexual relations without being married. I thought it was sinful, so I wanted to get married to Tom. He also wanted to get married, so we made our plans. I didn't think it was too fast, because I was in love." The first two months of their marriage were very good. Tom filed the immigration papers on Martha's behalf so she would be able to stay with him in the United States.

Soon after, Tom's behavior began to change. First, he cheated on Martha. When she confronted him, he said, "I don't love you anymore; I love somebody else." Martha was "crushed." Tom left and was gone for days. When he returned home, he did not care about her feelings. "I was very upset, but it didn't matter to him. He began to treat me very bad all the time. I was very sad and couldn't understand why my husband was doing that to me. Eventually things got so bad that I thought the best option would be to get a divorce." As soon as Martha told Tom, he began to threaten her with her immigration status. She recalled:

> He would say that he was going to call immigration to cancel my papers, and that they would come to pick me up and ship me back to Africa. I didn't care about his threats. I didn't want to be in a relationship like that anymore; it was too painful. I preferred to go back to my country rather than stay here with Tom treating me so poorly.

I proceeded to file for a divorce. I couldn't take his abuse anymore; he would curse at me, he would go out to strip clubs and tell me about it, and he would use my debit card to buy things for other women. It was terrible. I couldn't take it anymore.

Martha separated from Tom, but he began to stalk her at the apartment where she was living and at her workplace (he would scream, "Immigration's coming! Don't you want to come back to me?"). He also retrieved her application to become a legal permanent resident in the United States. However, the day of the last hearing of their divorce, Tom begged Martha for forgiveness, saying that "he had given his life to Christ and that he was going through deep change. He promised me that he was committed to improving his behavior." Martha accepted his apologies, and they moved back in together. Their reunion was positive: "My husband was the perfect man—he respected me and treated me well." He also resubmitted her immigration paperwork for her to be able to stay legally in this country. Martha was pleased to see that he had changed for the better, especially after she found out that they were expecting a baby. Tom was caring during Martha's pregnancy. "We were very happy," she said.

Seven months after their daughter was born, Tom's behavior began to change. First, he would get annoyed with the baby. Then, he began to have issues with his ex-wife because she did not like the fact that their son was spending so much time with Martha, Tom, and the baby girl in their apartment. Martha was treating Tom's son "as well as I was treating my own daughter because that was the right thing to do in my view." But, "I didn't want to cause any problems with the ex-wife, so I started spending less time with my stepson. Then that caused problems too, because Tom said that I hated his son." Martha "tried to explain that that wasn't true," but to no avail, and "Tom would react by getting angry." Finally, Tom started to spend more time with his ex-wife and son in their house than with Martha and their daughter, which "upset" Martha. "Every time that I tried to talk with him about my feelings, he would ignore me. Completely. I felt that he did not care for our daughter or for me. This made me feel worse." Soon, Martha and Tom began to argue all the time, and Tom would get very aggressive: "He would scream, curse, throw things around, and break and punch things. I reacted by keeping quiet and hoping that things would change. My daughter would see what was happening, and she would stay, 'Stop, Daddy!' over and over again. I soon realized that I didn't want her to grow up seeing this violence. I knew it wasn't a good environment for her."

With the intention of appeasing Tom, Martha would "go to church and pray for this nightmare to cease." She tried to stay calm whenever Tom was aggressive, even if his "violence and screams" drove her "crazy." He would get "extremely angry" and humiliate Martha whenever she talked with him about "money, our household, or other marital things." One night, as Martha was cooking dinner:

> Tom came to the kitchen and suddenly began to argue, scream, and hit things. I tried to stay calm and not to scream or get mad. My husband ended up hitting the glass lid of the pot in which I was cooking. He destroyed the glass lid. I had to throw the whole dinner out because it was filled with broken glass. It was a horrible moment, especially when I heard my daughter saying "No, Daddy! No, Daddy! Stop, Daddy!" I grabbed my daughter and took her with me to the bedroom. I was scared that he was going to harm us. My daughter had said on other occasions, "Daddy is so, so angry!" After he calmed down, I went back to the kitchen and cleaned everything up.

A friend of Martha's perceived her sadness and, after finding out about her problems, suggested that she go to a shelter for battered women. Initially, Martha resisted the idea because she thought that she had to have been a victim of physical abuse, and that her contact with the shelter would result in Tom being put in jail. Martha's friend reassured her that she should not be frightened and convinced her to reach out. The shelter welcomed Martha and gave her the contact information for ORA so she could arrange her immigration status. Martha did not move into the shelter because she used to work during the night and did not want to leave her daughter alone in the shelter while she was out at work. She did, however, call ORA. Martha had decided to move on with her life; while she applied for VAWA, she began divorce procedures and started to save money in order to move to an apartment with her daughter where they could live in a peaceful environment. Martha told me, "I wish I could stay in this country with my daughter because she was born here, and her father lives here. I want her to continue to be able to see her father, even if we are divorced." Martha's VAWA self-petition was completed at ORA and approved by USCIS in fourteen months; a few months later, she received her legal permanent residency.

Rosa

Rosa was originally from Mexico and had migrated to the United States to find a job that would allow her family to survive. After two years, she met Mateo, who also was from Mexico but had lived in Texas for several years and had obtained his legal permanent residency. Mateo and Rosa fell in love, got married, and had a baby. Mateo's aggression began soon afterward. Rosa and her baby had endured all kinds of abuse—physical, verbal, emotional, economic, and legal. One of the many violent incidents resulted in Mateo's arrest, which several months later led to his deportation. More than a year had passed when Rosa found out about ORA's services at an outreach session in her neighborhood's church. ORA took Rosa's case because she appeared to qualify under VAWA as an abused spouse of a resident. However, as soon as ORA found out that Mateo had lost his residency status and been deported, Rosa's case was closed. It was too late. Rosa missed the two-year window of opportunity to become a citizen through VAWA after her resident abuser had been deported, even if the deportation was somewhat related to domestic violence charges. In addition, she missed her chance to find relief through VTVPA because at the time of the violent incident, she did not get involved in the police investigation against Mateo. Rosa's quest for citizenship was finished.

Manuela

Also from Mexico, Manuela had found her way up north to escape poverty. Her mother and her daughter were still in Mexico and had been living off Manuela's remittances. Similar to the other women, Manuela met and fell in love with a man who had cared for her. José was Mexican, too, and had become a legal permanent resident years before meeting Manuela. Amid plans of bringing Manuela's mother and daughter they got married. The joyful times faded as José began abusing alcohol and drugs. Despite her disappointment and sadness, Manuela tried her best to appease José and help him fight his addictions. However, he remained physically, verbally, and emotionally abusive and threatened Manuela with deportation. Eventually, José abandoned them. As Manuela tried to make ends meet, a friend told her about another person who was in a similar situation and was being helped by ORA. Manuela approached the organization and completed and submitted her VAWA self-petition to USCIS. Months later, ORA received a denial of her application: José had lost his legal permanent residency status because of drug dealing and was deported between the time ORA had received a positive result to its routine check of residency status of the abuser and Manuela's self-petition was prepared and sent by ORA and processed by USCIS. That was the end of Manuela's chances to become a citizen of the United States.

Ana

Ana, an immigrant from Mexico looking for better opportunities for her and her family, had married Pedro, also an undocumented Mexican immigrant, in Texas. Ana had been enjoying her marriage for only two weeks when Pedro began to be abusive toward her. Pedro cheated on Ana, and when she expressed her wishes to divorce him, he held her hostage and hit, threatened, and raped her repeatedly. He lied to Ana and convinced her that she could not do anything about his behavior because she did not have documents. He told her that if she called the police, both of them would be deported, vowing that if they were sent back to Mexico, he would brutally punish her there. Ana had been isolated from her family and friends, and she was "in panic." At first, Pedro forbade Ana to work; later he forced her to work and kept her salary.

Ana tried to end the relationship several times, but Pedro never let her go. She became pregnant with Pedro's child from forced intercourse, but he accused her of cheating and did not believe that the baby was his (he threatened Ana that "he would do DNA tests to prove that he was right"). His family convinced him to take care of the baby, but he did so very poorly. Pedro "would hit me, pull my hair, undress me forcefully, and accuse me of being with other men. The baby would not stop crying. He would ignore him and let him cry and cry."

A year later, Ana got pregnant again against her will. She explained, "He used to hide my pills, and I ended up pregnant once again. He was not a good father; he was impatient and mistreated the kids. However, all he wanted me for was to have many kids, so I would stay home all the time. During the pregnancy he continued with his usual behavior: lies, screams, arguments, fights, alcohol." Ana's feeling of entrapment continued to grow not only because Pedro was violent toward her but also because his family deceived her as they protected Pedro, even if they knew about his violent behavior and his extramarital affairs, including the upcoming birth of a child from "one of the girls he was with." Ana recalled, "I was very depressed, I began to lose my patience with the kids; it was an awful time."

She wanted to end her relationship, but she was terrified and confused. Pedro "would threaten me that he was going to take the kids away from me, and I believed that he was able and was going to do so. Someone had told me that if I didn't have a job, money, and a house, he would be able to take the kids away from me." But soon, Ana reached her limit, found a job, and moved out with her children. At first, Pedro left her alone, but after several months, he became obsessed with her:

> He stalked me at work; he wanted to find out where I was living. He would wait for me at the bus stop. I kept changing my routes not to run into him. He found out where the kids were, so he would go there and wait for me. He wanted to see the kids, but I didn't want him to do so. The oldest one had been very much affected by the separation. I didn't want him to be with the kids. By then, I already knew that he could be punished for all his deeds, so I wasn't so fearful. I knew that I could get a divorce and stay with the kids, even though he would say that I was talking nonsense. He had brought me some papers for me to sign, but I didn't sign them and took them to a lawyer.

Ana began divorce proceedings. Pedro found out where she was living, and one night "he came to my apartment and raped me. I got pregnant again." The lawyer suggested that Ana "stop the divorce proceedings so the new baby would be legally his," but after the birth, Ana restarted the paperwork. Eventually, she got the divorce and obtained custody and supervision of her children. However, Pedro did not stop harassing her. After a couple of months:

> I went to pick up the kids, and there he was, with all of them. I went in the house to pay [his aunt for taking care of the children], and then he forced me into a room. I resisted. His aunt was in the living room, but she didn't pay attention; she thought we were talking. Once in the room, he raped me. As soon as I was able to leave, I ran away, I was very scared and upset. On my way out, I touched his aunt's hand and said, "Thank you." His aunt was in shock. I ran away from the house and told the kids to get in the car quickly. I was all beaten, and my clothes were torn. He ran toward the car and pulled my hair to stop me from leaving, but I managed to start the car and leave. The kids were confused; they were asking what happened. They were screaming to their dad to leave me alone. He gave the kids money.

The kids were crying on the ride back home. Once we arrived at the apartment, I showered and changed. Then, I took the kids to [a] pizza [parlor] to make them feel better. I was destroyed.

Ana called her lawyer, who put her in touch with a local shelter for battered women that also provided counseling. The psychologist at the shelter suggested that she call the police. Then, she made a report, which led her to find out about her immigration options. She got in touch with ORA and began to work on her U visa. Her successful cooperation with the police provided her with certification to request protection under VTVPA. After two years, Ana was granted U visa interim relief for three years. She renewed her employment authorization on a yearly basis, and once U visa regulations were released by USCIS in 2007, she applied for the visa.[21] If USCIS were to approve Ana's application, her U visa would be dated back to the time she received interim relief. Three years after that date, Ana would be able to apply for her legal permanent residency.[22]

Legacies of Racialized Citizenship

The cases of Angela, Laura, Martha, Rosa, Manuela, and Ana exemplify the gradation of benefits that battered immigrants may obtain depending on their abuser's citizenship status and their own national origin, and independently from their intimate violence experiences. This gradation reflects the long-lasting centrality of race and ethnicity in the United States' efforts to define its nationhood. Birthright, naturalization, and immigration laws overtly sustained race as a legitimate source of differentiation among individuals from the very beginnings of this country until 1965—a phase during which "being a 'white person' was a condition for acquiring citizenship."[23] Early examples are the 1790 congressional provision "to establish a uniform rule of naturalization for aliens who were 'free white males' and who had two years' residence," which excluded Native Americans, "indentured servants, slaves, and most women,"[24] and the 1798 Alien and Sedition Laws, aimed at protecting the nation from "foreign influence," largely targeted at "Irish immigrants and French refugees" with political views in line with the French Revolution.[25] During the nineteenth century, and parallel to the expansion of its frontiers, the new nation promoted immigration, emphasizing the "economic benefits of abundant immigration," with the enactment of the first comprehensive federal immigration law in 1864.[26] However, this welcoming spirit was targeted at "the *right kind* of immigrants";[27] "Irish and German Catholics on the East Coast and . . . Chinese and Mexicans on the West Coast"[28] generated xenophobic resistance that was reflected in nativist groups combating the "alien menace."[29] In 1870, the Chinese were "denied the opportunity to naturalize,"[30] and in 1875, Chinese women were "disallowed entry" because they had been brought as prostitutes.[31] The anti-Chinese sentiment and policies would culminate in the enactment of the Chinese Exclusion Act in 1882, which excluded workers for ten years and "effectively slammed the door on all Chinese immigration."[32] In 1908, a gentleman's agreement between the United States and Japan diplomatically set limits to Japanese immigration as anti-Japanese sentiment was growing along with Japan's strength. According to the agreement, Japan restricted immigration to the United States in exchange for permitting Japanese wives and children to reunite with their families in the United States.[33] In 1913, California passed the Alien Land Law (later copied by other ten states), which "prohibited 'aliens ineligible for citizenship' from owning land"[34] or "property," with the aim of deterring migration, principally from Japan.[35]

Exclusionary patterns were to be sealed for four decades with the enactment of the complementary immigration acts of 1917 and 1924. The former represented qualitative restrictions, requiring all newcomers "over sixteen years old, who were physically capable of reading, to be able to read English or some other language or dialect."[36] The latter represented quantitative restrictions; it "adopted a national origins formula that eventually based the quota of each nationality on the number of foreign-born persons of that national origin in the United States in 1890."[37] While both acts were targeted mostly at limiting "immigration from southern and eastern Europe," they also closed the doors to all Asian attempts to immigrate,[38] under the justification of "the racial superiority of Anglo-Saxons, the fact that immigrants would cause the lowering of wages, and the unassimilability of foreigners, while citing the usual threats to the nation's social unity and order posed by immigration."[39] Because of these restrictions, cheap and nearby Mexican labor was very much in demand; to maintain it, the "head tax and literacy requirement" of the 1917 act were "legally waived for Mexicans," who were allowed to immigrate to do various kinds of work, including agricultural labor, under the so-called Ninth Proviso.[40] After the stock market crash of 1929, Mexican laborers' luck changed as they were massively repatriated. In 1942, the United States instituted the labor importation program with Mexico (the so-called bracero program) aimed at regulating temporary agricultural migration. Under this program, which, along with its amendments, remained in place until 1964, Mexican "temporary workers enjoyed few of the protections that the law guaranteed them, and employer abuses ran rampant";[41] "even though the braceros were invited 'guests,' fears of a brown 'invasion' grew with their presence."[42] Anti-Mexican sentiments congealed in the so-called Operation Wetback, which "indiscriminately deported more than one million citizens and noncitizens in 1954 alone."[43] The McCarran-Walter Act of 1952 continued to prioritize Western European immigrants over all others,[44] adding specific measures against "un-American" immigrants, those who were subversives, communists, and/or homosexuals.[45]

By 1965, in resonance with the civil rights movement, immigration laws were amended to be stripped of racial- and ethnic-based exclusionary clauses, embracing "colorblindness in immigration admissions."[46] Besides immediate relatives of citizens entering as nonquota immigrants, the new Immigration Act allocated different quota slots, numerical limits, and preferences to the Eastern and Western Hemispheres. The former received 170,000 quota slots (80 percent for family members and 20 percent for employment seekers), with a maximum of 20,000 per country. The latter received 120,000 quota slots without country-specific numerical limitations or family or labor preferences.[47] These regulations abolished the national origins quotas, but ultimately, the quota restrictions negatively affected certain nations that had had and would have higher migration flows—Mexico and Asian countries (which have since then accumulated the largest backlogs in family reunification categories). Mexico's situation was critical particularly after the amendments of 1976, which capped all Western Hemisphere countries to 20,000 as well—this resulted in the deportation of 781,000 Mexicans and fewer than 100,000 immigrants from the rest of the world in that year alone.[48] The implementation of massive deportation operations, such as Operation Cooperation of 1982, never seemed to solve "the problem of undocumented aliens,"[49] particularly from the "out of control"[50] southern border, and in 1986, the Immigration Reform and Control Act aimed to do so by different means. This act provided amnesty (legalization provisions) to undocumented immigrants who had been residing in the United States since before 1982 and to agricultural workers who had been working in this country for at least ninety days between 1985 and 1986. The legalization process was complicated and presented various exclusion grounds, and the number of applicants was lower than expected (the 2.7 million who applied represented "less than half of those who were actually eligible").[51] Mexican applicants were predominant under both the pre-1982 and the agricultural workers provisions (with 70 and 82 percent, respectively), distantly followed by Salvadorans (8 percent) and Guatemalans (3 percent) for pre-1982, and by Haitians (3.4 percent) and Salvadorans (2 percent) for farmworkers.[52] The act also imposed sanctions against employers who knowingly hired undocumented immigrants, but these measures were unsuccessful, particularly because they fostered high rates of discrimination against documented immigrants of color, mostly Latina/o and Asian.[53] Finally, the act implemented the so-called diversity programs to help immigration from countries that had been adversely affected by the 1965 Immigration Act—that is, those that had sent fewer immigrants to the United States after the act than before. These programs ended up promoting immigration from developed European countries, like Great Britain, Germany, and France, but not from any African countries, which had sent fewer immigrants than prior to 1965. Implicitly, the "diversity programs" counterbalanced the "undesired" influx of so many nonwhite, non-European immigrants.[54] All these measures to curb undocumented (nonwhite) immigration were strengthened with Border Patrol operations, that is, with the steep militarization of the U.S.-Mexico frontier, in the 1990s. These programs, like Operation Blockade (1993) in Texas, Operation Gatekeeper (1994) in California, Operation Safeguard (1994) in Arizona, and Operation Rio Grande (1997) in Texas, not only failed to reduce the flow of undocumented migration but also increased the fatalities of Mexican and other border-crossing immigrants;[55] indeed, the Border Patrol has "had a reputation for committing human rights abuses against immigrants and U.S. citizens of Mexican ancestry. . . . the Border Patrol has historically been plagued by reports of brutality, shootings, beatings, and killings."[56] In 1990, with Asian and Latina/o (documented and undocumented) immigration continuing to predominate regardless of all measures taken to curtail it, a new immigration act concentrated on attracting skilled workers from *other* parts of the world by creating new categories for employment- and investment-based immigration.[57]

All in all, since 1965, racial and ethnic bars to citizenship have remained implicit in regulations with "seemingly neutral"[58] language or "nonracial terms, but their effects usually [have] disadvantaged nationals from certain countries."[59] As Hill Collins maintains:

Whites constitute the most valuable citizens. In this racialized nation-state, Native Americans, African-Americans, Mexican-Americans, and Puerto Ricans become second-class citizens, whereas people of color from the Caribbean, Asia, Latin America, and Africa encounter more difficulty becoming naturalized citizens than immigrants from European nations. Because all of these groups are not White and thereby lack appropriate blood ties, they are deemed to be less-worthy actual and potential U.S. citizens.[60]

Moreover, racial and ethnic bars have survived in the "simultaneously ignorant and informed"[61] racist practices of immigration and law enforcement officers, legal providers, and laymen, which obliquely exclude certain groups of people.[62] Contemporary racial and ethnic discrimination is based on "subtle, institutional and apparently nonracial"[63] practices and mechanisms feeding the new "dominant racial ideology"[64]—a "color-blind racism" that "otherizes softly" while maintaining "white privilege . . . without naming those who it subjects and those who it rewards," as theorized by Bonilla-Silva.[65]

Just as they do not escape the pervasiveness of gender and sexual discrimination, VAWA and VTVPA are permeated by ideologies and practices of racialized citizenship.[66] First, if abusers are U.S. citizens by birth or naturalization, their victims can obtain legal permanent residency as soon as their VAWA applications are approved, and can apply for citizenship three years later. This was the case for Angela, who received her and her sons' residency within four months of the approval of her VAWA self-petition. Second, if abusers are legal permanent residents, their victims can also obtain legal permanent residency and apply for citizenship three years later. However, the waiting period to obtain residency varies depending on the nationality of the battered immigrant, ranging from less than one year to more than eight, depending on the size of USCIS's backlog in processing all kinds of petitions from the applicant's country of origin. The longer a petitioner has to wait for her residency, the longer the path toward citizenship. Laura's and Martha's cases illustrate this point. Laura, originally from Mexico and married to an abusive legal permanent resident, had to wait between five and eight years to obtain her residency after her VAWA petition was approved. Until then, she could not travel outside the United States, even if she had obtained deferred action (which meant that she could not be deported), and had an employment authorization (which she had to renew and pay for on a yearly basis). Laura was going to be able to apply for citizenship between eight and eleven years after the approval of her VAWA self-petition. In contrast, Martha, originally from Nigeria, and also married to an abusive legal permanent resident, had to wait less than one year after the approval of her VAWA application to obtain her residency. Martha did not have to renew her employment authorization, was able to travel abroad within a year of the approval of her VAWA self-petition, and could apply for citizenship three years later, that is, four years after the approval of her self-petition.

The noncitizen status of the abusers damages their victims not only in terms of the length of the process but also in terms of its certainty. On the one hand, if the abusive resident is deported (i.e., loses his status as legal permanent resident) due to an incident of domestic violence, the survivor has two years to file a VAWA self-petition or else her chances to gain legal status perish—as in the case of Rosa, a Mexican survivor of abuse committed by a legal permanent resident who had been deported too long before she was able to initiate her VAWA self-petition. On the other hand, if the abusive resident is deported due to other reasons before the VAWA application of the battered immigrant is approved by USCIS, all chances to gain legal status for the applicant perish instantaneously, as in the case of Manuela, a Mexican survivor of an abusive legal permanent resident who was deported because of drug dealing and lost his status.

Third, if abusers are neither U.S. citizens nor legal permanent residents, victims cannot apply for VAWA but instead can apply for a U visa under VTVPA. This was the case for Ana, originally from Mexico and married to an undocumented immigrant from the same country. To change her undocumented status, Ana had to collaborate with the police on the scrutiny of her abuser's deeds against her. The police had to certify to USCIS that Ana had been victimized and had been helpful to law enforcement. Ana had succeeded in proving her goodwill and good behavior, and after two years of working on her application, she was able to obtain U visa interim relief.[67] She was allowed to stay in the United States without fear of deportation and was permitted to work legally for up to three years. After U visa regulations were released in 2007, Ana applied for the visa. If her application were to be approved by USCIS, Ana would be able to apply for residency after three years from the date her interim relief was granted. USCIS would then evaluate her eligibility for legal permanent residency on two key points: her lawfulness (applicants are supposed to have a "clean" criminal record) and her resourcefulness (applicants are supposed to be economically independent, that is, not living on state funding, such as social welfare and the like). While all battered immigrants must satisfy these two major parameters when applying for legal permanent residency, the closer in time it is to their abusive treatment, the easier it is for USCIS to contextualize crimes or economic vulnerability within their domestic violence experiences and, perhaps, to be more lenient in granting them residency. Moreover, U visa holders who seek legal permanent residency probably will have to wait for a decision depending on the backlog USCIS has in processing applications from their country of origin (ranging from less than one year to more than eight for spouses). In this regard, survivors of violence perpetrated by undocumented immigrants are similar to survivors of violence by abusive residents—both of whom are at a disadvantage compared with survivors of violence perpetrated by U.S. citizens.

The disparities between the cases of Angela, Laura, Martha, Rosa, Manuela, and Ana reveal how the law prioritizes the abusers' nationality and immigration status over the immigrant survivors of violence and the wrongdoings against them. No matter the intensity of the abuse, if the perpetrator is not a citizen, the length and certainty of the path to citizenship are negatively affected. All in all, the battered immigrant provisions included in VAWA and VTVPA do not apply equally to all survivors. In reflecting the long-standing discriminatory character of immigration laws, VAWA and VTVPA add to the mechanisms through which the United States reinforces its ideals of Americanness along racial and ethnic hierarchies—exclusionist hierarchies that have sustained "a Eurocentric (originally western Eurocentric) vision of America that [has] idealized the *true* American as white, Anglo-Saxon, English-speaking, and Christian."[68] While racial, ethnic, gender, and sexual orientation biases have jeopardized access to citizenship for battered immigrants, it is their intersection with class that clearly reveals the incidence of the stratified structure of immigration laws.

Class Discrimination

Also in contradiction to these laws' spirit of shielding all survivors of violence, regardless of their background or status, the requirements for filing a VAWA self-petition or a U visa application under VTVPA end up excluding the most destitute immigrants. Even if advocates have struggled to remove economic barriers from poor survivors' access to citizenship by requesting fee waivers from USCIS and creating nonprofit legal organizations, the poorest immigrants continue to find the process unaffordable and, thus, unattainable. The case of Susana illustrates this aspect.

Susana

Susana, a Mexican immigrant, came to the intake appointment with her two-year-old daughter. "Gisella was born prematurely," Susana informed me. "That's why she doesn't look her age. She's been sick since she was born. But now she's sleeping, so she won't bother us." I told Susana not to worry about the baby disturbing us, and we began with the routine questionnaire. Susana and her baby had been exposed to extreme violence and cruelty from her husband, Ivan, a legal permanent resident originally from Mexico. Due to her father's abuse and neglect, Gisella was born earlier than expected. As Susana recalled, "He never took care of me while I was pregnant, never went with me to the doctor, even if I was ill. He used to hit me, curse at me. He would not allow me to work and would not give me money, both before and after Gisella's birth." Ivan neglected and abused Susana and their daughter to the point of locking them up in "a one-bedroom apartment infested with rats, without food or heat during part of the winter." If Susana asked for help, he would say, "How come? Isn't it that women always manage as mothers? You should take care of yourself and your baby. What a shame!" Still, Ivan prohibited Susana from leaving the apartment to work or to do whatever else she needed to "be able to manage." One time, Susana told Ivan that she was going to press charges against him in order to get child support, but "he reacted so violently that I discarded the idea and never reported the abuse to the police." Susana was visibly depressed and upset, particularly because of her daughter's poor health. She had left Ivan. She found shelter with family members, but she was still living in very poor conditions.

As Gisella was waking up, I told Susana that she seemed to be eligible to apply for VAWA and that, in a matter of days, I would be able to tell her if the lawyer thought so too and accepted her as a client at ORA. Susana wanted to know exactly what that meant, so I explained the steps she would have to follow and the benefits of obtaining VAWA protections. For a second, Susana was hopeful, smiling. But when I went through the list of paperwork she would have to bring to complete her VAWA application, she looked serious and concerned. While rocking Gisella, she explained: "I do not have those documents. . . . How much will I have to pay? I don't have that kind of money. I'm barely making ends meet. . . .

Letters of support from friends and relatives? I don't think I can get any. I know I won't. . . . Counseling, I don't know, I'm afraid. Do I have to do it? Is it expensive? How many times do I have to come over here, to this office? How long does the whole process take?" Susana had to go; she had to work, and the baby was restless and hungry. She promised to call us in a week to find out if her case had been approved by ORA (I would have called her myself except that Susana did not have a phone or any person who could serve as a trustworthy contact between her and ORA).

ORA took her case; there were no doubts about Susana's eligibility to apply for VAWA. However, Susana did not go through the daunting application process. She explained, "I will not be able to get all the necessary documentation, or the money. I don't have the time either. And Gisella, I have to take care of her. . . . Maybe in a while I can do it, but not now. Now, I can't." Susana never returned to ORA.

Hidden Classism

Susana's case poignantly illustrates the hidden classism of the immigration portions of VAWA and VTVPA and how these reflect the immigration system as a whole. Even if critical analyses of the immigration system have mostly emphasized its racial, ethnic, gender, and sexual aspects, class has historically played a major discriminatory role as well.[69] As Hing put it, "The Statue of Liberty's 'give us your tired, your poor' refrain written by political dissenter Emma Lazarus in 1883 was definitely not the philosophy of the colonies, nor it is today's philosophy, as modern laws exclude those immigrants who are 'likely to become a public charge.'"[70] More specifically, the United States has had a history of, on the one hand, welcoming poor immigrants as long as they arrived to become part of an inexpensive (exploitable and disposable) labor force while, on the other hand, objecting to poor immigrants as soon as they sought to be incorporated into the polity as residents or citizens.[71] This double standard in regard to class was applied to migratory flows from all over the world; however, in its intersections with race, ethnicity, gender, and sexual orientation, it tended to prioritize white, Anglo-Saxon, Protestant men and heterosexuals—an order that has been maintained through the selective allocation of citizenship and labor rights, as Glenn has documented.[72]

In the 1780s, colonists feared that "Europe was using the New World as a dumping ground for the lazy and disabled,"[73] and "paupers were disqualified because their neediness rendered them unable to know and act for the common good."[74] In the 1870s, resistance to the massive arrival of poor foreigners emerged mostly from nativist pressures fearing that the domestic workforce would be displaced by cheaper immigrant labor, culminating in the Chinese Exclusion Act in 1882.[75] All immigrants who were "deemed likely to become public charges" were excluded through the Immigration Act of 1891,[76] and immigrant laborers who had not come from such destitute conditions and/or had achieved a higher working-class status in the United States, like the Japanese, faced fierce resentment from white, native workers who also felt threatened by their presence and achievements, eventually resulting in labor laws curbing foreign labor, the gentleman's agreement of 1908, and the Alien Land Laws of 1913.[77] "Adult immigrants unable to read a simple passage in some language" were denied entry through the literacy law of 1917, which even if it was aimed racially and ethnically at curbing southern and eastern European immigration, affected the poorer newcomers, that is, those who were illiterate.[78] Refusal to include the poor as part of the polity was also reflected in calls during the 1930s for the exclusion of "hardworking, submissive and reliable" Filipino workers (which eventually occurred as the Philippines gained independence as a country in 1946, meaning that Filipinos in the United States lost their noncitizen national status, and those willing to immigrate were restricted by a quota of fifty visas per year).[79] The massive repatriation of Mexican laborers in the 1930s, followed by the bracero program in the 1940s, also reasserted the disposability of immigrant labor (when needed, immigrant workers were welcomed and exploited; when not needed, they were rejected and repatriated).[80] The termination of the bracero program in 1964 together with the application of quotas restricting Mexican immigration in the 1970s ended up keeping "Mexican migrant workers outside the American working class and outside the national body"[81] and making the exploitation of cheap labor an "exclusively undocumented" affair,[82] "a condition that has endured into the twenty-first century."[83] Indeed, since the act of 1965, foreigners seeking to migrate to the United States for labor reasons have had to get approval from the Department of Labor,[84] a measure that, although intended to protect the domestic labor force, resulted in increasing the number of poorer immigrants who entered without documents. These kinds of controlling policies have had counter-effects, as exemplified by the sophisticated legalization process offered by the Immigration Reform and Control Act of 1986, which weeded out the most destitute immigrants, who may have been able to afford the costs of the process but were daunted by its complexity,[85] and the Immigration and Naturalization Act of 1990, which privileged permanent skilled workers and investors (able both economically and intellectually to complete all bureaucratic procedures) with 185,000 visas per year,[86] and restricted temporary unskilled (poorer) work migrants to only 10,000 visas per year, to be granted "for jobs for which qualified American workers were not available."[87] Needless to say, these formal restrictions have not stopped the flow of poor immigrants into the United States, particularly from Mexico (the economic differentials between these two countries have continued to increase, as has the demand for cheap labor in the United States).

To obtain the proper documentation to enter and stay in the United States, immigrants must have certain economic, cultural, and social capital in order to gather the right information, follow the procedure, and pay for its costs. This premise has resulted in the creation of two distinct groups of immigrants: those who are capable of navigating the system (the documented and documented-to-be), and those who are not (the undocumented). VAWA and U visa applications illustrate this phenomenon. The costs associated with these applications represent an apparent barrier for low-income immigrants. Nonprofit organizations and pro bono lawyers have tried to address this problem by offering free legal assistance to individuals who qualify by having incomes under the official poverty line (i.e., with annual earnings lower than $17,500 for a household of two in 2008)[88] and by requesting fee waivers from USCIS. While these measures have facilitated the application process for many low-income immigrants, not all costs are waived, and therefore they remain too high for the immigrants with the fewest resources and the most demands: the ability to save money on a tight budget depends not only on immigrants' income but also on the stability of their job, knowledge about how to efficiently distribute and save money, and number of children and other dependent family members. Often, the cost of the required passport photographs, criminal background checks, birth, marriage, divorce, and other certificates, medical evaluations, health tests, and vaccines, and the strongly recommended psychological counseling (all of which add up to at least $2,000 for one person if counseling is free) either slows down the application process or directly weeds out those who need the most help.

Moreover, VAWA and U visa applications require immigrants not only to possess birth certificates for the applicant and her children, the applicant's marriage certificate, divorce decrees for the applicant and her spouse, if applicable, rental or leasing contracts for all the locations where the applicant and the abuser lived together, bills for the services they contracted while living together as husband and wife, such as utilities, gas, telephone, and cable TV, and tax declarations but also to provide these documents in a very specific fashion. This list of documents must be complete, and the leasing contracts and bills must be chronologically ordered, without any gaps, to show that the applicant lived with the abusive spouse and was married "in good faith." Both the possession of and the ability to compile these documents represent a burden for immigrants; often, an abusive spouse may control access to documentation, and applicants also may not be used to systematically filing these kinds of documents (which is a regular practice for middle- and upper-class citizens but not necessarily for lower-class immigrants). Moreover, low-income immigrants (who account for the majority of the VAWA applicants, especially if they are undocumented) tend to have informal living arrangements, without leasing contracts or receipts for their weekly or monthly payments, and therefore often are unable to compile the required documentation to prove common residency with their spouse.

Besides these documents, VAWA applications must include police reports of domestic violence and/or psychological reports proving that the petitioner has been a victim of violence (sometimes police reports are enough evidence, but legal practitioners tend to request psychological reports as well to strengthen the case), and U visa petitions must be based on the battered immigrant's collaboration with the police in the investigation of the crime committed against her. These requirements are intimidating to the most destitute immigrants. On the one hand, the majority of battered immigrants trying to apply for VAWA entered the country without the proper immigration documentation and as such are considered undocumented or "illegal" individuals, which instantaneously translates to fear of official authorities (be they police or immigration officers). The fear is based on the risk of deportation and on previous negative experiences with authorities both in the United States and in the immigrant's country of origin (since the most marginal populations tend to be the most mistreated by law enforcement officers). Their fear is fed by their abusers' threats of calling the police or immigration authorities to have them deported to their countries of origin. Immigrants often believe these threats, and when they try to defy their abusers by calling the police, the abusers are quickly able to deter them from doing so, claiming that the officer will listen only to the abuser, who is the citizen or resident, head of the household, and an English speaker. Some battered immigrants who are able to break through and call the police on their abusers are lucky to have responsive and trained officers who will make sure to speak separately with each spouse and request a translator if necessary. However, my field-work revealed that many battered immigrants who call the police find their abuser's threats to be true: the police tend to talk with the English-speaking member of the household and even call immigration officials to report the undocumented individual (even if by law they are not supposed to do so). Moreover, the police tend to be more responsive if there is clear evidence of physical violence, which represents only a part of family violence cases, which always involve nonvisible psychological violence (verbal and emotional) and sometimes also include nonvisible economic abuse.

On the other hand, the majority of undocumented battered immigrants find psychological counseling a foreign, threatening, and demanding practice. While some middle- and upper-class American citizens and foreigners from certain countries may consider psychological counseling a useful tool to overcome stressful situations, working-class and poor citizens and foreigners tend not to trust or count on this tool. Religious practices instead seem to be a more common avenue to relieve stress and find explanations for undesirable situations. While some battered immigrants agree to try psychological counseling, they soon find it very demanding. Even if a battered immigrant might be able to make use of free services, she must attend an average of ten sessions for the nonprofit organization to request a report about her experiences from the counselor. In order to attend at least ten sessions, the immigrant must be consistent and able to manage her work and personal schedule around the appointments, which is very difficult due to the unstable nature of the jobs held by most undocumented immigrants. Moreover, if the battered immigrant is still living with the abuser (as is often the case), making up excuses to leave every week at the same time is also risky due to the controlling and mistrustful behavior of abusive individuals. Battered immigrants applying for VAWA or a U visa must also attend their legal assistance appointments regularly in order to move forward with their cases. While the times of these appointments tend to be during regular business hours (as opposed to the free psychological services, which tend to be available in the evenings), immigrants must be able to balance all their needs (generating their own income for themselves and their children, taking care of their children and themselves, particularly if they are still living with the abusers, and, finally, trying to gain legal status). In general, even if their VAWA or U visa application is one of their highest priorities, battered immigrants tend to put their children and jobs first, which affects their consistency in keeping psychological and legal appointments and, in turn, jeopardizes their chances to advance their applications.

Overall, following bureaucratic requests, such as gathering basic documentation, responding to and relying on official authorities, and attending appointments, usually weeds out the neediest, who "encounter serious difficulties when they attempt to understand or to cope with" these normative orders.[89] As Crenshaw puts it, "Immigrant women who are socially, culturally, or economically privileged are more likely to be able to marshal all the resources needed to satisfy the . . . requirements."[90] Poor, undocumented, battered immigrants like Claudia, Luisa, or Susana were indeed unable to overcome these class-based barriers: Claudia was fearful of the police; Luisa did not meet the police standards because she did not have a steady residence, job, or phone access; and Susana did not possess the required documentation, was not able to afford the costs, and could not fathom the idea that she would have to spend so much time preparing the application while her daughter's survival needs were so urgent that she had to prioritize making a living over anything else. Among the poor immigrants who were able to go through the VAWA or U visa application process at ORA, I observed that those with a higher economic, social, and cultural standing were consistently able to navigate it quicker than those with a lower economic, social, and cultural standing. Finally, I believe that most of the battered immigrants who never dared to approach ORA or other community organizations, because of misinformation, constraint, or fear, are the ones living under extremely poor conditions.

All in all, VAWA and VTVPA have not escaped the historic selective character of the immigration system in the United States or the inequalities of U.S. society, which continues to privilege male, heterosexual, white, Protestant, middle- to upper-class citizens. The spirit of these laws, which is to protect all survivors of intimate partner violence regardless of their gender, sexual orientation, race, ethnicity, class, or immigration status, is tainted with long-lasting discriminatory ideas and institutions, which, while some may argue are unavoidable, others may find testament to the need for furthering our understanding of how these inequalities are reproduced and could be challenged. In the latter vein, chapter 4 explores the informal ways in which these insidious differences are maintained at the nonprofit level; then, chapter 5 looks into the capacity that battered immigrants and advocates have to defy such pervasive inequalities.

4

Informal Barriers
to Citizenship

Having uncovered the parameters that the state employs to determine whether a battered immigrant is worthy or unworthy to become a citizen of the United States, I now look into how attorneys, legal assistants, and other immigrants' advocates act as mediators between the state and the immigrants. Do they conform to or contest immigration regulations and citizenship ideals and disciplines? Do they alter or reproduce the stratified structure of American society in their daily practice? In this chapter, I will focus first on the history and institutional development of the Organization for Refugees of America/Organización para Refugiados de América, the nonprofit organization where I spent two years working as a volunteer intern in the program to assist battered immigrants. Then, I will share the cases of immigrant survivors Clara, Silvana, Rosario, Mónica, Samuel,[1] Yolanda, Patricia, Ramona, and Leticia to illustrate ORA's role as a broker of citizenship between the state and the immigrants—what I will call a gatekeeper.

ORA's History and Institutional Development

Gender, sexual, racial, ethnic, and class barriers to citizenship embedded in the immigration system were inherited by VAWA and VTVPA. ORA staff perceived these matters, particularly the legacies of coverture, as unfortunate, but they were not committed to overcoming them. Instead, these barriers were taken as part of reality, as rules of the game, and thus were not questioned in practice. ORA staff were devoted to providing free legal services to those who could qualify within the margins of the existing legislation and were not actively advocating for changes in the law that intended to get rid of this discriminatory baggage. Arguably, their compliance reproduced the inherited inequalities. However, the fact that ORA was providing services to those who did qualify counterbalanced their political passivity (or apathy); they were working within real constraints with the aim of at least helping people in need who deserved and could access justice. ORA's exclusive focus on providing legal services was a problematic but conscious decision that had marked a shift in the history of the organization.

In 1987, when "the nature of people doing public immigration law changed from nonpolitical to very political, because of the changing origin and reasons why immigrants left their countries,"[2] the three lawyers who later formed ORA worked on a volunteer basis together with three other organizations in Texas. One was a religious group that was the first to declare sanctuary to asylum seekers in the city (and eventually was granted funds from the National Sanctuary Defense Fund), another, a shelter for Central American asylum seekers, and the third, the local chapter of the National Lawyers Guild. "Committed to advancing human rights in foreign and immigration policies,"[3] as Sophia, one of the founding lawyers told me, ORA's original mission was to provide legal assistance free of cost to Central American immigrants in Texas who had been arrested in very poor conditions in the United States and had been placed in deportation procedures. While these immigrants were deportable according to immigration laws, international conventions that applied to the United States permitted them to request asylum on the basis of reasonable fear of persecution based on race, religion, nationality, political opinion, or membership with a particular social group in their home countries. The passage of the Refugee Act of 1980 was pivotal because it brought "U.S. law into conformity with" the United Nations Protocol Relating to the Status of Refugees of 1967, eliminated special preferences to people "fleeing from communist-dominated countries or countries of the Middle-East," and differentiated between refugees and asylees.[4] However, this act had been applied selectively according to the political logic of the Cold War. The government supported Nicaraguan asylum seekers (who were supposed to be right-wing "freedom fighters" against the leftist ruling Sandinistas) "at a higher rate than most, and deportation was not enforced against Nicaraguans who were denied asylum or who simply wanted to remain in the United States."[5] On the contrary, the government labeled Guatemalan and Salvadoran asylum seekers (who were supposed to be left-wing *guerilleros* against the right-wing U.S.-supported governments of their countries) as "'economic migrants,' who were generally denied asylum and deported."[6] The government bias against Salvadorans and Guatemalans (through immigration, Border Patrol, and asylum corps officers) was further evidenced in a lawsuit filed against the Immigration and Naturalization Service (INS, which was transformed to USCIS after 2003), *Orantes-Hernandez v. Smith*, and a class action filed on their behalf, *American Baptist Churches v. Thornburgh*, both of which intended to rectify the mistreatment and provided new asylum opportunities.[7] ORA's founding lawyers struggled legally to make sure that the increasing number of Central American immigrants who were crossing the border would be included as asylees in this country, despite the Cold War political inclinations of the United States. ORA's work developed in this "very politicized" context, as Sophia explained to me, "to ensure justice for all asylum seekers."[8] Valerie, another founding lawyer of ORA, asserted:

> We were playing by the rules, but we were playing very differently; we wanted to make sure that immigration laws were serving a good purpose, so instead of accepting courts' decisions without logical arguing, we fought for the meaning of every single word of the law. Central American immigrants in the eighties were fleeing persecution and war—a war that had been financed by the United States government—and had been arrested in horrible conditions in places like *El Corralón* (the large corral) in Texas, where human rights were not respected. We were convinced that these immigrants deserved to be treated fairly; jail and deportation were not the solution. We were working for a grand cause, ideological and politically, within the broader Sanctuary movement and other nonviolent leftist organizations which believed in the supremacy of human rights over any other rights.[9]

From the very beginning, ORA's volunteer lawyers were flooded with cases, which attested to the need for free legal services for asylum seekers and other destitute immigrants. ORA's volunteers were working out of their own houses and would meet to review cases and make organizational decisions at local cafés and restaurants. In 1990, ORA was incorporated as an independent nonprofit organization, which allowed it to obtain grants from the Texas Equal Access to Justice Foundation and the Dougherty Foundation. These grants paid for a full-time director and a full-time attorney, but as ORA grew, it continued to run as a volunteer-based organization (for instance, Valerie always worked as a volunteer lawyer, and ORA actively called for and heavily relied on the work of volunteer attorneys, paralegal interviewers, researchers to substantiate the claims of asylum seekers, document translators, interpreters, court monitors, brief writers, fund-raisers, and office helpers).[10] ORA's founding lawyers eventually were able to rent a small office located in a low-income, immigrant neighborhood.

As the sociopolitical context and laws changed in the 1990s, with the end of the Cold War, the peace accords in Central America, and the change of immigration provisions for Central American asylees resulting from the *American Baptist Church v. Thornburgh* settlement agreement of 1991 and the Nicaraguan Adjustment and Central American Relief Act (NACARA) of 1997, ORA began to offer other legal services to underprivileged immigrant populations, such as representation for battered immigrants under VAWA, first enacted in 1994. In order to survive institutionally, ORA continued to apply for grants, despite increasing competition as similar organizations gained legitimacy by the state in the middle and late 1990s. While these grants ensured institutional presence, they curtailed the organization's freedom. In general, funding is accompanied by certain requirements; thus, when ORA is granted funds, its lawyers must set priorities to meet the grantor's expectations in terms of the quantity, quality, and type of cases solved. For instance, as a recipient of the Interest on Lawyers Trust Accounts (IOLTA) grant, ORA has not been allowed to do any class action suits. The enabling yet constraining power of grants has been critically analyzed, particularly in the context of nonprofit organizations as long as the restrictions have tended to moderate the radical character of grassroots movements that became institutionalized and funded or, as some have argued, co-opted.[11]

With the development and growth of the organization, its volunteer members and staff diversified. This diversification brought political conflicts and ideological differences in terms of institutional management. The executive director of ORA at the time, herself an immigrant who had worked there for twelve years, and the founding lawyers of ORA left the organization around 2003 as it grew away from its original radical character and mission. A new executive director with a nonprofit management background was hired, and ORA moved to a larger office. By 2005, ORA numbered ten employees, including three full-time attorneys. While ORA continued to rely on volunteers to take care of certain tasks, such as translation, it had gradually become an employee-based organization. The staff was unionized, and ORA's political activism was formally framed within certain limitations. While ORA staff was identified with the mission of providing justice for immigrants, my participant observation and interviews reflected the workers' political moderation. When asked to describe their jobs, employees from the 1990s to 2003 tended to emphasize the political rather than the bureaucratic aspects of their jobs, whereas those hired after 2003 tended to do the contrary.

For example, Carlos was originally a Salvadoran asylum client of ORA in 1991, who later worked as a volunteer at the organization as a means of expressing his gratitude; eventually, he became a paid employee. Carlos believed that working at ORA was a great way to "help his own."[12] Carlos worked as the organization's receptionist and also did intakes for family-based applications; he was "committed to the immigrants' cause," that is, "to the humanist reason to help immigrants, whether by offering them legal assistance or, if that were not possible, other kind of help. To struggle to help those who come to the United States in search of a better future."[13] Marina had migrated from Mexico to the United States as a child along with her parents, who were farmworkers. She became interested in working at ORA because while she was taking a course about Central America in college, a volunteer from ORA gave a guest lecture about immigrants from this region and the organization's goal of providing them with free legal assistance and justice. Marina thought it was a great mission and decided to get involved with the organization to help the immigrant community. She was "ORA's volunteer coordinator and also did outreach activities to the community, other immigrants' advocates, and law enforcement officers to educate about legal remedies for immigrants and services provided by ORA."[14]

Conversely, Jenna, Maggie, Courtney, Cathy, and John emphasized the administrative aspects of their jobs. Jenna described herself as "a legal caseworker working with, assisting, immigrants in filing petitions with immigration" and claimed that her job was "to abide by what immigration is requiring of us and the clients in order to help them obtain the benefits they are entitled to."[15] Jenna was the daughter of two Philippine immigrants, had earned a college degree in sociology, and, before being employed at ORA, had worked as a volunteer at a shelter for immigrants and as a social worker at a shelter for battered women. She emphasized that having immigrant parents was one reason, but not the main reason, she became interested in working with immigrants. Her curiosity grew from her experience as a foreign student in Mexico, where her host brother suggested to her that he was going to try to cross the border and stay in the United States. After four years or so, Jenna resigned from her job to take a trip around the world with her husband.

Maggie said that she was "part social worker, part office worker, and part advocate," and that sometimes she thought of her role "as a circus ringleader saying, 'OK, now, jump through this loop, then, jump through this one . . .', or like a chauffeur driving immigrants through this road to legality."[16] Maggie applied for the legal assistant position at ORA because she was "attracted by its mission and had tremendous respect for the organization," where some of her friends had worked. She was very excited to be able to apply her academic knowledge, since she had a college degree in Latin American studies and had learned Spanish "by doing projects in Bolivia and Ecuador." Born to U.S. citizens, she had lived in Ecuador until she was one year old.[17] Maggie worked at ORA for two years, after which she left to join a U.S. community service program for poor communities in Latin America for one year. Upon her return to the United States, Maggie began to work at a nonprofit organization on the West Coast that provides support for refugee women micro-entrepreneurship. Similarly, Courtney applied for a position at ORA because she had a friend who did this kind of work and found it interesting, and because she wanted to make use of her college degree in Spanish and international studies. Self-described as an "upper-middle-class white woman,"[18] Courtney thought that working as a legal assistant would help her if she decided to apply to law school in the future. Courtney specialized in VTVPA clients, assisting "immigrants who are victims of crime to apply for legal status in the United States."[19] Courtney left ORA after working there for more than five years and traveled through Africa. After she returned to the United States, she moved back to the same city and took a similar job at another nonprofit organization providing services for poor immigrant families.

Cathy was a lawyer, but "because it was immigration work, she did a lot of filing immigration forms and figuring out people's past immigration history."[20] As the lawyer at ORA, she supervised the legal assistants and accredited representatives by reviewing their cases and doing legal research when necessary. Cathy was an immigrant herself, born in Korea, who had gone through the naturalization process when she was eighteen years old. Her immigration status had deeply affected her development and how she saw herself in comparison to other people. As she explained, "I was always very conscious of what other people think of me, how do I sound like, what I do for a living, and all of those things, especially because I grew up in a very white community, and every time I interacted and explained what I did, that I was a citizen, it impacted my life very much."[21] Cathy had known that she wanted to work on domestic violence issues since she was in college; when she entered law school, she decided to specialize in immigration matters and to work at a nonprofit organization.

John, ORA's executive director, explained that his job was "to oversee the staff, work with the board to make sure that the organization is sound financially, is raising the money, getting the grants, serving the clients, doing the things that our mission says that we are supposed to do, and really what ORA is all about is promoting justice to immigrants."[22] John, who never referred to his own racial, ethnic, immigrant, or ideological background, became part of ORA because

> I really was wanting to move to [central Texas] and was applying for jobs. I come from a nonprofit management background, so when I saw the ad for ORA, and thought, I don't know a whole lot about immigration and absolutely nothing about law, but I'll send my resume and see . . . and they called me. The board member I talked with was so enthusiastic that I started researching what was going on with immigration and immigration law and was absolutely appalled, and thought, Oh, my God, something has to be done about this, and now I thought, I not only want this job because I want to move to [central Texas] but I want this job because I want this job![23]

Around 2005, ORA was focused on achieving excellence as a legal nonprofit organization. As the population it served expanded beyond Central America, ORA created new programs to represent immigrant survivors of a variety of forms of abuse, such as trafficking and domestic violence. Moreover, it also offered low-cost services for immigrants who were filing for family-based visa petitions, adjustment of status, and U.S. citizenship. On its website, ORA described its mission and services as follows: "to offer safety and hope for a new life to hundreds of immigrants, refugees and asylum seekers, by empowering them to advocate for themselves and their families, and keeping them informed about their rights and responsibilities, and by educating law enforcement, the legal community, and other advocates on how to use social and legal resources to uphold the law in Central Texas."[24] During the two years that I spent as a volunteer and researcher at ORA, the organization worked on revising its public appearance, changing its motto, logo, website, newsletters, fund-raising tactics, and ultimately even its name. The original motto, "No human being is illegal/*Ningún hermano es ilegal*," was dropped. The logo, which had been drawn by a volunteer artist of the immigrant community and since 1999 had consisted of a bird of peace in black and white (previously, it had consisted of a man and a woman sitting on the floor, holding their knees, and hiding their faces, as if they were tired, resting, or crying), was changed to a colorful icon that read ORA, Organization for Refugees of America, designed by a team of marketing students from a local university. ORA's website reflected these color changes and was redesigned as well with the aim of "making it look more professional," as expressed in a staff meeting with the marketing students. ORA's newsletters also reflected this shift: originally, the colorful newsletters were filled with legal, political, and social news of relevance to the immigrant community (announcing changes in immigration regulations, the schedules of legal aid clinics, free primary health care, and English as a second language classes, as well as promoting events organized for and by the immigrant community); more recently, neat black-and-white "environment-friendly" electronic files have been dominated by short pieces directed at potential private donors (providing quotes from ORA's clients reading, "I found my freedom" and "America for me is the opportunity to make our dreams come true," and explaining what a donation would pay for, such as, "$50 will educate 10 immigrants on their legal rights and responsibilities in the U.S."). The fund-raising activities were also altered: from plant sales, garage sales, silent auctions, musical events, and potlucks at the volunteer attorneys' backyards and community venues, and *peñas* at affordable local Hispanic restaurants, to dinners at museums and five-stars hotels that cost more than seventy dollars per participant, with the titles Ambassador, Consul, Diplomat, and Attaché awarded to donors depending on the amount of money contributed.

Finally, the organization changed its name from Organization for Refugees of America/Organización para Refugiados de América to Freedom Path. The former name was purposely chosen to be translatable into Spanish and have an acronym that was simple to say for Spanish speakers. Also, when written in newsletters, letterheads, and websites, the organization's name always appeared in both languages. In contrast, the new name was purposely chosen not to be translatable into Spanish or have an acronym at all, with the aim of changing the image of the organization to reach a wider audience and make it more attractive for private donors.[25] The organization had been discussing the name change for more than a year. First, the same students who redesigned the webpage suggested some changes, including the option of retaining the acronym ORA as a name on its own with the goal of keeping the twenty-year-long identity of the organization while erasing the term *refugees*, which, on the one hand, did not reflect the variety of services that the organization offered to all kinds of low-income immigrants, and, on the other hand (and more important for the board), appeared to be a deterrent for private donors. But, in the face of opposition from certain members of the executive board, a professional marketing company was designated to do more research on the name change. This company conducted focus groups and found that Freedom Path was the best name to attract funding from private donors because it conveyed the idea that the organization was working for immigrants without causing confusion about which kind of immigrants (donors felt "funny" about giving their money for refugees because they "were not sure about what refugees were exactly"). Freedom Path also transmitted a clear message about embracing the idea that the United State is the "land of opportunity." The company also suggested using the name Freedom Path only in English to avoid the possibility of donors associating the organization with protecting undocumented Mexican and other Hispanic immigrants.

The reactions to these practical and ideological changes were negative for almost all the people I was able to get in touch with after the name change officially occurred and the new website was launched. Current ORA staff were disappointed and "had had a difficult time even using the name—I still use ORA," Cathy told me.[26] Former ORA staff expressed disbelief. "Is it really true?" Courtney asked Cathy by e-mail; later, when we met, she told me that in her view the name change reflected "that ORA was clueless and that it had lost its identity."[27] Former founding members were not happy about it either. Valerie, for example, posted a blurb on her current nonprofit organization's website explaining that "ORA used to be what Freedom Path denies being—an organization advocating and actively defending immigrants' rights."[28] She was so far from sharing the renamed ORA's current ideology that she found it necessary to clarify that at the time she was associated with ORA, the organization was something else, something that coincided with her inclusive and activist political views. Valerie had been very disappointed with ORA's twists; in one of our interviews, she expressed, "I cannot even go to the offices where ORA is now operating. They look like they belong to a large corporation. It is awful, I can't take it!"[29] Current members disagreed with views such as Valerie's. They did not believe that the changes were losses; instead, they welcomed them and saw them as inevitable trade-offs of institutional survival. As Kathy said:

I can't stand the complaints of previous ORA lawyers. They did a great job, but they have been unable to understand what it takes to have a successful working organization. We need to follow internal rules and have archives in order to provide good services for immigrants. They don't understand that we could no longer work out of tiny offices without logistics, personnel, or space to handle the amount of cases we have now.[30]

Valerie's and Kathy's views could be considered romantic and practical, respectively, but this quick labeling would overlook the fact that Valerie's romanticism was certainly accompanied by a practical sense, as she and her colleagues were able to build an organization and provide services for immigrants while pushing for pathbreaking jurisprudence. The question remained as to why the current ORA staff were so convinced that legal and social activism would hinder their provision of services. As I mentioned earlier, ORA's transformation from a social change to a social service organization is typical of a general shift among nonprofit organizations, particularly those that emerged in the spirit of the 1960s social movements. Many grassroots groups that had organized to take action on a particular issue lost their radical character as they became nonprofit organizations funded by private foundations and state grants, both of which ultimately represented and preserved the interests of the power elite.[31] While these nonprofits have been able to provide social services to marginalized communities, they have had to work within constraints that have preempted "the radical work so urgently needed from a social justice movement."[32] Aware of this trade-off, some nonprofit groups have been strategic about adapting a "corporate culture and developing business skills"[33] while transforming their "internal cultures and practices in ways that are more congruent with the objectives of radical change,"[34] like Sisters in Action for Power, an organization based in Portland, Oregon; Project South in Atlanta, Georgia, which developed community-based, grassroots economic strategies to counterbalance its dependence on private foundations;[35] Communities against Rape and Abuse in Seattle, Washington, which re-created itself to be able to maintain "an ethic of resistance and creativity" within the nonprofit structure;[36] or Arte Sana in Austin, Texas, which has consistently advocated for the rights of battered immigrants of color, predominantly Latinas, reflecting on the racial and ethnic disparities of providing services, and resisting co-optation forces of state and private grantors, which often denied funding because the organization's work was "too marginal, not mainstream enough."[37] However, other nonprofits seemed to have succumbed to the logics of state and corporate co-optation while "intentionally or inadvertently working to maintain the status quo."[38]

So far, ORA seemed to have followed the latter faith. In complying with public and private grantors' requirements, ORA had focused on the provision of services to the kind and number of immigrants that fit the grants' profile, or, as Courtney claimed, ORA staff were "trained to fulfill legal services only and to achieve a certain volume of cases."[39] Moreover, ORA had ceased to aim to develop groundbreaking jurisprudence and had eliminated any kind of direct political activism. While ORA staff were permitted to engage in political causes independently from the organization, they tended to be reluctant to do so. ORA's workers view their own daily work as their way to act upon their personal politics. ORA's institutionalized advocacy could be seen, for example, in the workers' indifference to immigration reform debates and protests held throughout the United States and in their hometowns in April and May 2006. In my interviews with ORA staff, some expressed ignorance about the immigration dispute. "To be honest, I'm not following the debate," Jenna confessed.[40] Some expressed their preference to work on their clients' cases rather than engaging in popular protests. "We do enough," Courtney claimed.[41] "We have to select our battles, we can't do everything," Maggie expressed.[42] Simultaneously, ORA's staff reflected the organization's political moderation and institutionalization in its daily work practices as it followed a set of informal parameters that coded which immigrants promised to become "good clients" and, in turn, good applicants in the eyes of USCIS—both of which helped ORA fulfill grant requirements. As a whole, ORA's acquiescence with the formal legacies of discrimination along gender, sexual, racial, ethnic, and class lines that I mentioned at the beginning of this section, together with its political passivity and its informal parameters (discussed later) to satisfy its grantors, had transformed it into a gatekeeper, a nongovernmental arm of state ideals and disciplines of citizenship that excluded the most destitute immigrants.[43]

ORA's Informal Parameters

The cases of immigrants Clara, Silvana, Rosario, Mónica, Samuel, Yolanda, Patricia, Ramona, and Leticia, compared with cases presented in previous chapters, illustrate the role that ORA played as a gatekeeper of citizenship ideals and disciplines. My fieldwork revealed informal parameters that ORA staff used on a daily basis to select immigrants and treat clients, parameters that reflected embedded notions of normalcy and defined who constituted a "good client" (who in turn promised to become a good applicant and a good citizen in the eyes of USCIS). ORA staff expected their clients to present themselves and behave in particular ways in their frequent interactions with them and in their potential interactions with official authorities. While, of course, there were no written rules about what constituted a good client in the eyes of ORA, its staff's daily practices, thoughts, emotions, and case management decisions reflected these parameters. I found that immigrants who were compliant, tidy, constant, resolute, autonomous, responsible, deferent, considerate, discreet, redeemable, considerably recovered from the battering, and "good parents" (when applicable) were prioritized by nonprofit staff, independently from their traumatic past and eligibility under VAWA or VTVPA. For instance, Angela, Laura, Manuela, and Ana satisfied all these informal standards and were considered good clients, "sweethearts," "wonderful, courageous women," and "tremendous mothers." Julia and Martha were on the verge of becoming "trouble clients." Julia was at risk because she was not autonomous enough, but as I took care of obtaining her civil status documentation, and she was also a "good client," her case moved along well. Martha's standing was shaky because she was perceived as not deferential enough—Maggie would often express her annoyance about Martha's "too demanding" attitude, doubted Martha's motives, and wondered if these just reflected "cultural differences." Luisa was labeled a "needy client" as soon as ORA staff found out that the intake appointment had lasted more than two hours, and she was perceived as inconsiderate as soon as ORA staff heard that she had not gone to the shelter as planned. Moreover, ORA was not sure about Luisa being redeemable: her abusive relationship had occurred while she was still legally married, and she seemed uncaring toward her children. Regarding the cases that I will present in the following, Clara was considered disrespectful of ORA staff; Silvana was "high-maintenance," messy, insensitive, and "a crier"; Rosario was disorganized and dependent; Mónica was untrustworthy, Samuel, unreliable, and both Mónica and Samuel, unredeemable (as opposed to Yolanda); Patricia was inconsiderate and her kids bothersome; Ramona was indiscreet; and Leticia, with her "messy boy," was almost unredeemable. All in all, the informal standards of ORA staff discriminated against the most destitute immigrants who approached the organization and, in turn, ended up either with significantly longer application processes (because their "files would be pushed down the pile")[44] or, in worse cases, with nothing at all (because ORA would decide not to represent their cases).

Clara

Clara was a battered Venezuelan immigrant who was married to an abusive U.S. citizen. Clara had written her own affidavit, which needed to be improved by clarifying and detailing events. Maggie, the legal assistant in charge of training me as an intern, had assigned me to work with Clara on her affidavit under Maggie's supervision. The day of the appointment with Clara, I went to ORA one hour in advance to review the client's entire file in order to be informed about her case, as well as to prepare questions about her affidavit for our meeting.

Clara had two teenage daughters from a previous marriage back in Venezuela. She had been married for more than two years to Mark, a U.S. citizen. She had met him casually in the street and "had fallen in love with him right away." They got married very soon after they met, and their problems began soon afterward. He had been emotionally, sexually, and economically abusive. Clara had first gotten in touch with ORA soon after the violence began, approximately two years before this meeting. However, she had dropped the case on several occasions. Maggie was frustrated about Clara's "back-and-forth" behavior (typical of survivors of intimate partner violence), and while she hoped that this time Clara would go through the VAWA application process in its entirety, she was "doubtful" about it. Maggie warned me, "Clara is very opinionated. She does not care about making it to her appointments on time, and she tends to show up whenever she wants." Also, Maggie explained to me "how to handle this kind of client": "I told Clara that I could not take care of her case on her schedule because I would be disregarding other women who had waited long for their scheduled appointments."

Ten minutes after the scheduled time for the appointment, Maggie came to the office where I was going to meet Clara and said, "I would not be surprised if the client does not show up due to her nature." Ten minutes later, Maggie came back to the office again and told me that she was going to call the client because it was already too late. When Clara answered Maggie's call, Maggie rolled her eyes and said, "We are waiting for you. You have a scheduled appointment." Clara apologized for the delay and promised to arrive at the office in thirty or forty minutes. Maggie put her on hold and asked me whether I wanted to wait for her or not; she suggested that it would be better to reschedule for another day because "clients have to understand that they cannot show up whenever they want. They have to learn to respect the staff and volunteers' schedules." I told

Maggie that I did not mind waiting, but that she should make the decision. Maggie pushed the hold button once again and began explaining to Clara, "The volunteer cannot wait for you. We must reschedule your appointment. What about next Monday?" Clara agreed. Maggie hung up the phone and sighed, "Finally! At least, this time, she apologized!"

Clara came to her rescheduled appointment on time, bringing along her youngest daughter; I was not sure if it was all right to have her daughter coming in, but even before I asked, Clara told me that it was fine with her. Clara and her daughter were both Afro-Venezuelan by birth, and Mark was African American. I asked Clara several of the questions that I had written down about her affidavit, but it was hard to follow her responses. Her narrative was disjointed, she had difficulty completing phrases, and she tended to mix up events. Clara was very upset about the poor manner in which Mark and his son had treated her daughters. Also, she had had problems communicating with her husband because she knew very little English and Mark did not speak any Spanish, which would trigger fights. Her daughter was quiet, but she expressed a few opinions about some of the episodes, particularly those that involved her directly. Her body language showed her to be tired and sad about the abusive incidents. Clara asked her daughter to step out of the room when I pointed to a part of her affidavit related to sexually transmitted diseases. Once her daughter was outside, she clarified how she found out that her husband had transmitted these illnesses to her. Almost two hours later, we scheduled another appointment to continue working on her affidavit.

Clara did not come to her next appointment, but this time she called in advance to let us know. She was going on a trip, and she told us that she would get in touch with us after she returned. Clara did not contact us for a while, so Maggie tried to reach her. Clara told Maggie, "I am now doing fine with Mark. Everything is OK. I am going to put the VAWA application on hold." Maggie was very frustrated but not at all surprised and was glad that I had not spent more time working on Clara's affidavit (by translating or typing it). "Put her file away," she told me. "I don't think she's coming back." Maggie closed Clara's case a month later.

A year and a half later, one of ORA's legal assistants got in touch with me to let me know that Clara had returned to ORA to reopen her case. For Clara, her VAWA application seemed to have worked as an insurance policy, which she could use to either get out of the relationship or renegotiate the relationship terms with her husband. Maggie was not working at ORA any longer, so the new legal assistant, Lucy, wanted to talk about the case with me. Lucy began by saying, "She's a difficult one, a no-show, right?" As I heard these words, I felt for Clara's fate at ORA. From the very beginning, she had not fit the organization's informal standards of being a good client. Clara's missing appointments and her indecision about leaving or staying with her abusive husband were red flags for the staff working on her case. The case notes were explicit enough to result in Lucy's labeling her as a difficult, inconsistent client. While I could not predict how these characteristics would affect Lucy's attitude toward Clara, our short conversation about Clara and the fact that Lucy took one month between appointments to get back to Clara with information on her case reflected that she was not being treated as a preferred client.

Silvana

Originally from Colombia, Silvana had married Paul, a U.S. citizen. He had begun to do her immigration paperwork but had been threatening to retrieve the application and cease his sponsorship. "You owe me. I gave you legal status. Now, you're tied to me for seven years," Paul said in his efforts to manipulate Silvana. He had stopped working and had forced Silvana to give him her paycheck to take care of all their bills. Silvana had a bachelor's degree in advertising from her country and was working as a salesperson at a local department store. She was desperate; she could not believe that Paul had become such a hurtful person. He constantly screamed at, belittled, and insulted her. He had abused her sexually and economically. Silvana was very scared of Paul and had been trying to escape his controlling behavior. The day of the intake appointment, Silvana was nervous that Paul might appear at ORA—he used to follow her around. She had been getting ready for this meeting for a long time and brought plenty of documentation: a pad with her own notes about abusive episodes she had been through, and a tape with a recording of one of their fights in which he had threatened her with deportation and had degraded her as a foreigner. Silvana was anxious, upset, and overwhelmed. Her documentation covered the desk of the conference room, which seated eight people, and as she was trying to show me the evidence, she cried, inconsolably several times. During the two-hour-long appointment, she revealed her trauma on repeated occasions. Although she claimed, "I have ambitions. I want to be independent. I can do it," she would shake her head and, crying, confess, "I don't know if I will be able to survive without Paul." As the end of the appointment was approaching, Silvana showed signs that she did not want to leave the office; she felt protected at ORA. She wanted to know exactly what was going to happen, to obtain a solution right at that moment, even though she knew that was not possible. Before leaving the office, Silvana gave me a strong hug and thanked me once, twice, and more.

As I walked out of the conference room, Maggie, the legal assistant who had done Silvana's screening interview, was grateful that I had taken care of her, saying, "I could not have dealt with her at all. I saw the papers all over the desk. And she was crying too, right? That's why you got more tissues, right?" Later that week, when I reviewed the case with ORA staff for the lawyer to determine whether or not Silvana could be accepted as a client they referred to her as "high-maintenance" and asked around the table to see who would be willing to take care of such a client. The lawyer assigned Jenna to the case and allowed me to assist her throughout (Silvana qualified to apply for the removal of conditions on her legal permanent residency under VAWA).[45] I was very happy for Silvana and called her friend, our point of contact, to ask her to call ORA as soon as possible. It took Silvana several weeks to find out about the good news because she had been able to contact ORA only during off-hours—Jenna and Silvana had been playing phone tag. When she was finally able to talk with Jenna, the next burden emerged: Silvana had trouble setting up an appointment because of the maneuvers she had to go through to get out of Paul's sight. Silvana missed several of the scheduled appointments and then showed up at the office unannounced. None of the legal assistants or lawyers at ORA took clients without appointments, and they were all very uncomfortable (visibly annoyed) with this kind of behavior (particularly if the client had missed scheduled appointments without notice, as was true in her case, regardless of the reasons appointments were missed, which usually were inherent to battered immigrants' life conditions). All of these meant that Silvana's case was moving at a very slow pace, including the transfer of the management of her case: Jenna decided to pass the case to Cathy, the lawyer, because "Silvana was too much. Jenna could not handle her." Cathy, on the contrary, was able "to handle Silvana." She was stricter and straightforward, saying, "If you show up unannounced, I won't see you. And when you come for scheduled appointments, you must have things organized." If Silvana was being too unfocused during an appointment, Cathy would "end it and schedule another meeting with the specific objective of having Silvana come back with her mind set for it." Cathy could not "waste" her time.

Silvana did not fit ORA's standards of a good, desirable client. She was perceived as "chaotic," "high-maintenance," "a crier," "demanding," and "inconsiderate," and neither the legal assistants nor the lawyer wanted to be responsible for her case. Even if Silvana had not been dismissed as a client, her case had been flagged as a difficult one, which would follow its own course at whatever pace possible. Silvana's path to independence had been elongated not only because her abuser was too controlling and Silvana was distressed but also because ORA staff had been bothered by her demeanor and behavior. Indeed, Silvana's case took almost three years after her intake appointment until she received the news from USCIS that her conditions had been removed; she had become a legal permanent resident free from her abusive citizen spouse.[46]

Rosario

Rosario came to ORA with her mother, who accompanied her during the intake as well. They were both very nervous. Rosario, originally from Mexico, had come to the United States when she was a young teenager and had been living in this country for more than ten years. She had gotten married to a U.S.-born Mexican American, who abused her emotionally and economically. Rosario was terrified by the idea of being deported to Mexico because her father, who was still living there, had abused her when she was a child. Rosario's mother had been traveling back and forth between the United States and Mexico with a visa, and she wanted to make sure that Rosario's abuse and legal situation were taken care of before she had to head back to Mexico. Rosario's mother had been her confidant and, as such, was aware of what had happened to her daughter. During the appointment, however, she was not intrusive and let Rosario answer the questions on her own. She intervened only if Rosario asked her a question or if she realized that her daughter had forgotten to mention something important (she would remind her, and then Rosario would talk about it).

Rosario's abusive husband had initiated her immigration paperwork, from which Rosario obtained her legal conditional residency (as opposed to a legal permanent residency because at the time of the adjustment of her immigration status, they had been married for less than two years). The date to remove the conditions on her residency in order to make it permanent was approaching, but Rosario was not going to be able to complete the process without her husband, who had stated that he would not support her petition any longer and had left her without any notice.[47] Rosario asked several times, "Is there anything I can do to avoid going back to Mexico?" I explained that she might be eligible to apply for VAWA to remove the conditions on her residency based on the abuse she had experienced. We proceeded with the intake to gather as much information as possible to evaluate her eligibility.

The first tense moment in the appointment arose with the questions related to how Rosario had come to the United States. Both she and her mother were very worried about saying that she had come without a permit, especially because during the days of the appointment, lawmakers were pushing for anti-immigration policies, and anti-immigration sentiments were rising. Once she expressed that she had had no contact with immigration officers, I explained that, then, her immigration history would not be a problem. She was somewhat relieved, but her fears of deportation were very much present throughout the appointment. The second tense moment arose with the questions about her abuse, which distressed her greatly. She began to cry and could not calm down. "I cannot believe that all these things are happening to me," she reiterated. I told Rosario to take a breath. We paused until she felt better. I decided not to go through the long list of detailed questions about the abuse because of Rosario's reaction. Instead, I just asked her to describe her experience in her own words.

Before ending the appointment, I told Rosario that because the abuse she had gone through was mostly emotional and economic, ORA was going to recommend she attend psychological counseling to support her application. I also told her that USCIS would check if she was economically self-sufficient, to which she quickly replied that she had her employment authorization and was going to look for a job now that her husband was not preventing her from leaving the house, working, or keeping her own income. "I have been babysitting, but I need to earn more money," she explained. "I want to get a full-time job. But I have been feeling so bad that I have not been able to begin the search. But I will." Finally, I told Rosario that she was going to be asked to bring specific documentation to support her application, such as her birth and marriage certificates, her conditional residency papers, photos of the marriage, leases, and bills to prove that she had been married in good faith. At that moment, Rosario bent down to pick up the large shoe box she had brought with her. "Here, I have everything, everything," she said, and she opened the box.

Rosario's box was full of papers, from pictures of herself as a baby to the next cell phone bill that was due. The papers were all mixed up, so it was difficult to find the necessary documents. We spent more than half an hour looking for the most basic ones: her birth and marriage certificates and her proof of conditional residency. I made copies of those three and, in following ORA's informal parameters, told Rosario to try to organize her bills by type and date to speed up her application process. Rosario and her mother left the office promising to organize the papers and saying they hoped to hear back from me as soon as ORA made a decision on her case.

During case review, I reported on Rosario's situation. Maggie interrupted me to ask, "Is she the one with the shoe box?" I was puzzled by her inquiry. Maggie explained, "I saw it through the window of the conference room as I was passing by while you were doing the intake. Were all of those her papers?" Maggie, Jenna, Courtney, and Cathy began to complain about "clients who did that—bring all their papers for us to organize them." They said that even if it was "harsh," they told "clients to take care of their things on their own." When I explained that I had helped Rosario find the most basic documents and then suggested she try to organize her papers for next time, they were relieved. "We can't spend time doing those kinds of things with clients. For volunteers it might be easier to do so because they don't have the time constraints, but we, the legal assistants, have to manage our time. It is amazing, these women are not aware of time issues," Courtney explained, while Maggie, Jenna, and Cathy assented. ORA accepted Rosario's case, with the hope that "she would take care of her own things, that she would do her job."

Rosario's vulnerability and apparent disorganization were taken as part of the information regarding her case. While the legal assistants knew that domestic violence victims are traumatized, generally depressed, and consequently prone to cry and to have difficulties getting things done, they had very demanding standards of behavior. Crying during intake and affidavit appointments was fine, as long as the clients could calm down and proceed with the task at hand. "Criers" were dreadful. Deciding to go through the application process was an "admirable sign of courage," as expressed many times by Maggie and Jenna, but the courage had to be accompanied by determination and organization. Having the required documentation was indispensable but not enough; clients had to be able to present that documentation in an orderly manner and to obtain it on their own if it was missing (which required going to different offices, asking for copies of past receipts, and sometimes paying for the paperwork). At ORA, pity was as common as strictness; pity and strictness were as common as annoyance and frustration; and all these feelings clearly tinted staff-client relationships.

Mónica

Mónica, who was from Mexico, had three children; the youngest one, a newborn baby, was with her during our intake appointment. Her husband, a U.S. citizen, had physically, sexually, economically, and psychologically mistreated Mónica. Her civil status and abusive experience made her seem eligible to apply for VAWA. However, her criminal background, critical to show that she has been a person of "good moral character" in the eyes of USCIS, got in the way. Mónica had been detained for possession and sale of drugs, but she explained, "My husband forced me to do the work for him. I did it only once. I never did it again." ORA had to check her criminal background because it could be a deterrent for USCIS to grant her legal permanent resident status. From Mónica's comments, I got the feeling that she had information about VAWA and other legal procedures. First, she insisted that her past criminal history was related to the abuse, which meant that ORA could make the case in order to obtain pardon from USCIS. Second, she had brought plenty of crucial supporting documentation, including photos of her after being beaten by her husband, and hospital and police reports related to the abuse. Third, she claimed that she would not be a burden on the state if she were to become a citizen because she was "a young, self-sufficient, hard worker." Fourth, she told me that she was a person who wanted to know "from 1 to 10" what her chances were of getting the legal permanent residency, and clarified that she did not want to "waste time waiting for nothing." Mónica was savvy and demanding, two characteristics that, based on my experience at ORA, were uncommon among ORA's battered clients.

When I presented Mónica's case at our weekly review, Cathy said that we needed the papers from her arrest to investigate her criminal past. I called Mónica and asked her to bring these papers. Frustrated, she responded, "I have been waiting for your call." I explained to her that I could not call her earlier because I had to wait for the lawyer's opinion. Once I asked her for the papers, she asked me again, "What are the chances from 1 to 10 for me to get the residency?" I replied that, until the lawyer investigated her case, we were not going to be able to tell her, and she promised, "I will bring the arrest papers in two days."

Our next meeting was during the first time slot in the morning. When I arrived at the office, Mónica was already there, waiting for me. She was sitting in the waiting room with her jacket covering her chest. I greeted her and asked if she had brought the papers for me to copy. When she moved to get the papers, I saw that she was breastfeeding her child beneath her jacket. Instantly, I remembered how bad I had felt when during our previous meeting she told her child that he was like his father because he had slapped her, trying to get her attention.

After Mónica gave me the papers, I asked her to wait while I copied them. While I was in the copy room, I noticed her at the door. When she saw me there making copies, she remained silent and went back to the waiting room. I perceived her mistrust; it seemed like she was checking on me. As soon as I finished her copies, I returned the originals to her and told her that I would call her back once I had news. Once again, Mónica asked me about her chances. After I repeated that we would not know until the lawyer looked over her case, she left.

Cathy reviewed Mónica's arrest papers, which revealed not only possession and dealing of drugs but also a sentence that included her deportation. Cathy realized that Mónica had approached ORA several years earlier, so she took her file out of storage and reviewed it. Cathy decided to offer Mónica to do further criminal and immigration background checks and to get the final disposition from the court where she had been sentenced to see if she would be eligible. I was happy about Cathy's determination to investigate in depth before making a final decision.

I met with Mónica to sign authorizations to release information so ORA could move on with her case. Mónica came to the appointment with her child, who spent the entire time screaming, banging, and throwing things all over the desk and the office. He got on top of the desk and began to scream right next to my face. Mónica would arbitrarily say, "Shut up! Stop!" but the child continued to cry loudly. When she had to sign a paper, she grabbed him forcefully and put him down. After the appointment, I went to Cathy's office to give her Mónica's papers. "Are you all right, Roberta?" Cathy asked. Overwhelmed, I replied, "I'm so tired. The screams . . . " Cathy finished my sentence, "Yes, I could hear the screams from my office." Her office was two doors down the hall from where I had been meeting with Mónica.

Cathy sent out the papers to further the investigation and then waited several weeks for the results. In the meantime, Mónica called only once to check on the status of her case. A month and a half later, Cathy made her final decision: ORA was not going to be able to take Mónica's case because of her drug-related criminal charges and her earlier deportation charges. Cathy prepared a letter for Mónica in which she explained that ORA did not have the resources to take care of her case at the time and gave contact information for lawyers who might be able to help her out. Mónica could get in touch with ORA with her questions if she wished to do so, but the decision was clearly negative and final. I clarified with Cathy the reasons ORA denied the case because I wanted to be ready to explain them to Mónica in the case she called back. Cathy put it in very simple terms: "Drug dealing and deportation complicate the case too much. It has very few chances to go through. ORA is overloaded with cases of people who deserve assistance and are clearly eligible."

Mónica's case revealed contradictions within ORA. While its mission was to provide justice to underprivileged immigrants, its standards of practice prioritized immigrants who were deserving of justice, but also who promised to have easy cases leading to successful resolutions. Immigrants with complicated histories tended to be dismissed because, on the one hand, their cases would be too labor intensive, that is, would require too many hours of work that instead could be allotted to at least double the number of immigrants who also deserved services but had easier cases to represent before USCIS; on the other hand, they were not a certain call, that is, the probabilities of getting the cases approved by USCIS were lower, which in turn affected ORA's records of successful cases, necessary for raising funds and keeping grants. Mónica seemed unredeemable and, at the same time, had been flagged as a potential demanding client, insensitive toward ORA's staff, with a "wild" child; three aspects that influenced ORA's final decision not to take her case.

Samuel

Samuel was a male survivor of domestic violence (one of the only two who approached ORA's battered immigrant assistance program during my two years of fieldwork). He was from Mexico, and his abusive wife was a U.S. citizen. They had a five-month-old baby who was being taken care of by Child Protective Services (CPS); Samuel's wife had two older daughters who were also under the care of CPS because she had a criminal record and severe addictions to alcohol and drugs. Samuel was fighting for custody of his baby, and the struggle had been very difficult. Samuel and his wife had had several violent episodes that involved the police. The most recent one had resulted in Samuel's incarceration because it was assumed that he was the perpetrator of violence, when in fact he was the victim. Samuel's wife was incarcerated later on. The judge and lawyer for his baby's case suggested that Samuel approach ORA to legalize his immigration status so he would have a chance at obtaining custody. Samuel was also attending domestic violence and parenting classes offered by the state.

At the beginning of the appointment, Samuel was very nervous; he had a bandana in his hands, which he folded and unfolded repeatedly. Later on, he relaxed. Samuel had brought photos of his wife, their baby, and himself. "When I met my wife, she was trying to stop consuming drugs. And she stopped. But when she got pregnant, she began to consume again." Samuel had tried to stop her, but "she would react violently" (curses, screams, punches, shoves, kicks). On many occasions, she threatened him with deportation and told him that "he was never going to be able to obtain custody because he was illegal and handicapped" (Samuel had a physical disability, and she used to abuse him about that as well). He had decided to leave her but was trying to figure out the best way to do it in order to remain in charge of their baby.

Maggie and I did the intake together (she had expressed her interest in working with a male victim and had invited me to participate because she thought it would be "interesting"). After going through the questionnaire, Maggie told Samuel that we would get in touch with him after reviewing the case with the lawyer. Samuel did not know much about VAWA, but he was eager to know if ORA would help him obtain custody of his baby, which was clearly his main concern. When he left, I asked Maggie if she thought ORA was going to accept the case. She responded, "He seems eligible; plus, his mistaken incarceration will probably work as proof of his victimhood."

Samuel's case was accepted by ORA. Maggie was in charge, and I assisted her. We met with Samuel to begin the application paperwork and sign the contract for services from ORA. Samuel was positive about it but still doubtful because he did not know if the application would result in his legalization and acquisition of custody. Samuel had gone to the Texas Bureau of Vital Statistics to get the birth certificate of his child after Maggie had given him the list of documents he needed to gather to apply for VAWA. Samuel told us that the bureau "did not want to give him the certificate"; Maggie could not understand why, but she said that she would request it via mail, which should not be a problem. Then Samuel explained how difficult it had been to be treated properly by CPS personnel, who automatically talked to the mother of the child and excluded him from the conversations. Samuel had told them, "I know I have equal rights over my child. You have to include me in every conversation and decision in regard to my child." Then he explained, "I know that I have been treated poorly because I don't have immigration documents. That is why . . . that is why I want to legalize my status, because of my child. . . . And, if I am deported, I would come back for my child right away." Samuel's paternal sense was as strong as the strongest maternal sense of some of the battered immigrant women I had met at ORA.

Samuel arrived late to our next appointment saying, "I am so sorry. My car did not start, so I had to take the bus." Maggie told him not to worry about it, then gave him an update on the state of his case: "ORA is in touch with the CPS caseworker, who will send ORA your court and psychological records. We also received the police reports, which show you only once as a victim, and more than once as the aggressor. We will have to clarify this, Samuel." He was very curious to see the reports because he had never understood why he had domestic violence charges when he was the victim—he had asked for the reports from the judge and the police, both of whom refused to show them to him. "The police were always on the side of my wife," he said. "She spoke in English, she is American. The police always assumed that I was the aggressor." We asked him about his lawyer, and Samuel said that he had not gotten an explanation from him either. Samuel gave us the attorney's contact information, and just from looking at the business card, it seemed like the lawyer was a charlatan, making a profit from people in a bind. Maggie and I went through the police reports, translated them into Spanish, and tried to explain as much as possible. Then Maggie suggested that Samuel apply for crime victims compensation, which would help defray the costs related to the abuse. He thanked her but explained, "I'd like to do it, but I don't think that I have the time to take care of something else. I work during the day, and at night I have to go to the CPS classes. And now, I have to come here, to these appointments."

Maggie moved on and began to ask him about his employment history, which is included in VAWA applications to show that a person is a reliable worker promising not to become "a burden" on the state as an unemployed subject or welfare recipient. Samuel had been in the United

States for more than ten years. He was deported once but came back after five months and resettled. He could not afford to stay in Mexico; Samuel knew that in the United States he could work and send money back to his family, so he decided to cross the border again, regardless of its risks. ORA would have to look into the deportation because it could affect his VAWA application. Maggie explained to me, "We will have to include all possible clarifications about the problematic aspects of Samuel's case in his application. This is going to be a tricky one, but it should be fine."

We met with Samuel a couple more times to work on his affidavit, which was a clear statement of his survival of not only domestic violence but also racial, ethnic, class, and gender discrimination. Samuel brought his fingerprints for us to send out for the FBI background check, another crucial piece of the VAWA application. Three months later, ORA received the results of Samuel's FBI check, and Maggie introduced the news during case review: "Well, I received the FBI check of my sweet male client. He was deported because of 'illegal import of persons for immoral purposes.' What are we supposed to do next?" Cathy suggested that Maggie request a Freedom of Information Act (FOIA) report from USCIS to figure out exactly what had happened, "now that we don't trust in his story." Maggie expressed frustration that Samuel had never mentioned the incident. A FOIA request was sent.

A couple of months later, the FOIA report arrived, and Maggie met with Cathy to look into Samuel's case. Weeks later, I found out that they had decided to close it "because it was too complicated." I asked Maggie if she or Cathy had been able to find out further details about Samuel's charge of "importing a person with immoral purposes," but they had not been able to do so. "It is not clear. But it is compromising enough for ORA not to proceed with his case," Maggie explained. ORA never asked Samuel about the alleged incident. He was sent a closure letter together with referrals to other lawyers in case he wanted to pursue his case further.

The "complications" had changed ORA's overwhelmingly positive attitude toward Samuel. From being a "sweetheart" and a "poor thing," he became an untrustworthy suspect. From being considered a first step toward the diversification of ORA's predominantly female clientele, he was dismissed as a "typical guy" ("What do you mean? Was he driving in from Mexico with a prostitute?" ORA staff wondered about the FOIA report). Besides gender matters, ORA's attitude toward Samuel was similar to Claudia's case; they both had complicated backgrounds that would require a good deal of work and could result in a denial by USCIS. ORA's prioritization of smooth, irreproachable cases accompanied the organization's departure from its original reason for existence: imparting justice to underprivileged immigrants. In this case, Samuel, an immigrant who not only deserved due process but also had faced (and was going to face) endless obstacles in his search for justice, ended up with nothing.

Yolanda

While Mónica and Samuel were initially welcomed in different ways, both were dismissed because of their problematic criminal and immigration backgrounds. Yolanda's case reveals another layer of ORA's preferences, showing that not all problematic cases were the same; some were better received and were deemed deserving of ORA's support.

Back in Mexico, Yolanda used to work at a brothel, where she met the man, a "regular client," who would become her abusive U.S. citizen spouse. Yolanda's past was unquestioned by ORA staff, and no doubts were expressed regarding her occupation in Texas. According to Yolanda, "I came to this country because my husband promised me a better future. He promised me that I would not have to work like that ever again." While prostitution, drug dealing, and importation of persons for immoral purposes were all crimes, they were viewed differently by ORA staff. Yolanda's history of abuse in the United States was as traumatic as the history of the other two clients (physical, sexual, psychological, and economic intimate partner violence), so why was Yolanda better suited as a client than Mónica and Samuel? There were both formal and informal reasons. Formally, the fact that Yolanda was believed to have left her "problematic past" back in Mexico made her eligible as an applicant according to USCIS because her "moral character" would be evaluated on the basis of her criminal history in the United States alone. If Yolanda were engaged in prostitution on U.S. soil, her eligibility would have been jeopardized. Moreover, unlike Mónica and Samuel, Yolanda did not have charges from her undocumented immigration status (she had not ignored deportation mandates, like Claudia, or been deported, like Samuel). Informally, Yolanda had been tagged as a good client. She had been "tricked" by the promises of an abusive sex client who was incarcerated for domestic violence. ORA's determination to provide justice to this woman was emphasized by the perceived ill fate of her life as a poor sex worker. Everyone (not only the legal assistant and volunteer in charge of the case, but all the staff) was aware of her case and felt sorry for her. Yolanda was always referred as "the ex- . . . hmm . . . you know who." She was described as "very brave and resourceful," particularly after she brought documentation proving that she had been living with her abuser (Maggie thought she was not going to be able to prove common residency because Yolanda's abuser had never included her name on any bill, service, or contract; however, Yolanda's name and address appeared on the monthly receipts for the money orders she had sent to her family back in Mexico).

In all my experience at ORA, Yolanda was the only one person who could miss five appointments in a row or show up two hours later than her scheduled time and not create resentment on the part of ORA staff. Her past as a sex worker and her present as a domestic violence survivor had sanctified her in a very peculiar way. ORA decided to help her, with uncommon passion. The organization's tacit values were revealed once again: a good client could have a criminal past, but the crime had to be a "fair" and "redeemable" one. Prostitution, in the end, was "the ultimate expression of patriarchy," as Maggie expressed, especially in its combination with domestic violence. If one looks at Yolanda's case alone, ORA's determination and efforts to defend it were not questionable. However, with the added perspective of the other cases, they were. Mónica's or Samuel's experiences were as unjust and reflected as much oppression as Yolanda's; however, these two cases were dismissed because of the bureaucratic complications they could have brought to ORA and the unsatisfactory demeanor of the immigrants. ORA, on the contrary, handled all the complications that Yolanda's case brought.

Patricia

Another bar against which battered immigrants were measured was the manner in which they cared for their children. Angela, Claudia, Julia, Luisa, Laura, Martha, Rosa, Manuela, Ana, Susana, Clara, Mónica, and Samuel all had children, and their relationship with them was taken into account when they were being informally evaluated as clients or potential clients. For instance, the fact that Luisa did not show concern about her children in Mexico, Clara's decision to include her daughter during her affidavit appointment, and Mónica's choice not to control or calm down her baby boy during appointments were negatively perceived by ORA staff. On the contrary, Angela, Julia, and Martha's devotion to their children, Laura's plan to surprise her children by "fixing the papers," and Samuel's struggle to gain custody of his newborn son were taken as positive signs by ORA staff. In general, good parents were considered good clients who, in turn, promised to become good citizens. However, what constituted a good parent? Patricia's case illuminates this quandary.

Patricia was from Mexico, but she had lived in the United States since she was four years old. Patricia spoke fluent English, and we proceeded with the intake in that language because she preferred to do so. Her abusive husband, a U.S. citizen, was in jail because of pending charges for driving while intoxicated and drug possession (he was an alcohol, marijuana, and methamphetamine addict who had been sent to rehabilitation). He had abused Patricia physically, economically, and psychologically. He also had threatened her with deportation and with taking away their children. They had two very young children and, as I found out four months later, another one on the way.

Patricia cried during the entire intake appointment, which lasted almost two hours. She was very depressed and angry about all the things that had happened to her. Patricia had lived at a shelter for battered women after her husband tried to run her over with his truck. Then she moved in with her aunt and, finally, with her mother. She seemed to be eligible, but as usual, I had to first review the case with the lawyer to see if ORA was going to accept it. At the very end of our meeting, she said, "I am glad it is over. My children have been waiting for too long." I asked her if she had left her children with her mother or aunt, and to my surprise, she said, "No, they are right here, in the waiting room with their grandma. I'm sorry that I brought them with me, but I couldn't arrange for anything else." In response to my confused expression, she clarified that the person she had made the appointment with had told her that she could not bring her children to the office because ORA did not have a child care center. I was appalled and apologized. I remember my thoughts—it was such an unreasonable request: these women were living in poverty, they tended to be isolated and at risk, their work demands were priorities, babysitting was not always an option—and wondered who had told her something like that. I felt terrible about it; Patricia had had to reschedule her intake appointment several times because she could not make child care arrangements. I told her that if it was easier for her, she could bring her children to the appointments. There were pros and cons to allowing this—for example, certain affidavit appointments could be very traumatic for the mother and consequently could have a negative effect on the children. However, I knew that we could work around this and try to balance moving forward with her case while taking care of her children. Later that day, I tried to find out who had told Patricia not to bring her children. Marina had done so and was very proud of it because she had started to take care of VAWA cases and was "very much bothered by the children." Moreover, she expressed that Courtney and Cathy had been doing the same. I told her that I did not mind immigrants who brought their children because most of the time, they could not attend the appointments otherwise, and I asked her that if she was to schedule appointments for me, to never tell the clients they could not bring their children along. Marina agreed to my request but was clearly bothered by my reaction.

ORA accepted Patricia's case, and in our next appointment, I explained all the steps and procedures related to her VAWA application. Patricia had come with her children and her mother again because she did not want to bother ORA. I wanted to do everything I could to lift the burden that was put on her about coming to the appointments "childless," so we agreed that she could send me paperwork in the mail to save her trips to the office. Patricia promised to begin writing her own affidavit and left.

I received a message from her right before our next scheduled meeting in which she apologized profusely: "My son got sick. I have to take him to the hospital. I am very sorry but I can't come to ORA." Patricia arrived fifteen minutes early to our rescheduled appointment and apologized because she had brought her son and daughter with her. I repeated that it was not a problem. She brought supporting documents, including photos of her family. When she opened the photo album, her son got very excited, particularly when he saw a picture of his father, whom he was missing greatly. He got very upset when Patricia turned the album's pages and "Daddy!" was not there any longer. The children ran around the room for the remainder of the appointment, which we finished just as they were becoming tired and restless.

When Patricia and her children left, I gathered all the documents, took them to the filing room, and closed the conference room where I had been having the appointment. As I was coming out of the filing room, one of the lawyers stopped me to ask if I had just had an appointment in the conference room. To my positive reply, he shook his head and said, "Please, leave the door open to air out the room. It smells bad! Were there children in there?" The children "might have had dirty diapers," I said, laughingly. But the lawyer and Cathy, who was passing by, had expressions of disgust on their faces. Cathy said, "It stinks!" They quickly walked into their offices and pushed their doors shut.

Patricia and I met one more time to work on her affidavit. She had left the children at home with her mother because she knew how upset she became when talking about her story. Indeed, she had begun to write it down and could not manage to get through the description of the violence. "I would start crying, and the paper would get all wet and ruined," she explained. "I tried several times, but I couldn't. I'm sorry." I told Patricia that if it was so difficult to write it on her own, we could do it together, so at least when she cried, I would be the one holding the paper. Patricia laughed and, with relief, began to talk. We worked for almost an hour, and then she had to leave to pick up her children.

Patricia missed a couple of appointments because she had to go to the hospital with her children again. The last time she came to ORA she was with her husband, who had just been released from jail, and her children. I was not there, so Cathy took care of the appointment and later told me all about it:

> I saw your client, Patricia, in the waiting room, with a guy. I asked her to come to my office alone for a second, and asked who that man was. Then, when she told me it was her husband, I asked her if he knew why she was there. She said that he did not, and that she didn't think he would hurt her. Then, I told Patricia to leave right away, and to never come back with her husband, because even if she might feel safe with him, nobody else at the office did.

Patricia apologized and said that I had not explained that to her before, and that she had come with him because she did not have anybody else to leave her children with. Cathy emphasized that if she came back to the office with her husband, ORA would "not represent her any longer." Patricia left and said that she would call to schedule another appointment.

After the incident, we had to wait for her to get back to us because we could not call her while she was living with her abuser. Patricia called back after seven months. She left a message saying that she had given birth to her baby and could start coming back again. ORA staff asked if she had left her husband, but she had not, so she was reminded that she could not bring him to the office. Patricia did not return to ORA.

Patricia's case illustrates ORA's contradictory measures of good parenthood. ORA staff seemed to evaluate parenthood based on their own social standards, which ignored the living conditions of poor bat-tered immigrants and prioritized ORA's comfort and safety. Children playing, running around, or being loud and babies crying, breastfeed-ing, or soiling their diapers on ORA's premises were not only "annoy-ing" but also "unacceptable." Even if some of the legal assistants had a few toys for the children to play with during appointments (so if chil-dren came along, "at least they had something to do"), most ORA staff thought that having toys sent "a wrong and unprofessional message" because clients would think it was okay to bring the children whereas, in fact, it was not. All staff had expressed frustration at how difficult it was to "work on legal applications while dealing with children." Chil-dren could be disturbing, and oftentimes affidavit appointments could affect children as well. However, ORA staff did not recognize the eco-nomic burden and risks that babysitting could bring for poor, battered immigrants, instead emphasizing their own annoyance and the proper functioning of the organization over the children's and immigrants' well-being. ORA's informal policy toward children was also a shift from the initial workings of the organization. Valerie recalls, "Toys, crayons, children's laughter . . . always. Most immigrants had children and of course, they brought them to the appointments. If there was something that gave the immigrants and us strength to move on, well, that was it—children. Because they made us realize that there was a purpose. That the efforts were worthy."[48] The case of Patricia prob-lematizes ORA's standards. She had left her husband because she felt that her children's lives and her own were at risk, she had prioritized her children's health over her application process to become a legal permanent resident, she had made all possible arrangements not to leave her children alone while she was at ORA, and she had tried not to violate ORA's policies regarding children. However, her children's presence and their sounds and smells annoyed ORA staff, even those who were not handling her case. Finally, the fact that she came to the office with her husband was interpreted as imprudent behavior; even if Patricia thought that she had things under control and that her chil-dren were better accompanied by their father than left alone, it had put ORA staff at risk. Patricia was perceived as a disorganized mother, an irresponsible client, and insensitive of the staff's safety. ORA dis-credited Patricia's behavior, and her chances to obtain legal services from ORA had been seriously jeopardized.

Ramona

Patricia's appearance in the office with her abuser illuminates another of ORA's criteria to measure a good client: discretion. Ramona's intake appointment clarifies ORA's practices regarding security and reveals, once again, certain inconsistencies. Ramona was a twenty-one-year-old Mexican survivor of domestic violence whose husband was a U.S. citizen. She had missed her previous intake appointment, for which I had been told to be ready to take photos of the marks her husband had left on her body. Ramona had called three weeks later to schedule a new appointment; she had just separated from her spouse. Ramona was six months pregnant and claimed that she did not want to deal with his violence anymore.

While I was waiting for Ramona to show up, Jenna came to my office, scared and disconcerted, saying, "Ramona is here. But I think she's with her husband. . . . I'm not sure how we should proceed. . . . I think you should call Ramona to your office and if you see that her husband tries to come in the office as well, you should tell him that the meeting was personal." I was puzzled, having never experienced such a situation firsthand. I followed Jenna's instructions. When I called Ramona into my office, she told her husband to stay in the waiting room. He asked, "Why can't I come in with you? I'm your husband!" Ramona calmly explained, "It is an appointment for the baby and me. Don't you worry. . . . You never come in to my doctor appointments, anyway." He was not convinced, and as he was standing up to walk in with Ramona, Jenna intervened, "If you do not agree, we have to cancel the appointment." Ramona's husband said that he was not comfortable with his wife going in alone, but Ramona said that it was perfectly fine and managed to convince him to leave her at ORA and pick her up an hour later. Jenna came to the office with us and told Ramona that if her husband tried to come into the room, we would call the police; Jenna explained that Ramona should not come to ORA with her spouse because it was dangerous for her and for ORA staff. Shaking her head, Ramona said, "Don't worry. He's not going to do anything."

After this prelude, I was nervous about her husband interrupting, but Ramona was very calm, so we began with the intake. Ramona had been a victim of physical and psychological violence. In one of the episodes, which ended with her calling the police, her husband was so angry that he destroyed their living room couch with a kitchen knife. As we were about to finish with the detailed questions about the abuse, somebody knocked at the door. As soon as I heard the knocking, I hid all the papers because I thought it could be her husband, and I did not want him to find out what Ramona was really doing at ORA. Fortunately, it was not her spouse but Jenna and ORA's executive director, John, who were coming to let Ramona know that her husband was back and wanted to take her away. John told Ramona that it was unsafe to proceed with the interview. We arranged another meeting with her for the following morning. A taxi would pick her up to bring her to the office on her own. Ramona left us her documents to avoid having her husband try to retrieve them from her. Jenna reminded her that she could call the police if her husband tried to hit her. Ramona thanked us and apologized.

After Ramona left, I was shocked about the entire episode, particularly about the way in which ORA had handled it. I told Jenna that I thought that it was a bad idea to have the appointment after her husband had accompanied her and expressed that he was not comfortable with her staying on her own because I thought that her husband was going to be mad at her, which could obviously result in violence. Jenna said that maybe I was right, and that they should have a set policy about this kind of occurrences because they were also unsafe for us.

I was so worried about Ramona that I could barely sleep that night. I had told Jenna that if Ramona did not come back the following morning, I was going to do a welfare check on her because I felt responsible. Jenna tried to dissuade me by saying that I was not responsible, but that we could talk about the situation with Cathy and John, who were ultimately in charge. Luckily, Ramona came to her appointment. She seemed untroubled and said to me that she thought it was "funny" how careful we were. I noticed that she was wearing a large T-shirt that covered almost all of her chest and arms, and I wondered if she was hiding bruises. I asked her about how her day ended, and she did not mention any particular event. She just said, "Here I am," implying survival. During the appointment she cried as she talked about the abuse. It was clear that Ramona was depressed, and I thought that one of her survival strategies was to deny or minimize her husband's aggression. I gave her as much information as possible about her legal options, and she promised to call us back to schedule another appointment (we could not call her because she could not provide us with any safe contact numbers).

I was greatly relieved that Ramona had come back, but I was still appalled by ORA's treatment of the case. I met with Cathy to talk about it, and she seemed to have a concrete idea about the steps that ORA should have taken. First, she said that her policy was not to have an appointment if the abuser was at the office. I asked her if that was ORA's general policy, and she said that it should be. Second, she said that ORA staff could always call 911 if there was an imminent threat and claim that a person was trespassing, and that if a client did not come to an appointment and we were suspicious, we could do a welfare check through the police. However, reporting the abuse to the police remained the client's decision, unless the abuse involved minors (in which case, we had to remain anonymous because we could not breach the client's confidentiality). Cathy's answers were more satisfactory, yet they contradicted the events related to Ramona. I felt that the organization had failed in providing security, and ultimately in facilitating justice, for Ramona. She never called or came back to ORA after the second appointment.

Ramona's and Patricia's cases illustrate ORA's concern with safety. The uncertainty with which Ramona's case was handled was overcome at the time of Patricia's case, which reflected an improvement in ORA's cohesion in dealing with this kind of episode. However, it also reflected that ORA stressed the security of its personnel more than that of the clients: the clients were free to do whatever they wanted about their abusers except when they were on ORA's premises; they could decide to endanger their own lives, but they could not put ORA staff at risk. The preservation of ORA staff as an institutional policy was also a new development in the history of the organization. Besides safety procedures, ORA had implemented strategies to prevent its personnel from burning out, such as closing the office to the public one day per week, allowing staff to use flextime to take care of themselves, planning recreational outdoor activities once a month, regularly hiring a massage therapist to provide in-house services, and providing optional stress-management/counseling sessions for the staff. The latter in particular would reveal another divide between ORA staff and immigrants, as illustrated by Leticia's case.

Leticia

Leticia, in her early twenties, had been born in Mexico and had come to the United States without proper immigration documents in search of better life chances. She married Clark, a U.S. citizen and first-generation Mexican American, who had been sexually and psychologically abusive. By the time Leticia approached ORA, Clark had been separated from her for a couple of months, was living with another woman, who had threatened Leticia with deportation, and also was on probation. Leticia did not speak any English and had received a ninth-grade education back in Mexico. She earned $600 per month, which barely covered living expenses for her and her ten-month-old baby. ORA took Leticia as a client and assigned me to her case under Cathy's supervision. The lawyer told me to "proceed as usual," collecting all the supporting documentation, including medical records and criminal background, and to work on her affidavit. In my meeting with Leticia, I emphasized that the length of the process would also depend on her: if she was able to bring documentation promptly and meet with me consistently, it was going to take us less time to get the application ready to be sent out to USCIS. Leticia was eager to start. She smiled at several opportunities, but she was never very expressive; Leticia was reserved and sad. As promised, she brought supporting documents and her written affidavit to our next appointment.

Her affidavit was a good start; but we had to meet several times to work on it with the aim of satisfying USCIS (and ORA) expectations. Affidavits had to include as many details about the abuse as possible, particularly in cases like Leticia's, dominated by emotional abuse and without police reports. Her affidavit would delve into abusive episodes, her feelings, and her contraction of a sexually transmitted disease from her husband (the latter would be documented by medical records as well). Leticia tended to be very quiet during the affidavit appointments, and her answers were short, so I had to ask many questions to get enough depth in the narration of her experiences. The role that ORA staff played in the preparation of affidavits was crucial: affidavits had to be translated not only into English but, more important, into USCIS's "language" (i.e., affidavits had to be written in a manner that satisfied the expectations of immigration laws and officers about battered immigrants' experiences). I had to make sure to get more details about the abusive aspects and her traumatic feelings about her past relationship; without them, her story could have been read as simply a bad (as opposed to abusive) marriage. Also in following ORA's guidelines, I had suggested that Leticia attend counseling sessions for battered women because a psychological report from the counselor certifying the abuse would further strengthen her application. Like many other immigrants, Leticia agreed to seek services without enthusiasm. Every time I met with her, I asked if she had been able to get an appointment, but Leticia always had difficulty in doing so. Once, she told me that "the line was busy"; another time she explained that "there were no individual appointments available at the moment." In following my suggestion to attend group sessions, she told me that these sessions were "at night," and, as she expressed, "I cannot leave my son alone. Even if I were able to find someone to look after him, it would take me a very long time to get there and come back home. I don't have a car, and I would have to take more than one bus to get there." Finally, Leticia claimed that the alternative of going to a counselor other than this kind of free community services was not going to work out, simply because "I cannot afford to pay for a counselor."

These were not Leticia's "private troubles" but a "public issue":[49] free or low-cost counseling in town (and across the country) was very limited, especially for non–English speakers and/or domestic violence survivors. In addition to language, specialization in battering was known to be a fundamental characteristic in a counselor not only for the credibility of the specialist's report in the eyes of USCIS but also for the well-being of battered immigrants: prejudice, expressed as doubts regarding their marriage motives and endurance of abuse, was widespread in nonexpert service providers for low-income communities. Presenting Leticia's case to ORA staff as an example, I offered to look into this issue in order to mitigate the lack of appropriate services available.

Counseling was vital to strengthen VAWA and U visa applications; however, it was controversial for low-income battered immigrants. Besides its scarcity and bias, counseling was usually perceived as a foreign practice, threatening (particularly for immigrants still embedded in violence and fear), and demanding (the length of the treatment was prohibitive to many battered immigrants due to their work schedules, family circumstances, and remote residences). ORA had lost touch with these constraints and often pushed immigrants into undertaking counseling, except that the long wait for an initial appointment would significantly delay their path to citizenship. While I tried to develop contacts with alternative counseling options for low-income battered immigrants, including internship programs with graduate students about to get matriculated in the field, Maggie announced that she had set stress-management sessions for ORA staff. "Fortunately," Maggie commented, "the counselor is not going to charge us. She's so wonderful." When I asked if this counselor would provide (or help us find) services for the immigrants, I received elusive answers. As I attended the stress-management sessions, I understood that the elusiveness reflected ORA staff's will to separate themselves from "the clients." Stress management was about self-care; it was about having a space to "vent" and get useful tools to feel better despite the immigrants' tragedies. Even if institutional matters (like "mothers with wild children" and "clients who cry during affidavit appointments") were brought up and discussed during these sessions, they were never acted on. ORA's workers were satisfied with attending these meetings because they were able to express their own frustrations and "avoid allowing work matters to affect their private lives," while they did not care about the fact that they did not implement actions to improve services for clients. Stress-management sessions, however, were contradictory because of the particular moment when these were implemented (a time when the number of cases put on hold was rapidly increasing because of the scarcity of counseling services for battered immigrants). While ORA did not find any obstacles to arrange for a free counselor to take care of its stressed staff, it never pursued alternatives to find free or low-cost counselors for its battered clients, who, on the one hand, were strongly recommended to attend counseling in order to apply for VAWA and U visas, and, on the other hand, had to wait between six and eight months to get an appointment. The prioritization of the staff over the clients reinforced the stratifying role that the organization had in moving immigrants in or out the realm of legitimacy in the United States.

While ORA staff went to free stress-management sessions, Leticia waited six months to attend sessions for battered women in Spanish; in the meantime, she continued to work on her VAWA application, which we completed three months before her first counseling appointment. As soon as it was ready, I gave Leticia's file to Cathy, who reviewed it, added some questions about the abuse described in her affidavit, and wrote a memo that read, "Weak case. Not enough proofs of abuse. Strongly suggest bringing more letters of support and going to counseling." I was disturbed by Cathy's observations because they meant at least a six-month waiting period to send out Leticia's application (approximately three months for an appointment and three more months to get a supporting letter from the counselor).

I arranged a meeting with Leticia to work on finalizing her affidavit by including as much evidence as possible about her abuse with the aim of convincing Cathy to send out the application without waiting so long for counseling (I knew that similar cases had been sent out before). Leticia brought more letters of support, and also her son, to the appointment. We met in Cathy's office (Cathy was going to be out until later that day). Leticia was preoccupied with her young son, who wanted to run around the office and play with everything that looked appealing: papers, cables, cardboard, fish tanks, and candles. Leticia was very nervous about his behavior and could not calm him down. She would grab him forcefully and implore him to be quiet, threatened to hit him, and also said that I "was going to get mad at him." I was trying to help her calm down her son. I tried to talk with him, put him on my lap, and gave him something to write with. Later, Leticia tried to feed him (she thought that would appease him), but when she got the bottle out of her purse, she spilled the milk all over Cathy's chair. Leticia was very embarrassed about it, saying, "I will never bring him again. He is trouble." She tried to clean up the milk, first, with a T-shirt that she had in her purse, and then with tissues I had handed to her. Her son refused to eat; he only wanted to play in the office, and Leticia could not prevent him from doing so without him crying. In the meantime, I was trying to ask her questions about the affidavit, some of which Leticia answered in a focused and quick manner, and some of which she asked me to repeat because she was distracted. Leticia became emotional at many of the questions but recovered quickly. She did not break down in front of her son, who was giving her "strength and reasons to apply for the papers, because I want to be able to stay with him in this country and to provide a better future for him." I ended the appointment and scheduled another one as Leticia repeated to her son, "We are about to leave now. Right now. It's OK. . . . Don't worry. We're going." Leticia had answered most of my questions, so it was unnecessary to try to keep them in the office. As I said good-bye to Leticia and her son, she promised, "Next time, I'll come alone. I'm so sorry."

After they left, I tried to straighten up Cathy's office, but the milk smell was pungent. I went to the kitchen to get some paper towels, but when I got back to the office, Cathy was already there. She told me not to worry about cleaning the stain because she had gotten rid of the chair. Cathy was shaking her head and expressed her frustration with clients bringing their children to appointments. The legal assistants joined the commotion, and all showed irritation with these kinds of episodes. I apologized, but Cathy quickly said that it was all right and then continued to express her aggravation with "messy children and noncontrolling moms." Then she told me that when she knew that a client's children were messy, she asked the client not to bring them to the appointments. I told her I did not follow that policy because I thought it was unrealistic for ORA's clients who had financial burdens and had to rely on family and friends to leave their children while they went to their appointments. Then I tried to lighten up the mood, saying, "There was a moment during the appointment that I realized that Cathy's fishes looked very quiet. Minutes later I saw that the aerator of the fishbowl had been unplugged! I plugged in the aerator right away and saved the fishes' lives!" Everybody was laughing, and the momentary tension began to disappear.

After my next appointment with Leticia, I was able to strengthen her file, including a note to the lawyer about the reasons Leticia had not been able to attend counseling yet. This time, Cathy approved the case, saying, "The affidavit is better and the STD medical records should be enough. However, we must be ready to get a request for further evidence from USCIS. Counseling certification should be sent then." Six months later, ORA received the approval of Leticia's case from USCIS, without a request for further evidence. I was glad to see that her case had overcome ORA's informal and USCIS's formal barriers. Leticia was in shock that she had obtained her residency; she could stay with her son "without fears."

ORA as a Gatekeeper

ORA staff's informal selective parameters helped them satisfy the goal of the program to assist battered immigrants by successfully serving the largest number of cases possible. This goal, linked to central requirements of the organization's grants, was sustained both practically and ideologically. On the practical end, ORA staff strove for efficiency and success, which were equated with obtaining USCIS approval for the largest number of cases possible (the more docile the clients, the greater the chances ORA had to make them fit within USCIS's formal selective standards). On the ideological end, ORA staff believed that having a large number of approved cases was an ideal indicator of success, regardless of its consequences (i.e., relegating "trouble clients" and excluding the most destitute immigrants). Staff were deeply and openly concerned with ORA's institutional success. They were proud of providing only legal services as opposed to social or holistic services for immigrants. "We are not social workers. We don't do social work. We are not counselors. This is a legal office," Courtney usually claimed. "We only provide immigration legal services; we don't have the necessary expertise to inform you in any other matters," was the explanation Maggie used if her clients requested services that were "out of ORA's boundaries." If immigrants broke down during intake or affidavit appointments or showed signs of not having recovered from the battering, ORA staff insisted on "bringing the clients back" to addressing their legal matters.

"I know they have issues, but we have forms to file, and other clients waiting. We can't do counseling. We can't spend time with people crying or venting," Cathy explained. After "stressful" appointments, ORA staff would insist that immigrants seek counseling services and clarify that they were legal advocates who did not do the same kind of work that counselors did.

While this distinction was not problematic per se, its implications were relevant. First, it reflected ORA's institutional shift to a co-opted/corporate nonprofit model, focused exclusively on the orderly provision of legal services within the existing formal parameters, unlike its original intentions to provoke "radical change"[50] (i.e., to push for more inclusive immigration policies in the United States). Second, it allowed ORA staff to separate from the pain, misery, and complications of their clients' lives, which were systematically objectified as legal cases, easily framed within bureaucratic tasks; this separation allowed them to "do their work," but at the same time it highlighted the social gap between staff and clients, that is, citizens and immigrants. Third, it showed incomprehension and ultimately disregard of the social conditions and personal circumstances of its clientele, both of which would have at least explained their "faulty" demeanor. The combination of these three phenomena fed exclusionary processes, which ultimately delegitimized certain immigrants: those who did not satisfy formal immigration law hierarchies and/or informal nonprofit expectations. The most destitute immigrants were deemed unworthy of "ORA's resources," as it was usually manifested. ORA had become a gatekeeper of the governmental means to monitor access to citizenship in the United States, means intended to protect a particular social order along ideals of patriarchy, heteronormativity, whiteness, American-ness, middle-class lifestyle, and hardworking, self-sufficient, law-abiding, healthy citizenry. ORA's role as a gatekeeper exemplified the interaction of the three dimensions of domination: ideological, institutional, and personal. In this case, nationhood ideologies defining who is worthy to become a citizen of the United States were articulated institutionally in immigration laws and policies (including grants for service providers), enforced by immigration officers in governmental bureaucracies, implemented by immigrants' advocates in nonprofit organizations, and reinforced through personal interactions between immigrants and advocates. While subversion was possible, particularly at the nongovernmental level of policy implementation and personal interactions, in the case of ORA, it was dismissed.

ORA had not escaped the dynamics of the institutionalization of grassroots movements, which included the moderation of its politics and the adoption of mainstream or normal practices to pursue their interests (as opposed to the original noninstitutionalized and radical manner to raise demands).[51] ORA was not an exception within the nonprofit world, which particularly since the 1970s had "stepped up to fill a service void" created by the shrinking of the state under neoliberal ideologies of governance, which tightly tied the so-called third sector organizations with market logics and state surveillance.[52] Like most nonprofits, ORA became more and more professionalized, eventually recruited a specialized manager, and gradually developed a devoted, obedient workforce, genuinely interested in social service while cautious about social change. ORA staff felt trapped in a "soul-dropping"[53] quandary: to accept the rules of the game and serve "clients who otherwise would have nowhere to go,"[54] or to challenge the system and risk not obtaining enough resources to provide services at all. ORA's institutional expansion and survival meant a departure from its original grassroots commitment to do whatever possible to provide justice for the most underserved immigrant populations. ORA's success came to be measured by the number of cases successfully approved by immigration, which required an efficient, safe, and nonstressed staff, able to select clients who promised to follow the legal application path as smoothly and independently as possible. ORA had been able to build and maintain a public reputation as a highly efficient nonprofit legal organization, which offered a unique set of services to the immigrant community, and was overloaded with demands of services. However, a closer look revealed that the most underprivileged people (those who could not satisfy ORA's informal standards to behave as good clients) tended to either be given low priority as clients or not be selected as clients at all, regardless of their traumatic past and formal eligibility under VAWA or VTVPA. Learning about ORA's ambivalent functionality may contribute to continuing the struggle to make immigration policies, and concomitantly society, more inclusive in this country. Skeptics may believe that systemic forces will continue to prevent change. Anti-immigration folk may believe that co-optation has worked as a controlling tool. Activists may agree that the struggle has not ended. In the latter spirit, I turn to how structural constraints have been and could be negotiated.

5

Resisting Inequality

How did battered immigrants and ORA staff negotiate intersecting gender, sexual, racial, ethnic, and class structural forces? How can the paradoxes of the system and the pervasiveness of inequality be resisted and overcome? As opposed to the previous two chapters, which focused on the power of immigration laws over nonprofit organizations and their workers over immigrants' actions, this chapter focuses on the capacity of battered women and advocates to cope with, legitimize, or defy these constraints. While battered immigrants seemed to be at the mercy of gatekeepers, and ORA staff seemed to be co-opted, they still had a say in these processes. These encounters between structural and individual wills and actions embody the theoretical debate around the issue of human agency versus structural forces, that is, between order and change. In this last chapter I will address the structure/agency theoretical debate, analyze immigrants' agency by bringing in the cases of immigrants presented in previous chapters,[1] share ORA staff's thoughts about their role as gatekeepers, and propose alternative actions toward change.

Structure/Agency Debate

Ever since sociology was founded as a discipline, and continuing with a long-standing philosophical dilemma, theorists and researchers have been dealing with a fundamental threefold puzzle: Do individuals have power to act independently of constraining social structures? How are these structures constituted? How can they be changed? Answers to these questions have spanned a continuum at whose extremes authors have emphasized either the oppressive character of social structures over individuals[2] or the capable nature of people to overcome oppression individually and/or collectively.[3] In the middle, one finds theories that propose that structures are not only constraining but also enabling of human agency,[4] and that structural power not only oppresses but also generates individuals' power.[5] To better understand the structure/agency conundrum with social equality as the end goal, feminists of color suggest questioning abstract notions of agency and social structures by emphasizing their sociohistorical, multifaceted, and often contradictory character.[6] One should "think of agency not as a synonym for resistance to relations of domination, but as a capacity for action that historically specific relations of subordination enable and create."[7] Interlocking structures of domination like race, ethnicity, gender, sexuality, and social class allow for various kinds and degrees of individual and collective action, which must be disentangled to further comprehend the dynamics and effects of power relations.[8] Most authors, at both extremes and in the middle of the structure/agency debate, have developed universal theories (applicable to a fictitious uniform "all") from above (without incorporating or getting involved with the research subjects) based on a binary system of thought (powerful/powerless, black/white, male/female, rich/poor, etc.). This standpoint ignored the multiplicity of experiences and the actual views of the oppressed and, in turn, reproduced the social hierarchies being studied. Feminists of color make an effort to break this perverse cycle by developing knowledge from below based on incorporating the views and voices of the subjects about whom the research is being developed, because "without them, the myriad individual and collective histories that simultaneously run parallel to official accounts of historic events and are their sequel, almost inevitably get submerged"[9] and become invisible.[10] Accordingly, the manner in which these voices are brought into the analysis is central: their mere inclusion is not enough and does not automatically provoke a change in the understanding of otherness. It is not only about including but also about how to include; it is not only about voicing but also about listening: the question "may not be whether the subaltern can speak so much as whether she can be heard to be speaking in a given set of materials and what, indeed, has been made of her voice by colonial and postcolonial historiography."[11]

By uncovering the ways in which Latina battered immigrants and ORA staff are affected by and negotiate specific intersecting structural forces, I propose that agency is nuanced.[12] Initially, agency does not occur in a vacuum but is always structurally limited and relative to others' agency. These relative limitations should be considered in order to fully understand the degrees of agency possible and how agency is expressed as individuals interact with one another within structural constraints. Accordingly, agency does not always equal resistance (i.e., expressed by breaking free from oppressive conditions, such as battered women leaving their abusers, undocumented immigrants becoming legal permanent residents, or ORA staff defying immigration laws); instead, agency may be compliant (i.e., expressed by following norms, rules, regulations, ideals, and expectations, such as battered immigrants following the prescribed citizenship application process, showing up on time for scheduled appointments, and arranging for child care, and ORA staff adhering to USCIS formal expectations for VAWA and U visas applications). Finally, agency may be the result of conscious, strategic planning (such as battered immigrants' tactics to keep their citizenship application process a secret from their abusive husbands, or ORA's goal to successfully assist the largest number of battered immigrants possible), but agency also may be unintended (such as battered immigrants casually blending in or clashing with informal selective parameters of nonprofit organizations, or ORA staff's assumption that their values regarding motherhood and civil responsibility are universal).[13] When looking at battered immigrants and ORA staff in this light, one is able to arrive at a more accurate comprehension of the diversity of their experiences, which may initially appear to be contradictory, and to elaborate more suitable routes of action, programs, and policies for immigrant survivors of gender violence.

Immigrants' Agency

Angela, Claudia, Julia, Luisa, Laura, Martha, Rosa, Manuela, Ana, Susana, Clara, Silvana, Rosario, Mónica, Samuel, Yolanda, Patricia, Ramona, and Leticia walked different paths toward or away from citizenship. While they were all affected by the formal and informal frames of action, each immigrant expressed her or his agency in varying degrees and multiple ways. Formally, as elaborated in chapter 3, battered immigrants' agency was framed along VAWA's and VTVPA's gender, sexual, racial, ethnic, and class lines. In mirroring the family-based immigration system, VAWA and the clauses for battered immigrants in VTVPA are still influenced by the legacies of the English common-law doctrine of coverture, which result in male and heterosexual privilege. For instance, Claudia's, Julia's, and Luisa's agency was predominantly limited by this bias. Claudia was a battered immigrant from Mexico and a mother of seven children, three living in Mexico, three in the United States, and one who had recently passed away. Claudia had been a victim of domestic violence since she was very young, and one of her daughters had also been victimized when she was four years old. Claudia had been abused by her current partner, a U.S. citizen, who punched, cursed, and screamed at her; pulled her hair; cut her; prevented her from working and from having or spending any money; and threatened her with deportation, separation from her children, and death. However, the fact that Claudia was not married to her abusive partner or had not engaged with her partner in a common-law union made her ineligible for VAWA. She could try to apply for a U visa if she called the police on her abuser and cooperated with the authorities in the investigation of the crime.

Julia was also a battered immigrant originally from Mexico, a mother of seven who had been abused physically, sexually, and psychologically. Unlike Claudia, however, Julia was married to a legal permanent resident who had left her three years before the date of the appointment and had been living with another woman for almost as long. Julia's husband had used almost all the abusive techniques mentioned in the ORA intake questionnaire,[14] including the ones used by Claudia's abuser. Moreover, Julia had had a miscarriage related to her husband's ill-treatment. Her husband had stopped seeing the children and sending money for them very soon after he had left her. Julia made $300 per month by picking up temporary work cleaning houses. Initially, she seemed to be eligible to apply for VAWA, but ORA had to know her exact civil status: if her husband had filed for divorce without her knowledge more than two years before the estimated application date, she could not apply for VAWA.

Like Claudia and Julia, Luisa had migrated from Mexico to escape extreme poverty. Her abuser was a U.S. citizen with whom she had cohabitated for a couple of years and who was incarcerated at the moment because of the last violent episode that he had committed against her. Besides physical attacks, Luisa's abuser had threatened her with deportation, prohibited her from managing the money she earned through her occasional temporary jobs, and therefore prevented her from sending money back to her sons in Mexico. Luisa was not married to her abuser because she had not legally divorced her original husband, who still resided in Mexico. Because of her marital status, Luisa could not apply for VAWA but rather petitioned for a U visa.

Despite Claudia's, Julia's, and Luisa's histories of abuse and their willingness to become citizens in the United States independently from their abusers, the legacies of coverture embedded in the immigration laws shaped their future. Claudia, upon ORA's suggestion that she should call the police and collaborate with the authorities in the investigation of her abusive partner, expressed fear and mistrust based on negative experiences of friends, relatives, and other immigrants in her community when dealing with the police, who either had contacted immigration officers to initiate deportation procedures or had prioritized the testimonies of English speakers over non–English speakers. Claudia never returned to ORA, which most likely meant that she did not apply for a U visa. Julia, on the contrary, was able to become a legal permanent resident once ORA resolved the enigma about her marital status: her husband, fortunately for Julia, had not filed for divorce, so she was able to seize the opportunity opened by VAWA. Luisa, unlike Claudia, decided to collaborate with the police, with whom she had been in touch when her abusive partner was incarcerated, and petitioned for a U visa. Luisa took the necessary steps suggested by ORA, but the police refused to certify her as a U visa applicant by claiming that she had not been cooperative enough because she had not returned their phone calls. Luisa had not been able to do so because she had moved to various temporary residences, without phone lines, due to her financial instability and the continuous threats from her abuser's family. Even though ORA complained to the police and requested a revision of their denial, the police once again refused to certify Luisa. ORA decided not to follow up on her case because of resource limitations, and so her opportunity to initiate her path to citizenship was blocked.

Besides the legacies of gender discrimination, VAWA and the options for battered immigrants of VTVPA were permeated with legacies of racial and ethnic discrimination. The national origin and immigration status of the abuser determine the options available for battered spouses through VAWA and VTVPA. These hierarchies were clearly visible in the cases of all the immigrants who approached ORA. For example, Angela, Laura, Martha, Rosa, Manuela, and Ana were all survivors of extreme physical, sexual, and psychological violence perpetrated by their respective husbands in the United States. However, their abusers' nationality and immigration status led each of these battered immigrants to significantly different paths to become citizens. If abusers are U.S. citizens by birth or naturalization, their victims can obtain legal permanent residency as soon as their VAWA applications are approved and can apply for citizenship three years later. This was the case for Angela, who received her and her sons' residency within four months of the approval of her VAWA petition. If abusers are legal permanent residents, their victims can also obtain legal permanent residency and apply for citizenship three years later. However, the waiting period to obtain residency varies depending on the nationality of the battered immigrant, ranging from less than one year to more than eight, depending on the size of the backlog that the USCIS has in processing petitions from the applicant's country of origin. The longer a petitioner has to wait for her residency, the longer the path toward citizenship. Laura's and Martha's cases illustrate this point.

Laura, originally from Mexico and married to a legal permanent resident, had to wait between six and eight years to obtain her residency after her VAWA petition was approved. Until then, Laura could not travel outside the United States, even if she had obtained deferred action (which meant that she could not be deported) and had an employment authorization (which she had to renew and pay for on a yearly basis). Laura was going to be able to apply for citizenship between eight and eleven years after the approval of her VAWA petition. In contrast, Martha, originally from Nigeria and also married to a legal permanent resident, had to wait less than one year after the approval of her VAWA application to obtain her residency. Martha did not have to renew her employment authorization, was able to travel abroad within a year of the approval of her VAWA petition, and could apply for citizenship three years later. The noncitizen status of the abusers damages their victims not only in terms of the length of the process but also in terms of its certainty. On the one hand, if the abusive resident is deported (i.e., loses his status as legal permanent resident) due to an incident of domestic violence, the survivor has two years to file a VAWA self-petition or else her chances to gain legal status perish, as in the case of Rosa, a survivor of physical and psychological abuse committed by a legal permanent resident who had been deported too long before she was able to initiate her VAWA application. On the other hand, if the abusive resident is deported for other reasons before the VAWA application of the battered immigrant is approved by USCIS, all chances to gain legal status for the applicant perish instantaneously, as in the case of Manuela, a survivor of psychological and sexual abuse committed by her husband, who lost his legal permanent residency status because of drug dealing and was deported.

If abusers are neither U.S. citizens nor legal permanent residents, their victims cannot apply for VAWA but rather for a U visa. This was the case for Ana, originally from Mexico and married to an undocumented immigrant also from Mexico. In order to change her undocumented status,

Ana had to collaborate with the police on the scrutiny of her abuser's deeds against her. The police had to certify to USCIS that Ana had been victimized and that she had been helpful with law enforcement personnel. Ana had succeeded in proving her goodwill and behavior, and after two years of working on her application, she was able to obtain her U visa (as opposed to Luisa's case, mentioned earlier, which was not successful). Ana was allowed to stay in the United States without fear of deportation for up to four years and was permitted to work legally for up to three years. After that time she could choose to apply for residency. The disparities between the cases of Angela, Laura, Martha, Rosa, Manuela, and Ana reveal how the law prioritizes the abusers' nationality and immigration status over the immigrant survivors of violence and the wrongdoings against them.

Gender, sexual, racial, and ethnic discriminatory parameters were accompanied by similar class-based parameters. The socioeconomic status of the immigrants influences their capacity to afford and complete the requirements to adjust their legal status through VAWA or VTVPA. On the one hand, the costs associated with the application process are high because of USCIS fees, the charges for supporting documentation, and the cost of legal representation. While this burden has been partially alleviated by the assistance of pro bono lawyers and nonprofit legal organizations like ORA, the costs that are not waived delay or impede the application process for the immigrants who are most in need. On the other hand, VAWA and VTVPA applications require immigrants to possess and provide documents, bills, receipts, and health reports and to trust authorities, such as policemen and government bureaucrats. These requirements weed out the neediest immigrants, who may lack the ability to collect personal documents and receipts to prove identity and common residency with the abusive spouse, may never have possessed such papers, or may not have been able to systematically file their papers or access them because of their controlling abusers. Simultaneously, police reports (or collaboration with the criminal investigation in the case of VTVPA) and the inclusion of psychological evaluations are a threatening obstacle for many applicants, who not only fear the police but also find counseling too foreign and demanding a practice. Battered immigrants like Luisa, Claudia, and Susana (whose abuser had kidnapped her and her newborn and held them in a rat-infested apartment without heat or food) were unable to overcome these class-based barriers: Claudia was fearful of the police; Luisa did not meet the police standards because she did not have a permanent residence, job, or phone access; and Susana did not posses the required documentation, was not able to afford the costs, and could not fathom the idea that she would have to spend so much time preparing the application while her daughter's survival needs were so urgent that she had to prioritize work over anything else.

In this way, VAWA and VTVPA have not escaped the historic discriminatory character of the immigration system in the United States or the inequalities of U.S. society. Implicit in the formalities of VAWA and VTVPA, gender, sexual, racial, ethnic, and class parameters have framed battered immigrants' agency. While some women had been prevented from accessing the citizenship rights to which, in principle, they were entitled (like Claudia, Luisa, Rosa, Manuela, and Susana), other women had been able to negotiate the constraints successfully (like Julia, Angela, Laura, Martha, and Ana). But how?

In order to elucidate battered immigrants' agency, one must contextualize their actions by taking into account not only the aforementioned formal constraints but also informal limitations that emerge from their interactions with nonprofit workers. Julia, Angela, Laura, Martha, and Ana were able to go through the entire long, complicated application process because they met both the formal requirements to become residents/citizens under VAWA or VTVPA and the informal qualifications to become clients at ORA. As I elaborated in chapter 4, my two years of activist research at ORA revealed that the battered immigrant women who were able to successfully navigate the process had certain characteristics: they were compliant, tidy, constant, resolute, autonomous, responsible, deferent, considerate, discreet, redeemable, considerably recovered from the battering, and "good" parents (when applicable) in the eyes of ORA staff. The combination of all these qualities allowed these women to express their agency in the *right* amount and the *right* way, which ORA staff perceived as their ability to be *good* clients who, in turn, could become *good* applicants in the eyes of USCIS (which would most probably approve their petitions because they promised to become *good* citizens, that is, citizens who would be self-sufficient, productive, and law-abiding).

Angela, Laura, and Ana behaved like good clients from beginning to end. They were compliant, following the formal and informal due process without any resistance, and also with resolution, constancy, autonomy, and order. For instance, they collected all the required paperwork promptly without the assistance of ORA staff and presented it in an orderly fashion. They did not miss any scheduled appointments, and they called in advance to reschedule if they could not keep an appointment. Their responsible attitude toward their application process and ORA was accompanied by deference: they were careful not to bother ORA staff, never phoning unless they were returning a call or had an emergency, such as detention, even if they had pressing questions about the status of their applications or related matters, and never brought their children unless they were quiet and well behaved (i.e., the women were "good parents"). These women were also considerate of ORA staff's safety: they managed to avoid bringing their abusers or their abusers' threatening relatives to the office, which meant that they had successfully kept their applications a secret, and had mastered the skill to dissipate or avoid danger. All these attributes revealed the immigrants' resilience: their ability to adapt to the circumstances and their significant recovery from the abuse. Last but not least, these women were redeemable in the eyes of ORA: they should and could be saved.

Unlike Angela, Laura, and Ana, Julia's, Leticia's, and Martha's application processes were temporarily at risk because the women did not meet these standards; eventually, they managed to overcome the impasses through their interactions with me. Julia did not comply with ORA's request to go to the Texas Bureau of Vital Statistics to ask for official evidence that her husband had not filed for divorce. She explained to me that she did not know how to do this: her reasons referred to language barriers, financial constraints, schedule conflicts, and mistrust of public offices. When she asked me for help, I suggested that I could accompany her. However, she would have to miss a day's work, so instead I asked the lawyer at ORA to make an exception to the organization's rules and allow me to get the documentation for Julia myself. Once the papers were received, Julia was able to continue with her application process.

Leticia's case was at risk because of her delay in attending counseling and her need to bring her son (who played with some file folders and once spilled milk on a chair) to some appointments. As in Julia's case, I mediated between Leticia and ORA staff: first, by explaining that despite her aversion to counseling, Leticia had called the local agency specialized in providing free services in Spanish to be added to the six-month waiting list for an appointment because she could not afford a private counselor on her meager monthly income; second, by contextualizing Leticia's choice to bring her son along to some appointments, thus downplaying ORA staff's perception of her as an "inadequate" mother with an "uncontrollable child." Martha's case was on the verge of being closed because at times she was "demanding" (she often inquired about the status of her application) and "defensive and mistrustful" (she often doubted the purpose of ORA's questioning about her past and present conditions). However, her awareness and her interest in making informed decisions offered a counterbalance; these qualities were very much valued by ORA because they fit the profile of an autonomous citizen, who would then be prioritized over the bothersome ones.

Julia's, Leticia's, and Martha's cases show the delicate balance of immigrants' agency. On a daily basis, battered immigrants who qualified to adjust their status under VAWA or VTVPA were either given a lower priority or discharged as clients because of their unsuitable demeanor at ORA. Both Claudia and Luisa (mentioned earlier) were eligible to apply for a U visa. However, Claudia was "too scared" of the police and, hence, not compliant or resolute enough; Luisa was "too needy" and, hence, not autonomous or responsible enough. Patricia, a Mexican survivor of physical, sexual, and psychological abuse by a U.S. citizen who was incarcerated, was eligible to apply for citizenship under VAWA. However, her two "loud" children, who often came along to the office, and, more important, her "imprudence" when her husband, once released from jail, accompanied her to ORA, put her application on hold as long as she "put ORA staff at risk by bringing her husband along." In other words, Patricia was not secretive, deferent, or resolute enough—and ended up not proceeding with her case at ORA. Ramona's fate was similar. A Mexican survivor of multiple kinds of violence perpetrated by her citizen husband, Ramona was dismissed from the office because "it was unsafe" due to her husband's presence, and despite her qualifications to apply for citizenship through VAWA, she did not return after her second appointment. Silvana, a Colombian survivor of multiple abuses from a citizen, also eligible to apply for citizenship under VAWA, was so "chaotic and high-maintenance" that no one in the office wanted to take her case, as expressed by the lawyer and one of the legal assistants, which consequently went forward at a very slow pace as appointments were not offered frequently enough to her. The case of Clara, a Venezuelan survivor of psychological abuse from a citizen, eligible under VAWA, was pushed down the pile of cases because she was "erratic and irresponsible," as described by her case manager. Rosario, a Mexican survivor of physical, sexual, and psychological abuse from a citizen, eligible under VAWA, was "too disorganized" and "cried too much"; she was advised to come back when she was truly ready to go through with the process because ORA could not "spend time organizing clients' papers or calming them down as they provided their affidavits about their abusive experiences." Finally, the cases of Mónica, Samuel, and Yolanda, all Mexican survivors of intimate partner violence perpetrated by U.S. citizens, show the interrelationship of formal and informal constraints. Their criminal history, a clear burden in the eyes of USCIS, put all their applications on hold. However, whereas Mónica's drug-dealing charges and deportation sentence, and Samuel's "importation of individuals for immoral purposes" and voluntary deportation stopped their chances with ORA, Yolanda's former occupation as a sex worker was downplayed and pardoned informally at the nonprofit level. Despite the applicant being documented or not, some crimes were redeemable—that is, ORA was invested in proving to USCIS that the immigrant had been involved in the criminal activity against her will and therefore the crime should be overlooked and the applicant protected by the state.

The question remains as to whether the capacity of battered immigrants to meet informal expectations was strategic or unintended. My field observations suggest that the latter was at least as common as the former. On many occasions, the ability of these immigrants to blend in successfully reflected their conscious efforts to do so, that is, to adapt to informal codes of behavior. However, many of the immigrants who managed to complete the application process had fit the "good client" profile from the very beginning. Did this mean, then, that these immigrants just happened to be fortunate enough to fit the mold? Not quite. Even if they possessed these qualities to begin with, they still had to retain these attributes in their interactions with ORA staff. While it was easier for these immigrants to complete the application process because of preexisting qualities, they still had to work at it.

Nevertheless, it is relevant to think about the conditions that allowed certain immigrants to fit the nonprofit's informal expectations. My field observations suggest that the most destitute immigrants (the ones who came from the poorest backgrounds and, accordingly, had not received any kind of formal education) had more trouble negotiating the process than those who had slightly higher allotments of social and cultural capital because of their achieved working-class status and their few years of formal education (typically, completion of elementary school). However, immigrants who came from or had achieved higher social status (lower middle class or middle class) and had higher levels of formal education (completion of high school or more) also had trouble negotiating the process because they were more demanding and somewhat critical. The difference, of course, was that the most destitute immigrants' search for citizenship through VAWA or VTVPA would begin and end at ORA, whereas lower-middle-class or middle-class immigrants' searches would move on to other (nonprofit or for-profit) organizations if truncated at ORA. Overall, these discrepancies illustrate the main argument of this section: that agency must be understood within structural constraints, situational conditions, and interactional dynamics in order to reveal its degrees and qualities.

So, do VAWA, VTVPA, and nonprofit organizations like ORA promote or hinder battered immigrants' exercise of agency? The cases of immigrants like Angela, Claudia, Julia, Luisa, Laura, Martha, Rosa, Manuela, Ana, Susana, Clara, Silvana, Rosario, Mónica, Samuel, Yolanda, Patricia, Ramona, and Leticia show that it depends. To begin with, the disadvantageous positionality of battered immigrants that gender violence–based legislation and nonprofits try to improve by offering immigration benefits and legal services is not completely mitigated. Both the legislation and the organizations are permeated by gender, sexual, racial, ethnic, and class discriminatory parameters that frame immigrants' agency. On the one hand, battered immigrant women who are (at least) working-class, slightly educated, heterosexual, married to U.S. citizens, and considerably restored from the battering are prioritized by the state, regardless of their history of abuse. On the other hand, battered immigrant women who fit ORA's informal standards of being a "good client" are prioritized by nonprofit staff, independently from their traumatic past. Battered immigrants' ability to negotiate these structural and interactional constraints depends on background, positionality, personality, and awareness: casual compliance is oftentimes their main asset when it comes to exercising their agency in order to become citizens under VAWA and VTVPA. Battered immigrants' passage through the formal and informal gates to citizenship can be both tentative and ruthless.

ORA Staff's Agency

The nuances of agency are also illustrated by the behaviors of nonprofit workers. ORA staff were structurally limited by immigration laws and regulations as well as by their public and private grantors: their agency was relative to the state, donors, and immigrants; their preference of compliance over defiance of legal standards was a conscious expression of their agency (not to challenge the status quo); and their selective behaviors toward immigrants were strategic. Here, I will focus on ORA staff responses to my analytical observations, which I was able to share with them in various ways. As soon as I completed a full-length write-up of my findings, I tried to organize a meeting with ORA staff, but because of coordination difficulties, I ended up sharing my analysis by writing. One year later, I was able to return to the organization to present a report to current and previous ORA staff, and to gather their reactions, I also did group and individual interviews with staff who used to work at ORA while I was doing my research. All of these corroborated my findings while adding a reflective layer from the perspective of ORA staff, critical to contextualizing and furthering the understanding of the processes at play at the organization. In my presentations and conversations with current and previous ORA staff, first, I talked about the particular vulnerabilities of battered immigrants; second, I articulated the role that VAWA, VTVPA, and nonprofits like ORA had in acknowledging these vulnerabilities by providing means to overcome them; third, I disclosed my understanding of immigration laws as national gates for accessing citizenship, and of immigration officers and nonprofit immigrants' advocates as gatekeepers; fourth, I went over the formal barriers embedded in VAWA and VTVPA and suggested strategies to skip and/or dismantle these obstacles; and, fifth, I explained the informal barriers that I found at work at ORA and posed a group discussion to think about strategies to deal with these. Overall, ORA staff found the analysis accurate and sensible, that is, they agreed with my observations in regard to structural barriers as well as their role as gatekeepers and their power to reproduce (or challenge) inequality. However, ORA staff were not interested in getting involved with defying unequal practices and institutions.

Cathy, Jenna, Maggie, and I discussed the report together. Maggie participated through a conference call because she had moved to the West Coast, where she was working at a nonprofit for the development of entrepreneurial projects for women refugees. Courtney was not able to attend the meeting because she could not cut her workday short (she still lived in the same city but was working at another nonprofit organization that provided services for low-income immigrant families as well); I met individually with Courtney the following week to talk about my findings. Although invited to participate, Marina, who was working in an administrative position at a local university, was not interested in coming to the meeting or doing an interview with me. Carlos was present at the general meeting with all current ORA staff, as were Lucy, the legal assistant who had replaced Maggie, and Cathy (Jenna was not able to stay because her relatives were visiting). Twelve people were present at this meeting. John, the executive director, did not attend or meet individually with me because of "time constraints and work priorities." I met with Sophia and Valerie, two of the founding members, separately, to obtain their feedback on my analysis as well. I had two personal conversations with Cathy, one before and one after the group meetings.

In my first conversation with Cathy, she told me that she had read my analysis, which "made sense, but it was very difficult to address when working—abstractly was OK, but practically was impossible."[15] When I suggested that there could be ways to address these issues practically, Cathy was skeptical, saying, "There are so many pressures at work already; it's too much."[16] Time and again, Cathy expressed her frustration with ORA, saying she felt

> drained, overwhelmed, stressed . . . having to deal with so many things . . . staff complaining about various things, from not having office conveniences, like post-it labels or colored filing folders, to my style of giving directions. New staff is younger and have less experience; their ideals changed once they got to see the hardships of the work—they get paid little, they come in with ideals of changing the world, and then they realize that this is hard work.[17]

Cathy, as opposed to the newer ORA staff, had been able to understand the "hardships," that is, the constraints of working at a nonprofit organization with a restricted budget, within the limits of immigration law and public and private funding agencies. Cathy seemed to have internalized these limitations to the point that when asked directly about feeling restrained, she would deny or moderate it. For example, regarding funding conditions, Cathy explained that they are "not limiting," and that, indeed, ORA staff were

> lucky that the executive director and board dealt with funding while ORA staff could focus on working. Plus, the executive director always asks me first: John would ask me, "If we applied for a grant that required ORA to do X, Y, and Z, would ORA be able to satisfy these?" Then, I say yes or no, and then, if we get the grant, I would set "case priorities" to make sure that we comply with X, Y, and Z (types of services, volume of cases, etc.).[18]

Cathy did not believe that setting case priorities to satisfy a grantor was limiting, despite the fact that to achieve these priorities, ORA staff had to filter immigrants according to the grant specifics, which left plenty of eligible immigrants without attention (as in the case of many of the VAWA and VTVPA applicants that I observed). Another instance in which Cathy showed a contradictory understanding of structural limitations was in regard to class actions and open political participation: part of the co-optation/corporatization process that most nonprofits went through resulted in public and private grantors' restrictions on grantees to participate in class actions (the main avenue that disfranchised groups have taken to fight for large-scale legal and policy changes) and support political causes. In this case, Cathy recognized that "not being allowed to do class actions or be directly supportive of political matters had reduced the radical potential of nonprofits like ORA," and that "her job makes her less of an activist, which is very sad. There is a gap between casework (services to the community) and impact work (impact cases to change policies)."[19] Cathy's struggle between the two was frustrating but not paralyzing for her. She was determined to excel as a caseworker and to make ORA an exemplary organization that complied with set standards, even if they "sucked."[20] While aware of these formal limitations, Cathy expressed her individual agency as a case manager and coordinator at ORA by adapting to restrictions and sticking to the provision of services. She would have liked "to be much more of an activist," but instead, she found "value in volume. We want to get as many people in the system as possible."[21] When confronted with ORA's informal selective practices, Cathy brought up the high volume issue to explain not only why had she been selective but also why she allowed this to happen institutionally across the board. Cathy sustained this informal organizational practice, which was not purposely planned or instituted from above but had emerged from below and casually blended with ORA's goal to successfully complete the largest possible number of applications. She explained, "We cannot lose time with clients who cry, are too disorganized, or miss appointments. Instead, we should use our resources on the clients that do their part."[22] While Cathy understood the problematic aspect of leaving "trouble clients" aside, she insisted on the value of helping "good clients" and expressed her satisfaction in leaving things as they were. Overall, Cathy's agency was structurally limited by immigration laws and by private and public grantors; it was relatively lower than that of the executive director and board and relatively higher than that of ORA staff and immigrants and was strategically expressed in a compliant mode.

Jenna's agency was similarly framed, relatively lower than that of the executive directors, board, and Cathy, her supervisor, and relatively higher than that of the immigrants. Jenna was also strategically compliant. Unlike Cathy, Jenna was not disappointed but comfortable with the political/activist restrictions at ORA: "I deal with what comes down the river. Let other people do it. I'm not an activist. I work on the ground. . . . There are different people for different roles. There is a difference between the big and the small picture. . . . I feel like I'm a social worker even if I'm doing legal work. The political aspect of ORA is fine, but it's not my thing."[23] Jenna believed that my analysis made sense, even if "it was hard to hear. . . . It is true that we are selecting the immigrants for whom we will spend resources. . . . Many times I hope that they [troublesome clients] will weed themselves out. They get pushed to the bottom of the pile, and then other clients can speed up their application process." However, Jenna did not think that change was necessary, saying, "We do a very good thing."[24]

Akin to Cathy, Jenna was puzzled by my explanation of VAWA's and VTVPA's gender bias. They could not see how these laws were skewed because men could also apply for benefits as battered immigrants. They doubted my more detailed explanation and insisted on taking advantage of the positive aspects of the laws by helping as many immigrants as possible to enter the system. Drawbacks within the law could be tackled by others, but they thought that it was not their responsibility. While they would not resist other advocates' efforts to make immigration policies more inclusive, they were not interested in joining the struggle. They added that if ORA staff were requested to engage in political activism, this work would have to be calculated as part of their labor as opposed to being unpaid.[25] If ORA paid them to do it and there was enough time put in by other workers to still take care of the same number of cases, then ORA staff interested in politics could become actively involved. So far, the slight political activism that ORA staff had engaged in (like signing online petitions or joining community rallies) had gone unpaid while their regular casework was put on hold. ORA staff felt that this trade-off was unfair to both their clients and themselves.

The one thing that Jenna and Cathy thought could be done was my suggestion to advise immigrants about the formal obstacles that could be skipped. For example, to inform immigrants about the two-year grace period for filing a VAWA petition after getting a divorce while clarifying that the completion of the application may well last one year or more so that applicants can strategize the date of filing divorce proceedings without putting their VAWA application at risk; or to explain to U visa applicants that they should keep their contact information updated with the police so they can be reached at all times and the possibility of getting a denial based on noncooperation with the investigation is reduced. While these suggestions were reasonable and seemed sensible to take on as a regular practice, ORA staff were often attached to a fast-paced bureaucratic routine that limited opportunities to spend extra time explaining these kinds of issues to immigrants (even if ignorance of these tips could result in an applicant losing the chance to become a citizen). Again, Cathy and Jenna were reluctant to commit to new responsibilities; as long as they were providing services and meeting funding expectations to successfully complete a high number of VAWA and VTVPA cases, they believed that they were doing "good enough."

Jenna and Cathy resisted my proposal to address the informal disparities at ORA. In my presentation, I had initially asked for ORA staff's opinion on the validity of my observations. To an overwhelmingly positive response, I suggested they evaluate whether these patterns were problematic and, if so, to think about ways to modify these practices. As examples, I recommended mechanisms that other nonprofit organizations had put in place to moderate the unintended effects of bureaucratization and co-optation, like setting regular meetings organizationally with the aim to focus on these kinds of issues and elaborate strategies to change what is identified as undesirable, or cultivating a constructive dialogue with other nonprofits with the aim of creating network solutions to troubles that may not be feasible to cope with institutionally. In disbelief, Cathy explained, "I don't think this would work. It wouldn't be welcomed. People would be like . . . 'What the fuck?!?' if I asked them to spend time talking about dropped cases while they have been working plenty on other cases that had been selected and approved." Amid laughter, Jenna agreed with Cathy. Again, even if they acknowledged that the informal practices of ORA staff resulted in weeding out the most destitute immigrants despite their eligibility, Cathy and Jenna thought that this problem was satisfactorily counterbalanced by the high volume of cases that were indeed completed at ORA and approved by USCIS. They seemed to have developed a utilitarian logic related to their job, that is, they had embraced the idea that a minority could be sacrificed for a majority's sake; if in order to achieve grant standards to keep the organization running, ORA staff had to concentrate resources on suitable clients who promised to become good applicants and citizens in the eyes of USCIS, the unsuitable clients who were left behind were a loss that could be tolerated (or ignored). ORA workers strongly believed that the organization was accomplishing a good cause and were thus disinclined to focus on the unfortunate side. While their rationale was common to other organizations (be they nonprofit, for-profit, public, or private) and legitimate, I think it deserves scrutiny because it not only conflicted with the original purpose of the organization but also reflected larger processes at play regarding the admittance of "others" into U.S. society. Which immigrants are worthy to be included? Who cares for the excluded? Are the most destitute immigrants "disposable beings"?[26] Why have workers at organizations designed to serve the disadvantaged become conscious, comfortable gatekeepers? What is to be done? With these questions in mind, I turn to the reactions of other ORA staff.

The reader may be wondering what Maggie said about these comments while listening to the conference call. Maggie was mostly quiet but expressed her "delight" at having a "conversation with such a group of smart women."[27] At times, she had trouble hearing because she was using her cell phone while shopping at an outdoor farmers' market, and "it was kind of loud." One of her observations was that her current work was much different from ORA's, and that most of these issues were absent because the organization did not have such a high demand for services. She explained, "We have to chase for clients here."[28] Maggie also felt disconnected from the discussion because "it had been such a long time ago" that she had worked at ORA.[29] Midway into the call, Maggie apologized because she had to run back to work and could not stay on the phone. Unsuccessfully, I tried to set up an individual phone interview with her to talk further about these issues. Like Maggie, Jenna preferred not to have another conversation with me because she "had said it all" during the group meeting and had a "full schedule" as she was getting ready to quit working at ORA (she was about to go on a long journey around the world with her husband).[30] Courtney, on the contrary, insisted on meeting with me. I was able to see her during her lunch hour. She was very interested and told me right away that she had read the report, which "made sense and brought up many issues that I had thought about and often wondered how to deal with."[31]

Courtney compared her current job at another local nonprofit organization providing services for low-income immigrants with her former job at ORA: "I do similar work, but it's so different because [my current organization's] mission is to help immigrant families and not only to provide legal services. At ORA I was trained to fulfill only legal services and to achieve a certain volume of cases."[32] Moreover, Courtney valued her new job's retreats for staff, which "were so good because even if the retreats were time-consuming, we were able to reflect on our jobs, and we felt better and more productive afterward. It also feels good to know that the organization where you work cares about its staff's well-being."[33] Courtney remembered how frustrated she felt the last year she worked at ORA: "When there were staff meetings regarding institutional issues, like changing the name of the organization or trying to come up with ways for the staff to feel less stressed and tired, I spoke up but always found that ORA was set on a mentality of getting the money that showed a lack of political identity."[34] In regard to stress-management sessions, Courtney found that these "did not really work" because only a few ORA staff attended the sessions, which never resulted in implementing change at the institutional level.[35] She felt that ORA staff "did not want to hear criticism because it would force them to change while they seemed to be satisfied with themselves."[36] According to Courtney, ORA's satisfaction was based on the "high demand for services" and its success in achieving grant-related goals, which assured more grants in the future, that is, organizational survival and job security.[37] She elaborated, "At the beginning, I wondered whether ORA should take money from grantors who think that 'illegals' don't deserve benefits unless they were victims of domestic violence. But then the dilemma was having or not having funding."[38] Funding conditions and the growing demand for services had changed ORA's attitude. Courtney explained:

> If ORA didn't get any more clients, the story would be different. I remember that at the very beginning of the U visa program at ORA, I had very few clients. I had to do a lot of outreach to get enough clients. But later on, I had so many that prioritizing or dropping clients didn't matter. There was a Nigerian woman, one of the first cases I had. . . . I had so much time on my hands that I did everything I could until I got the certification from the police. Later on, the case of this woman would have been dropped once her certification was denied in the first place—I would have thought, I tried hard enough and there are so many other clients waiting.[39]

It was in the latter context that Courtney had dealt with Luisa's case, and as we talked about it, and I shared with her my frustration about how she had let Luisa's case sit in the file cabinet for several months and later had stopped trying to convince the police to look further into it, Courtney added that "the fact that we were still helping many others made it hard to recognize these informal practices as problematic. There were also issues of self-preservation. For example, not getting too involved or sad with the clients' stories allowed me to distance myself from the immigrants and focus on doing business." Courtney and other ORA staff had developed thick skins in regard to the past and present lives of immigrants as a mechanism to keep up with productivity (measured in volume of cases and expedience) and preserve their own well-being (to avoid burning out). In this way, nonprofit workers were similar to governmental public service providers, or what Lipsky called "street-level bureaucrats," who often struggle with the gap between ideals and reality:

> Ideally, and by training, street-level bureaucrats respond to the individual needs or characteristics of the people they serve or confront. In practice, they must deal with clients on a mass basis, since work requirements prohibit individualized service. . . . At best, street-level bureaucrats invent benign modes of mass processing that more or less permit them to deal with the public fairly, appropriately, and successfully. At worst, they give in to favoritism, stereotyping, and routinizing—all of which serve private or agency purposes. Some street-level bureaucrats drop out or burn out relatively early in their careers. Those who stay on, to be sure, often grow in the jobs and perfect techniques, but not without adjusting their work habits and attitudes to reflect lower expectations of themselves, their clients, and the potential of public policy. Ultimately, these adjustments permit acceptance of the view that clients receive the best that can be provided under prevailing circumstances.[40]

ORA staff can be easily compared to street-level bureaucrats, particularly because the co-optation of grassroots movements into nonprofit organizations exacerbated their institutionalization in a context in which the state shrunk as a service provider and nonprofits were supposed to fill the void, forming what Wolch called "the shadow state,"[41] in which, Gilmore claims, "the work people set out to accomplish is vulnerable to becoming mission impossible under the sternly specific funding rubrics and structural prohibitions that situate grassroots groups both in the third sector's entanglements and in the shadow of the shadow state."[42]

However, by understanding how these processes of bureaucratization and professionalization work, I believe that change can be triggered because, as much as governmental and nongovernmental street-level bureaucrats may become more distant and apathetic, they may as well revisit their intentions and practices in order to close the gap between ideals and reality. Insofar as "the decisions of street-level bureaucrats, the routines they establish, and the devices they invent to cope with uncertainties and work pressures, effectively *become* the public policies they carry out,"[43] nonprofit workers such as those at ORA should be aware of their critical position in maintaining or transforming existing policies.

To revisit ORA staff's responsibility as a gatekeeper, Courtney believed that leadership was also important: "As staff, we also identified with our supervisor. So, for instance, Cathy was not fond of children or clients who cried too much. So, when we didn't like them either, this went unnoticed."[44] Her reflections help further debunk the myth of nonprofit organizations' immunity to the typical processes that hierarchical organizations cope with, such as bureaucratization, specialization, and verticalization.[45] In regard to the latter, while nonprofits tend to be structured along the principle of horizontality, they are not free of power relations and their concomitant conflicts, since "all organizations have inequality regimes."[46] Executive directors who serve as main links with executive boards cannot make up for the disconnection that staff tend to feel from those above. In the case of ORA, the two degrees of separation between legal assistants and the board were exponential. While communication among all parties was open, legal assistants interacted closely and daily with their supervising lawyer, Cathy, who represented them before the executive director, John, who was frequently in touch with executive board members. As Courtney expressed, "Boards can be problematic because oftentimes they don't know about the actual work staff do or because sometimes they are not active enough, yet they have so much power over us."[47] This view was shared by most ORA staff. For instance, Cathy had made various cautious remarks: "Some board members are great, but there are some who are not committed with the organization, so they don't know enough. . . . There are others, newer members, who are, like . . . well, they are good to get funding because they know how to convince other wealthy people to donate money, but . . . they don't know much about immigration policy issues."[48] Tensions within nonprofits like ORA were also rooted in the scarce nature of its material resources (even if ORA had been successful in terms of funding and had grown over the years, it could not be thought of as a rich organization). With the exception of Carlos, ORA staff had expressed their views on this topic. Maggie frequently said, "We're not earning a six-figure salary here";[49] Marina had to find another job because she could not afford to earn so little any longer;[50] Jenna explained, "Even if I had not been earning much, my husband and I made the effort to save money so we could do our dream trip around the world."[51] Courtney claimed:

> Nonprofits have to be able to offer competitive salaries and good benefits in order to have good workers, educated and motivated. Nonprofit employees must be compliant and efficient in order to keep their job. We know that we are replaceable; there are so many recent graduates that are willing to do these jobs for a while, even if the pay is little. Nonprofits treat us as if we were commodities. That is why we formed a union at ORA, to make sure that the rights of the nonprofit workers were protected.[52]

Cathy, who was hired on the premise that she would organize and run the union, expressed how hard it had been for her to play all roles, that of the legal supervisor/case manager, union leader, and employee (because of the contradictory interests of these roles and the heavy workload). Cathy, who had been the main recipient of staff complaints, explained:

> There are always complaints. They complain about having too many cases, working too many hours, not having enough office supplies, not having better-looking or more welcoming offices, not having enough trainings, not being taken care of, being told what to do and how to do it quickly and harshly, et cetera, et cetera. Then, when I do things to accommodate them, like I organize trainings, but they don't participate or ask questions, it's so frustrating. I also feel that I can't ask more from them because they are getting paid very little.[53]

Staff turnover at nonprofits is very high indeed and very common (advocates refer to this phenomenon as the "revolving door of nonprofits"). Most people enter the field as a short-term occupation to gain experience in order to get another, better-paying job in the future. The few people who are committed to doing this kind of work for a longer term usually feel frustrated with inexperienced and less committed coworkers. This was the case with the older and newer ORA staff. Cathy claimed, "The new staff is not the same," and Jenna assented, "They are not as involved."[54] During my report to the new group of ORA workers (which included, as mentioned earlier, Cathy, Carlos, and Lucy), however, I did not perceive new staff to be disinterested, but frustrated. Overall, ORA staff were attentive to my report, and their reaction was positive. The section on informal barriers truly caught their attention: amid laughter and jokes, they spoke up and collectively confirmed that they "dreaded working with clients who cried a lot, clients who brought and could not control their kids in appointments, clients who called too much (many times per week, more than once a day), clients who were too demanding (the ones with higher economic status)."[55] If the clients behaved in these ways, the staff "didn't rush to make appointments with them."[56] The consensus on this matter seemed to relieve their concerns about the consequences of leaving these clients unattended. One staff member shared that "even though I know that these clients cannot afford day care, I still feel annoyed by them bringing in their children."[57] This comment was followed by Lucy, who said, "I realize that these client preferences ended up reinforcing the barriers you are talking about (particularly social class). But, I'm not sure what we can do about it."[58]

To my suggestion of setting time aside to discuss these issues at the organizational level, ORA staff seemed enthusiastic. I offered to come back to continue with this workshop, but later on Cathy told me that "it would be weird to have an outsider moderating the discussion,"[59] an opinion that Jenna and Courtney shared. One of the new workers asked me if I had done this research somewhere else, and after sharing my experience in another nonprofit organization, I emphasized the importance of thinking about what was happening at ORA in the broader context of nonprofits. I offered articles, reports, and books about other nonprofits that had identified similar patterns and had been working on dealing with them, and also pointed out that fostering network communication through trainings or conferences with similar organizations could help as well. The contextualization of ORA among other nonprofits alleviated some of the anxiety resulting from hearing a critical report. Courtney articulated this feeling as well:

> It is hard but necessary to hear criticism in order to be able to change. It helps to know that other nonprofits are going through similar things—it would be great to be more collaborative between nonprofits (here [in central Texas] is difficult because nonprofits are competing for the same funding sources, but it would be nice to see more

collaboration). I believe that thinking about how the organization is doing is very important. Retreats can help—at a retreat staff could focus on what is happening and develop ways to deal with whatever is thought of as wrong. Another way to provide better services is to get thorough, constructive feedback from the clients (as opposed to the feedback that ORA collects right now, which is useless because the survey that clients complete provides set answers), as well as keeping and evaluating records of the flow of immigrants through the organization (even if these may require resources, I think it would be worthy). . . . Also, I see that even if it's hard, and one may be tired from working so much, it is very important to keep politics alive.[60]

Courtney, now an outsider to ORA, acknowledged the problems and believed in the value of both institutional reflection and self-reflection. Valerie, one of ORA's founding lawyers, also an outsider, had a similar reaction. She was very much invested in reading and hearing about my project in order to avoid the same kind of mistakes in her newly created nonprofit organization. As she commented:

It takes courage and it's tough because there is always discrimination in place. Still, change is possible and it is important to be aware, remain faithful to the organization's mission. Other nonprofits had done it—little by little. Once one is aware, change can happen. For example, think about disability: ten years ago few people thought of this. But slowly, things began to change. Are you aware of how unfriendly your own office may be to people with disabilities? Once you realize, then you can go ahead and do the appropriate changes: build a ramp, check that your hallways and doorways are wide enough. You know what I mean.[61]

Valerie's reaction was also consistent with her general approach to advocacy, grassroots work, which remained politicized throughout the years. In other words, becoming an outsider should not be thought of as a prerequisite for reevaluation or change as a nonprofit worker. Take the example of Sophia, one of the other founding lawyers of ORA, who was also an outsider at the time of my interview with her. Her reaction was similar to Cathy's; she expressed a pragmatic view of the current state of affairs and disenchantment regarding change. She thought that the current legislation, with all its faults, was "better than nothing" and stressed that the enactment of VAWA contributed to the institutionalization and depoliticization of grassroots movements and the growth of nonprofits like ORA, which have been restricted by funding but "at least existed."[62] Sophia defended ORA staff's concentration on legal work and emphasized the need to value ORA's work and "understand that they were making tough decisions" and that change would be very "hard."[63]

Indeed, ORA staff, both old and new, recognized that formal and informal barriers stood in the way of immigrants' search of citizenship, but they were not eager to revisit their own practices to shrink or dismantle these barriers. The various reactions that I obtained were indicative of the possibility of change: Courtney's contemplativeness came as a surprise given her highly institutionalized role as a worker at ORA (recall Courtney's detachment in dealing with Luisa, for example, and her defensiveness against immigrants' massive protests); Maggie's disinterest could have been explained by the fact that she had stopped working at ORA "too long ago," and her belief that her new job on the West Coast was "different," although her attitude could have been a continuation of her beliefs and practices while working at ORA (her insistence on taking time to "pamper" oneself to "keep sane," going to stress-management sessions to avoid burnout, and picking "your battles"); Cathy's protectiveness was bound to her leading position at ORA and also consistent with her pragmatism ("the system sucks, but you have to work with it"); Jenna's reluctance reflected her satisfaction with her work (and also her upcoming departure); and the rest of ORA staff's curiosity provided an opening that could have been followed up but was not (because, in line with ORA's overall institutional satisfaction with its large numbers of citizenship application approvals, neither the staff nor Cathy pushed the issue any further). Change was possible yet difficult—and in line with social movement theories, from Marx to Tilly, it needed consciousness-raising, organization, and leadership.[64] My research intends to contribute to raising consciousness with the aim of generating willpower at the nonprofit level toward change, but it would fall short if I ended my relationship with ORA and/or reduced my scope to this organization as opposed to opening it up to others (I have done this through participating in nonprofit networks like Arte Sana, keeping involved with the immigrant community by, for example, doing open workshops on rights for immigrant survivors of violence in which I make sure to include tips to avoid or surpass existing barriers, and also by writing this book).

Collective action, however, is tied to individual agency. What can be learned from ORA staff's daily practices and reactions to my report? As in the case of the immigrants, the agency of the ORA staff was nuanced. The relevance of taking into account the frame of agency becomes even more apparent when observing the different responses: the agency of all nonprofit staff was limited by the formal frame of legislation and funding conditions, and by the informal frame of their nonprofits' internal rules and interactional expectations. The informal frames were more or less conducive to political engagement (to modify unequal formal frames) and self-reflection (to alter unequal informal practices), which influenced the capacity and willingness of nonprofit workers to be more or less active in regard to inequality matters. Nonprofit staff's agency was also relative to others' agency, not only that of immigration and law enforcement officers, and immigrant clients, but also that of their supervisors and peers, all of which could foster or deter staff's inclinations to change. While Courtney's and Valerie's outsider positions and new jobs seemed to have allowed them to reflect and take on new practices, the rest seemed to be set in their ways. Theorists have tended to emphasize the defiant aspects of agency, but nonprofit staff's agency is better depicted if one acknowledges its compliant side: ORA's workers were obedient gatekeepers, that is, they respected existing formal laws and informal rules despite their respective biases in order to include as many suitable immigrants as possible in the system (as opposed to adopting a defiant position engaged in changing formal and informal policies to include more of the supposedly nonsuitable immigrants). My doubts regarding nonprofit workers' awareness of their role as gatekeepers were lifted after I had the opportunity to do the report and the interviews with them. While they may not have thought of themselves in those terms, they were all conscious of their power to include immigrants as citizens; the exclusion of those immigrants who did not fit in formally or informally was, on the contrary, a "side effect" that was minimized or overlooked. ORA staff's awareness of the problematic aspects of the law and their institutional practices illustrates that agency cannot be defined only as power to do otherwise because their agency was indeed their power *not* to do otherwise. Moreover, by taking into account the frames, relativity, intent, and consciousness of action, one is able to better comprehend what may seem insubstantial or contradictory behavior.

Through their reluctance to push for legal change or modify inequitable practices, ORA staff had been consciously reproducing a biased system that leaves out the most dispossessed. Then, where should the struggle for inclusion be directed or located? In the presentation of my work at *"Nuestras Voces*/Our Voices: Collaboration and Transformation *en la Comunidad,"* the 2008 Arte Sana national conference, I broadened the front. I conducted a workshop among Latina battered immigrants' advocates who identify with Arte Sana's grassroots mission to "help bridge the gaps in victim services by promoting the development of culturally competent programs and the active participation of the Latino community in anti-sexual violence work," with little to no "private or governmental financial support."[65] In my presentation, I emphasized that the processes I discovered while working as a volunteer at ORA were common to other nonprofit organizations subjected to similar legal and funding constraints, and that the objective of thinking about these issues was to develop more inclusive policies and practices for battered immigrants. Workshop participants (nonprofit and governmental immigrants' advocates) were asked to form groups, reflect about the formal and informal barriers that stand in the way of battered immigrants' search for citizenship, and propose means that they had used or could use to avoid or dismantle these barriers. Most participants mentioned the constraints attached to grants and seemed to be doubtful about overcoming these, mostly because of a tremendous need for resources. A few argued for developing alternative sources of funding to be able to serve a broader spectrum of the immigrant population in tandem with the nonprofits' inclusive missions. Common propositions included collaborating with other nonprofits, educating the community, increasing the number of bilingual advocates, and developing culturally competent services. While the strategy of pushing for policy changes was put in the context of grantors' constraints, participants recognized its importance and noted the fear that immigrants felt in regard to deportation due to increasing anti-immigrant sentiments in the country. Finally, regarding informal practices at the nonprofit level, most advocates pointed to their struggles between allocation of scarce resources and faithfulness to their organizations' missions. They also emphasized the need to connect and cooperate with other organizations and valued the possibility of thinking of and elaborating strategies to handle these issues at in-house and network meetings, trainings, and conferences. The diversity of the group of advocates at the workshop was exemplified by their main concerns: while victim services specialists from the police department felt constrained by bureaucratic red tape that significantly slowed the process to assist battered immigrants, recently hired advocates were surprised to find out that VAWA and VTVPA were permeated by gender, sexual, racial, ethnic, and class discrimination. The range of responses, however, stressed the need to take a proactive, comparative, and collaborative approach on the matter. As Laura Zárate, Arte Sana's founding executive director, stated in the conference's opening remarks: "We are very diverse. . . . We are a big family. . . . We are all experts. . . . We are all survivors,"[66] and in order to survive organizationally and struggle for the well-being of "newly arrived or third generation" immigrants, "we need to create ways to work together, include each other, refer each other, and support each other's efforts."[67] In this spirit, I propose alternative actions for change.

Alternative Actions for Change

Change is structurally limited yet possible and, in my view, overdue. It is overdue not only because the legislation and nonprofit organizations that were created to include battered immigrants became actual means of exclusion but also because the apparent disposability of the most destitute battered immigrants reflects a broader and deeply rooted discriminatory system of nation building and social organization in the United States. What is to be done? Although there is no magical solution, I believe that two fundamental principles can be conducive to inclusion and equality: first, to believe that change is possible; and second, to act upon it. New beliefs and understandings will then be reflected in individuals' social interactions and collective action, and eventually articulated in institutional and structural arrangements. Before trying to implement (more or less radical) reforms, ideas about "what can-and-should be" must be crafted and embraced for change to occur in the desired direction and be durable. Conflict and collaboration among advocates and activists will fuel the process together with their critical awareness, individual and collective action, and determination to defy entrenched beliefs and systems that seem to have developed an overpowering life of their own. After forty years, the battered women's movement shall be "reenergized and refocused"[68] to find a new balance between the provision of services and the struggle to change inequitable social conditions that stand in the way of ending violence against immigrant women.

Specifically, I suggest that a number of myths ought to be discredited in order to refresh the willingness and commitment for individual and collective action. Initially, immigrant advocates shall counter the myth that "nothing can be done against the powers that be," a fallacy that only protects an unfair status quo. While it is true that the current structure and ideology of power are potent, it is also true that "alternative futures"[69] are possible. Tied to this, immigrant advocates shall expose that the myth that "one's actions don't matter" also serves a conservative, oppressive motive to keep things as they are and "obscures the role we can play"[70] in challenging and transforming our societies. A revived conviction in the power of individuals' beliefs and actions, as well as of social mobilization, is critical.

The case presented in this book is a keen example: ORA staff seemed to have grown into the notion that all that could have been done to improve the immigration system had been exhausted and that working within this (unfair) system was the only possible way to include immigrants. The original political spirit of the organization was lost among co-opted successes, which moderated the nonprofit's ambitions by instilling a market-like competitive mentality oriented to winning grants and satisfying grantors' expectations, and by disassociating the provision of legal services from dedication to social change. In recognizing the pivotal role that nonprofit advocates play in the inclusion or exclusion of immigrants into American society, these interconnected myths shall be reverted. On the one hand, while collective movements need institutional organization and resources to survive and advance their cause, the terms by which each organization accumulates and distributes its riches do not need to be set unilaterally by grantors in such a conditional way that the organization loses its own identity. As activist Hawk claims, "Just by trying to keep funding and pay everyone's salaries, [people in nonprofits] start to unconsciously limit their imagination of what they *could* do."[71] While reclaiming economic independence may be difficult, it is particularly desirable if grantors have opposing values, and it is viable, as exemplified by organizations like Project South in Atlanta, Georgia,[72] Sisters in Action for Power in Portland, Oregon,[73] and Communities against Rape and Abuse in Seattle, Washington,[74] all of which reevaluated their definition of institutional success to see how much of it responded to grantors, staff, and constituency, recentered their relationship with the communities they were serving, and employed alternative funding tactics. On the other hand, while concentration on service provision may increase the organization's productivity measured by volume of cases and expedience, the lack of political engagement and commitment to contribute to social change counteracts the potential of grassroots advocacy, since this is reduced to a framed delivery of services that reproduces unequal social systems detrimental to the population that is supposed to be served.

The division of labor between case managers, legal assistants, and social workers may be positive, but this occupational divide should not be equated with a disregard for the broader picture: an immigrant is not a legal case or a social work case but a *person* whose past story and present circumstances reflect wider and interconnected personal and structural processes. In the particular case of battered immigrants, the legal aspects cannot be detached from the psychological or social aspects of their case; in other words, their citizenship applications are tied to their trauma and their gender, sexuality, race, ethnicity, social class, and immigrant status. An integrated understanding of battered immigrants will generate better individual assistance as well as better chances to challenge disadvantageous structural forces at a collective level if advocates act on their social and political responsibility.

A related myth that shall be addressed is that of "time constraints and resource wasting." The idea that taking the time and resources to address this kind of institutional or political issues hinders institutional productivity has been proved wrong again and again in the nonprofit as well as in the private and public sectors. Collective critical reflection has been celebrated for its positive effects on creativity and productivity because it is through this kind of practice that staff regain ownership of their labor and the organization revives its efforts, as recognized by Courtney,[75] expressed at Arte Sana's national conference,[76] and articulated by INCITE! Women of Color against Violence.[77] Critical and creative thinking has been historically resisted by those in power, with the aim of maintaining the status quo that privileges them. Hence, to challenge oppressive forces, it can only be beneficial to reclaim this type of pensive and proactive practice as a constitutive aspect of grassroots organizations to grow institutionally, honor inclusive missions, and ultimately advance the struggle to end violence against (immigrant) women.

In regard to privilege, another diverting myth shall be questioned: that of assuming that nonprofits and their workers are free of the influences of gender, sexual, racial, ethnic, class, and other social hierarchies. Part of the discriminatory informal practices at ORA and the staff's reluctance to change may be explained by broader systems of oppression embedded within the organization.[78] ORA staff, with their own interlocking gender, sexual, racial, ethnic, and class composition, were unquestionably in a

dominating position over the immigrants who approached the organization, or, as Courtney expressed, "They tell you that you and your client
are partners, but in the end, we have more power."[79] While the power differences may be unavoidable, ORA staff could explore the ways in which
these differences play out in order to make use of their privilege in an
inclusive fashion through workshops. The process of recognizing one's
privileges is not easy, particularly if one is among racial or ethnic groups
that have earned a higher social status (after generations of personal and
collective struggle) and, since being in a position of relative dominance
over underprivileged immigrants, have begun to adopt abusive attitudes
typical of those in hegemonic positions of power (who enjoy possessing
"an invisible package of unearned assets that [one] can count on cashing
in each day, but about which [one] was 'meant' to remain oblivious"),[80]
together with abusive attitudes resulting from internalized racism, sexism, and classism. In ORA's case, all the workers in the program to assist
battered immigrants were women, were citizens (some were white sec-
ond- or third-generation immigrants, and some were first-generation
immigrants of color), had a middle-class social standing, and were college
educated. None was a survivor of intimate partner violence, most were
heterosexual, and one was bisexual. The intersection of all these characteristics shaped their interactions with survivors, in which they (unconsciously or not) enacted their privileges by differentiating themselves
from the undocumented, foreigner, battered, poor, immigrant "clients"
of color. If ORA staff worked through these power dynamics, the benefits would be felt by the immigrant community and also by the nonprofit
workers, who would be set free from the contradictions of harming those
they mean to help.

If questioned whether these suggestions are "asking too much" from
the advocates, I propose that another myth that should be revisited is
that of limited expectations. Believing that nonprofit workers should not
be invited to engage in critical and creative practices (because they earn
relatively low salaries, may have become institutionalized activists, and,
ultimately, are already assisting an underserved population) is conde-
scending toward the staff and detrimental to the immigrant community.
As reflected in my interviews, and in line with other researchers of grassroots movements and organizations,[81] it is accurate to say that nonprofit
workers get involved in this kind of occupation because they believe they
can help improve the living conditions of disfranchised populations. As
articulated by Lipsky, the reduction of the labor to achieving bureaucratic

goals is demoralizing for the personnel, who may rationalize their "compromises in work habits and attitudes . . . as reflecting workers' greater maturity, their appreciation of practical and political realities, or their more realistic assessment of the nature of the problem. But these rationalizations only summarize the prevailing structural constraints on human service bureaucracies. They are not 'true' in an absolute sense."[82] If pushed to think critically and creatively in order to highlight the potential of their work, nonprofit staff will eventually regain a sense of pride and revitalize their commitment to social change.

When presented with the criticism of being "too romantic," I insist that in order to rally for change, one must believe in its feasibility and be conscious of the nuances of agency while embracing a historical perspective and developing a keen sense of social awareness.[83] Contemporary and historical examples of the power of individual and collective action are abundant, but the choice to minimize them is often made either because of a preference for the status quo or an internalized fear of change. All social movements began and succeeded because of the shared beliefs of their constituencies, their organization, and their resilience. The institutionalization and co-optation of these movements had been overturned when their members became aware of these processes (i.e., when they broke through their alienation, as theorized by Marx) and acted against them.[84] Accordingly, my suggestions for nonprofit workers like ORA staff begin with the ideological: in my humble intent to raise critical consciousness of the pervasive inequalities within the immigration system available for battered immigrants and the nonprofit organizations providing services, I hope to provide staff with a new perspective on their role as gatekeepers, which may trigger their willingness to change adverse practices and institutions. Similar to Naples's objective, my analysis "foregrounds how racism, class, sexism and other dimensions of social inequalities are manifest even in the most radical political projects. With this heightened analytical sensibility to the relations of ruling within progressive social movements and claims-making strategies, movement actors may become more effective in resisting the cooptation of movement frames for reactionary purposes."[85]

Practical effects will follow the ideological challenge. Although I can provide "strategies to skip or dismantle" formal and informal barriers to access citizenship, as I called them in my report to ORA and workshop at the Arte Sana national conference, the only way in which substantive change will occur is if nonprofit staff recognize the barriers as problematic, believe in their own potential to influence policy and modify counterproductive informal practices, and create their own interpretation and courses of action. All these will impact the individual, organizational, and structural levels. Individually, nonprofit workers will alter, at least partially, their attitudes and practices as they interact with immigrants and other members of the organization. Renewed social interactions will have an effect on overall outcomes. To offer an example, by understanding the implications of being intolerant of immigrants who cry while sharing their abuse stories or call repeatedly because they are anxious to know about the status of their application, individual staff will be able to transform their feelings and put into practice more patient and helpful means to assist survivors without jeopardizing their citizenship application process. For the shifts in individuals' attitudes and interactions to be durable and substantive, change at the organizational level must be articulated (if not, individual changes may succumb to old organizational practices and become anecdotal).

Organizationally, nonprofit staff shall work collectively to evaluate the advantages and disadvantages of the existing legislation and the labor practices at play through meetings, workshops, or retreats devoted to addressing these matters. Specifically, in regard to immigration and violence, does ORA (or whichever nonprofit organization) recognize gender, sexual, racial, ethnic, and class discriminatory legacies embedded in VAWA and VTVPA? And, in regard to informal practices, do nonprofit staff acknowledge the prioritization of certain immigrants over others despite their formal eligibility? If these two (and/or other issues that may come up from their collective reflection) are identified, nonprofit staff should then invest in creating ways to eliminate unequal institutions and detrimental practices. Attending network conferences and trainings like the Network to End Violence against Immigrant Women National Network Conference, the Arte Sana national conference, meetings of INCITE! Women of Color against Violence, or other regional or local network gatherings may be of much help, particularly if nonprofit staff meet after these events to think about and adapt the lessons learned to their own circumstances. Reading research elaborated on and/or by nonprofits may also be critical to contextualize a particular organization's experience and draw on other nonprofits' strategies, both of which would help improve services and reduce the anxiety of thinking that whatever may be happening at ORA is extraordinary or isolated.

Another useful tactic may be to distinguish between formal and informal barriers. In regard to formal/legal barriers, nonprofit staff could think on the practical and political levels. Practically, ORA or whichever nonprofit may decide on instituting an organizational policy to inform immigrants about legal twists and turns and provide advice on how to overcome the formal barriers that may be avoidable (e.g., by being transparent about the length and full cost of the application process, the need for and cost of providing supporting documentation, the advantages of being employed in some capacity and keeping a clean criminal record, the relevance of providing a stable, current mailing address, and the convenience of attending counseling sessions and reporting incidents to the police). Politically, the nonprofit organization may redefine its political stance and strategies to challenge biases in gender violence and immigration policies while remaining faithful to its inclusive mission and wise in regard to its financial solvency (which may require the renegotiation of its ties with public and private grantors).

Collaboration with other groups active in policy struggles may be one option to seek, with the ultimate intention of reforming the legal pillars that sustain inequality structurally. VAWA, VTVPA, and the immigration system as a whole have maintained (more or less overtly) a social hierarchy that prioritizes citizens over noncitizens, men over women, heterosexual over nonheterosexual, European (white) over non-European, and richer over poorer—a system that legitimizes exploitation under a discursive coat of equality for all. By advocating for change of the embedded discriminatory aspects of the immigration provisions of VAWA and VTVPA, nonprofit organizations would contribute to the struggle to eliminate nationalist, patriarchal, sexist, homophobic, racist, and classist legacies within gender violence legislation as well as immigration law. Advocates could push policy makers to change VAWA's and VTVPA's biased immigration provisions by, for example, (1) equalizing the kind of benefits available (and the application process to obtain them) for all survivors regardless of their marital status—this modification would diminish the importance of (heterosexual) marriage as an institution legitimizing intimate partner violence, which indeed occurs despite and beyond marriage; (2) making the benefits of these laws equally available to all survivors regardless of their sexual orientation—this change would include the now excluded immigrant survivors of same-sex intimate partner violence; (3) erasing the different routes to citizenship by providing every survivor with a process of the same length and certainty regardless of the citizenship and immigration status of the abuser (this includes eliminating U visas or, if this were nonnegotiable, making them equivalent in process to

VAWA self-petitions, that is, more accessible and less threatening)—this amendment would provide a more racially and ethnically fair treatment of immigrants together with making the penalties to abusers uniform regardless of their citizenship and immigration status; (4) eliminating the requirements and fees that make the application process inaccessible for the poorest survivors, and in the instances where this is nonnegotiable, assuring that full support is available for them to comply—this measure would help these policies reach the most destitute immigrant survivors, who not only are currently excluded but also tend to be the most unprotected and at the highest risk for victimization; (5) issuing an instant protected immigration status for all applicant survivors to avoid the risks of deportation during the long process of collecting documentation, sending out the application, and having it reviewed and approved by USCIS— this tool would be particularly beneficial for undocumented immigrant survivors whose abusers' status plays against their odds to get access to their rights as survivors of intimate partner violence under the existing legislation; (6) guaranteeing confidentiality (and making nonconfidentiality punishable) of immigrant survivors' immigration status, reports, and testimonies given to the police and civil providers—this would counter current biases against undocumented immigrants who suddenly find themselves in deportation procedures because the police or civil providers reported them to immigration officers; (7) increasing the budget available for service providers, particularly those devoted to the most destitute populations, and making the application process for these funds more accessible to allow organizations from within these communities to compete for resources—this mechanism would diversify and extend the current reach of public funding, which tends to concentrate among more privileged groups who are able to compete using mainstream means; (8) promoting (and funding) holistic social services and/or facilitating connections between organizations and specialists in the community for survivors to meet their various needs comprehensively—this would reduce the number of survivors who succumb in their efforts to leave their abusive relationships because they are unable to find employment or affordable and safe housing, among other vital conditions, to be able to provide for their families and/or themselves; (9) refreshing and creating new outreach programs and public education in regard to violence against immigrant women and rights of immigrant survivors, especially in underserved communities—this would help in lifting knowledge barriers that prevent people in more socially disadvantaged settings from accessing the rights that in principle they are entitled to; and (10) keeping policy makers and state officials in touch with the realities of survivors of intimate partner violence and service providers through frequent specialized trainings—this would allow policies to be adapted to fit the needs of survivors and keep survivors at the center of all measures. In all, these kinds of amendments would make the immigration provisions of VAWA and VTVPA less discriminatory and, as such, could be used as examples in the broader struggle against the biases that pervade immigration law as a whole. In this regard, advocates for battered immigrants may join forces to push for a comprehensive reform in order to establish a system that erases all legacies of oppression. Political awareness and activism are crucial in this matter, particularly because windows of opportunity for policy change may open from within or may be opened by outsiders; not to lose hope is as important as being able to negotiate in order to achieve change, even if incrementally (the battered women's movement, indeed, is an example of the worth of such an attitude: despite persisting problems, very much has been gained by maintaining a long, collective, active, and ongoing sociopolitical movement to end violence against women). I believe that in maintaining policy/political awareness and a critical sense of social responsibility, nonprofit organizations like ORA do not have anything to lose but much to gain for the organization and, most important, the immigrant community.

In regard to informal barriers, nonprofit advocates could evaluate the origins and effects of their selective work practices and think about strategies to address these. The origins, in my view, are to be found in the organizational structure of nonprofits (including institutional policy and ideology, resource limitations, bureaucratization, professionalization, co-optation, corporatization, network connections, and staff training and support) and in the social composition of their staff (i.e., their inherited intersecting gender, sexual, racial, ethnic, and class systems) in relation to that of the immigrants. In the particular case of ORA, when wondering about its staff's impatience with immigrants who make the process more difficult, slower, and uncertain (i.e., immigrants who do not satisfy the institutional informal standards of being a "good client"), the identification of the origins of their feelings will guide the search for solutions. For example, if ORA staff believe that funding constraints are a main explanation, ideas about renegotiating terms with grantors or developing alternative resources should be explored. If ORA staff think that their intolerance for "criers" and immigrants who change their mind about moving forward with their application is legitimate, further understanding of the psychological and social conditions framing survivors of violence (all of which lead to emotional distress), and assistance from social workers and specialized counselors may be arranged (these services may be offered on site on a pro bono basis or through an exchange with the school of social work or the psychology department of surrounding universities). If ORA staff believe that immigrants' failure to steadily follow the application process is related to a lack of knowledge about its intricacies, improved informational packages may be provided, and support sessions for applicants may be organized (volunteers could collaborate with these activities).

If ORA staff identify that fear of retaliation by immigrants' abusive partners is a deterrent to helping undecided survivors, institutional policies to safeguard staff and immigrants could be implemented (such as the design of safety rules and measures to prevent and intervene in violent episodes). If ORA staff find that immigrants' children are distracting, child care options should be tinkered with, given the low socioeconomic position of their public (such as creating a program to have volunteers take care of the children or organizing an area with toys in the waiting room). If ORA staff feel that their own gender, sexual orientation, race, ethnicity, and social class stand in the way of their relationships with immigrants (such as female staff feeling threatened by male immigrants, citizen staff feeling superior to undocumented immigrants, or middle-class staff looking down on the practices of lower-income immigrants), reflection and attitude change could be fostered at the institutional level (ORA could schedule sessions with network members who have been addressing these kinds of discriminatory practices by providing information and organizing workshops with the aim of recognizing and redirecting privilege).[86]

If ORA staff complain about immigrants' demands for services, a reassessment of staff-client relationships and the nature of nonprofit work may be useful (for instance, staff may evaluate whether their "clients" have a "right" to make demands on their services "even if they are getting it for free"; if their answer is that clients should not be demanding, staff may think about ways to express this to the immigrants, who could be told that because of the nature of the nonprofit, staff try to address their needs as efficiently as possible within limitations; if their answer is that immigrants still have a right to make demands, staff may think about better institutional ways to process these, such as taking notes of the verbal demands or having a suggestion box available for immigrants to express their needs, and then looking into these concerns at staff meetings to decide what to do about them). If ORA staff claim to be overwhelmed, stress-management, counseling, recreational, or other activities may be implemented to relieve the burden staff feel and presumably transfer to the immigrants. Finally, if ORA staff are comfortable with their informal selective practices, they may refer "trouble clients" to other nonprofit organizations known for their commitment to serve the most destitute and/or for their tolerant staff to avoid blocking the survivors' search for citizenship.

All in all, contrary to the argument that lifting informal barriers would be costly and unworthy, the measures I suggest here either cost nothing or else could be crafted through an exchange of services with community partners, their worth being, again, for both immigrants and nonprofit staff. Ultimately, the interest in performing these kinds of critical/creative activities will be tied to the advocates' change of mind-set and conscious work toward challenging a long-lasting, pervasive system of inequality. As activists suggest, advocates should "not make any assumptions about what a domestic violence *program* should look like, but instead ask: What would it take *to end violence against [immigrant] women of color*?"[87] The actions toward such a goal may be more or less subversive, more or less innovative, more or less effective, but ultimately all these actions may be taken to achieve the radical moment when violence against immigrant women will be a horror from the past.

So, to return to the original question that guided this chapter, I believe that the nuanced agency that battered immigrants and ORA staff had in negotiating oppressive structures could be redirected toward change. On the one hand, my research may guide violence against women and immigrants' activists and advocates in the direction of facilitating battered immigrants' access to citizenship by eroding formal and informal barriers. At the policy level, measures should be taken to reduce the impact of the discriminatory legacies of the immigration system in legislation related to violence against women (and, on a grand scale, to reform the system comprehensively and eliminate these kinds of discriminatory patterns altogether).[88] At the organizational level, reflection on institutional practices and priorities should be promoted to reduce the nonprofits' dependency on external (private and public) funding—which emphasizes the number of clients and petitions approved and curtails their political activism—and to revive their activism and commitment in the struggle for the inclusion of all immigrant survivors of violence, that is, to end violence against *all* women.

On the other hand, this research may guide battered immigrants' agency in their ability to overcome the formal and informal obstacles they may encounter on their path to citizenship in this country. This may come from advocates who are engaged in outreach programs as well as in the provision of services by including as much information as possible for the immigrants to skip formal and informal barriers along the way and to encourage them not to give up if stopped in the process. Other members of the community, including battered immigrants who went through the process, and other immigrants who may be aware of these issues may be of help, too, by becoming carriers of information and referral points for survivors. Without the need to be professional experts, basic information about rights for (battered) immigrants may be passed along, together with referral to community organizations providing specialized services. An example of battered immigrants' activism is Arte Sana's program Capacitadoras en Acción (Trainers in Action), which consists of training battered immigrants to become sexual violence educators in their communities and then train other immigrants to become community educators themselves. This grassroots program is bilingual and sensitive to the cultural identities of the immigrant community, with the aim of reducing the revictimization of Latina/o Spanish-speaking survivors of sexual violence, who often find language and cultural barriers in mainstream antiviolence organizations, and empowering "the participation of Latinas and Latinos in the prevention of violence against women, especially along the Texas-Mexico border."[89] Spreading knowledge is superlative; all the battered immigrants whom I met at ORA and in other contexts were surprised to learn that they indeed had rights and that they could do something to escape their violent situation. A small bit of information was often enough for battered immigrants to seek help and, in that way, begin to walk their own path toward autonomy, nonviolence, and citizenship. As Brabeck and Guzmán found in their study of Mexican-origin survivors,[90] the number of Latina immigrants seeking help and trying to leave their abusive relationships has been increasing partly because they were able to learn that the kind of relationship they had was abusive, that they had rights as survivors regardless of their immigration status, and that free services were available in their communities to help them overcome their violent and dependent situation. Most activists, advocates, and researchers of violence against immigrant women have recognized the relevance of the dissemination of such knowledge and have pushed for public outreach. Flyers describing safety rules as well as survivors' rights and contact information of community services for battered immigrant women have been written in various languages and widely distributed. On my end, I have focused on sharing and distributing information about the formal and informal intricacies of going through VAWA and VTVPA application processes with the aim of helping immigrant survivors avoid or overcome these obstacles.[91] I provide a comprehensive list of the requirements, length, and costs of the process and focus on how to cope with covert barriers by, for example, stressing the current importance of being married and, therefore, the strategic handling of divorce options, the current privilege of heterosexuality, and the thin but existing options for homosexuals through VTVPA, tactics to endure the application process in its various lengths depending on the abusers' nationality, means to save money to afford the remaining costs of the process, why and how to handle counseling services, how to interact with police and immigration officers, and how to be aware of nonprofit staff's preferences and ways to interact with them. When providing this information in the community, I also have the opportunity to record the experiences of other immigrants in other organizations, which inform me of other obstacles and means to achieve the end goal of nonviolence and independence. Also, as I provide this information, I try to remain sensitive to immigrants' perspectives and values as opposed to trying to "teach them how to do it"; my suggestions are not intended to discipline them but, instead, to give them extra tools to take on the challenge.[92]

We usually forget how much our actions matter to the maintenance and defiance of the social structures that surround us, but as Berger and Luckmann theorized, we all construct the reality in which we live.[93] Particularly in regard to the social inclusion and exclusion of immigrants, and, as Garfield claimed, "knowing what we know,"[94] we should recall that "formal laws and legal rulings create a structure that legitimates the granting or denial of recognition. However, the maintenance of boundaries relied on 'enforcement' not only by designated officials but also by so-called members of the public."[95] We are all responsible, and we can all take action. Taking an essentialist approach would be highly detrimental to the advance of the struggle for equality (i.e., thinking that only battered immigrants of color could do this work, as opposed to thinking that every person who is aware of the issues and keeps a critical and proactive attitude about the subtleties of discrimination could be of help).[96] In the end, to go back to the main quandary of this chapter, the value of the structure/agency sociological debate is given by its practical implications to challenge and overcome inequality. As feminists of color claim, in order to contribute to the struggle to end violence against immigrant women, one must "focus on the ways in which they experience exploitation, marginalization, powerlessness, cultural imperialism and violence,"[97] by truly listening to other voices, and working with them to do otherwise.

6

Conclusion

The Violence Against Women Act and the Victims of Trafficking and Violence Protection Act represent major achievements in the struggle to end violence against immigrant women as long as these laws acknowledge intimate partner violence as a social problem and provide a diverse array of support to survivors according to their particular vulnerabilities. However, by looking into the experiences of Latina battered immigrants in their search for nonviolence, autonomy, and citizenship at a nonprofit organization in Texas that provided legal services free of charge for poor immigrants, I found that not all survivors have been protected in the same way. The disparate fates of battered immigrants Angela, Claudia, Julia, Luisa, Laura, Martha, Rosa, Manuela, Ana, Susana, Clara, Silvana, Rosario, Mónica, Samuel, Yolanda, Patricia, Ramona, and Leticia reveal significant biases in the laws and the provision of services. Despite the good intentions of VAWA, VTVPA, and community organizations like ORA, immigrant survivors of violence who are women of color, extremely poor, with few years of formal education, undocumented, in relationships with residents or undocumented immigrants, originally from Mexico, homosexual, and/or unable to fit within "normal" standards of civil behavior tend to be discriminated against in (or barred from) the process of becoming U.S. citizens, independently from their histories of abuse. This unfair outcome contradicts the all-inclusive spirit of VAWA and VTVPA and counters the struggle of battered immigrant women activists to end violence against *all* women. In joining efforts to eliminate such conditions, I hope this book will further the understanding of the complexities beneath the lives of Latina immigrants as they traverse gender violence, social inequalities, and citizenship matters, as well as motivate individual and collective action against unfair practices and systems both within and beyond immigrant communities.

In chapter 2, I share the story of Angela, an undocumented Latina survivor of intimate partner violence, at length. Her story, together with those of the other eighteen battered immigrants presented in subsequent chapters, reflects the particular vulnerabilities and intricacies of violence against Latina immigrants. Their undocumented immigration status intersects with gender, sexual, racial, ethnic, and class discriminatory practices and systems in shaping the kind of violence perpetrated as well as the means available for survivors to escape their abusive relationship. Angela's migratory history adds an extra layer to the understanding of the reasons immigrants may endure the violence (both intimate and structural) that they encounter once they arrive in the United States (i.e., how much their poor background, needs of their family, and history of violence shape their expectations and tolerance). Moreover, Angela's case locates intimate partner violence against Latina immigrants in the broader context of the exploitation of poor Mexican immigrants in the United States (from unwelcoming immigration laws and unfair labor conditions to covert racism, sexism, and classism, and internalized histories of oppression), that heightens battered immigrants' dependency on their abusers, fear of deportation, mistrust, isolation, and ignorance of their rights as survivors of intimate partner violence. Angela's story also exemplifies the struggles survivors endure in their repeated efforts to break free from their intimate partners and, thus, counters the commonly held perception that survivors who stay with or come back to abusers are passive or pathological (particularly by showing the multiple traps within and against which undocumented immigrant survivors tend to act). At the same time, her story illustrates similarities between undocumented immigrant and other survivors of intimate partner violence, such as their tendency to believe that their perpetrators' aggressions are their fault; to internalize their abusers' demoralizing comments, lose hope, and consequently adjust their expectations to a life of abuse; to keep their experiences secret because of shame and often with the intention of preserving the safety of family members and friends who may have been threatened; to endure abusers' addictions, jealousy, and multiple and repeated expressions of violence (physical, sexual, economic, psychological); and to believe in their abusers' promises of change and love.

Angela's story, despite being disheartening, ends encouragingly. With determination and the support of a network of family members, friends, and community organizations like ORA, she was able to break free from her violent relationship by achieving legal and economic independence as a U.S. citizen. Her case celebrates the achievements of the existing legislation to protect immigrant survivors of gender violence, that is, VAWA and

VTVPA, as well as the good work of advocates in community organizations like ORA. Angela recovered the hope that "something good" could "still happen" once she learned that she had rights as a survivor of violence, regardless of her undocumented immigration status. She changed her perception of possibility as she went through the process of collecting the necessary documentation for her citizenship application process, particularly as she wrote her own history. Angela understood that her husband's behavior was not acceptable but abusive and that she was indeed a decent, valuable survivor of intimate partner violence, and a single mother who had tried to do the best for her children (even if these acts may have harmed them). At the end of the process, Angela was able to look back at her painful past and, feeling "relieved," look forward to the future.

However, not all battered immigrants who approached ORA were as fortunate as Angela in their search for protection through VAWA and VTVPA. In chapter 3, I share the stories of other immigrants with whom I worked at ORA with the double aim of continuing to learn about the intricacies of intimate partner violence against Latina immigrants and to analyze the obstacles that stand in the way of their search for nonviolence, autonomy, and citizenship. The cases of Claudia, Julia, Luisa, Laura, Martha, Rosa, Manuela, Ana, and Susana put gender violence–based legislation in perspective. As much as the immigration provisions in VAWA and VTVPA have made a positive impact on many survivors, I show that inherited biases from the broader immigration system have limited the reach of their help. Immigration laws are one of the mechanisms that the state utilizes to sustain its sovereignty (because they regulate which individuals are welcomed to form part of its population), build nationhood (because they set citizenship ideals), and control productivity (because they stimulate foreign laborers to legally join its workforce or prevent them from doing so) along gender, sexual, racial, ethnic, and class lines. In the United States, immigration laws have historically prioritized men over women, married over nonmarried, heterosexual over nonheterosexual, white over nonwhite, European over non-European, Christian over non-Christian, citizen over foreigner, and richer over poor. Framed within these laws, VAWA and VTVPA reproduce such hierarchies in their treatment of immigrant survivors; an outcome that counters their inclusive spirit.

The stories of Claudia, Julia, and Luisa (unlike Angela's) and the fact that in my two years of work at ORA I never learned of a nonheterosexual immigrant survivor of a crime seeking services exemplify the gender and sexual discriminatory parameters within which these laws work. In mirroring the family-based immigration system, VAWA and the clauses for battered immigrants married to undocumented immigrants in VTVPA are still influenced by the legacies of the English common-law doctrines of coverture and chastisement, which legitimized not only men's domination and violence against women but also heteronormativity. In practice, this means that the marital status and sexual orientation of the abused determine the options available for them: whereas married, heterosexual survivors of gender violence are fully protected, nonmarried, separated but not divorced, and nonheterosexual survivors are partially protected, since they find more obstacles than opportunities along the way. As long as survivors are treated differently along gender and sexual lines, VAWA's and VTVPA's efforts to end gender violence will be curtailed from within.

The cases of Laura, Martha, Rosa, Manuela, and Ana (again, unlike Angela's) reflect the racial and ethnic discriminatory parameters that pervade the immigrant provisions in VAWA and VTVPA. The national origin and immigration status of the abuser determine the options available for battered spouses: Angela found the shortest and safest route because her abusive husband was a U.S. citizen; Laura, Martha, Rosa, and Manuela found less certain (and, when available, longer) routes because their husbands were legal permanent residents; and Ana found the least certain and longest route because her abuser was an undocumented immigrant. These differences reflect the long-lasting centrality of race and ethnicity in the United States' history to build its nationhood. Birthright, naturalization, and immigration laws overtly sustained race and ethnicity as legitimate sources of differentiation among individuals from the very beginnings of this country until 1965, at which time, in resonance with the civil rights movement, immigration laws were amended to be stripped of race- and ethnicity-based exclusionary clauses. However, racial and ethnic bars to citizenship have remained implicit in regulations and thus continue to prioritize whiteness in a cultural context of color-blind racism. VAWA and VTVPA prioritize the abusers' nationality and immigration status over the immigrant survivors of violence and the wrongdoings against them: no matter the intensity of the abuse, if the perpetrator is not a citizen, the length and certainty of the path to citizenship are negatively affected. In such a way, VAWA and VTVPA reinforce ideals of Americanness along racial and ethnic hierarchies.

The case of Susana, together with Luisa's and Claudia's, illustrates how VAWA and VTVPA exclude battered immigrants along class lines.

The costs and demanding requisites to file a VAWA self-petition or a U visa under VTVPA end up excluding the most destitute immigrants, despite the fact that advocates have struggled to remove economic barriers from poor survivors' access to citizenship by requesting fee waivers from USCIS and creating nonprofit legal organizations. The poorest immigrants continue to find the process unaffordable, complicated, and thus unattainable. This kind of socioeconomic barrier also reflects a long-standing characteristic of the broader immigration system. The United States has a history of, on the one hand, welcoming poor immigrants as long as they arrived to become part of an inexpensive (exploitable and disposable) labor force while, on the other hand, objecting to the poor origins of immigrants as soon as they sought to be incorporated into the polity as residents or citizens. This double standard in regard to class was applied to migratory flows from all over the world; however, in its intersection with race, ethnicity, gender, and sexual orientation, it tended to prioritize white, Anglo-Saxon, Protestant men and heterosexuals—an order that has been maintained through the selective allocation of citizenship and labor rights. VAWA and VTVPA are not exceptions to such class-based selectivity, which also diminishes the positive effects of these laws particularly because most battered immigrant women are poor.

The spirit of VAWA and VTVPA, that is, to protect all survivors of intimate partner violence regardless of their gender, sexual orientation, race, ethnicity, class, or immigration status, is truncated by superseding exclusionary ideals and institutions. One may think that as long as the immigration provisions of VAWA and VTVPA exist within the broader immigration system, there is no way to avoid its exclusionary forces. However, one should recognize that as a result of the work of activists for battered immigrant women's rights, the laws have been modified to curb the impact of such discriminatory regulations. I hope that by furthering the understanding of how these inequalities permeate the formalities of current laws, activists and advocates will be better equipped to push for changes of VAWA, VTVPA, and the overall immigration system.

In chapter 4, I look beyond the formal barriers that stand in the way of battered immigrants' search for nonviolence, autonomy, and citizenship by focusing on the role that nonprofit organizations' workers play as mediators between the state (grantor of rights) and the immigrants (claimant of rights). Nonprofit advocates become brokers of citizenship, or gatekeepers, as I called them, as they facilitate or hinder the inclusion of immigrants into U.S. society. The cases of Clara, Silvana, Rosario, Mónica,

Samuel, Yolanda, Patricia, Ramona, and Leticia take one further into the specific vulnerabilities of battered immigrants particularly in regard to the kind of informal obstacles they may find in their interactions with advocates. ORA workers' power to guide immigrants through the application process was paired with their power to exclude immigrants beyond legal constraints. Through time, ORA had developed institutional policies and informal routines that ended up prioritizing certain immigrants over others. Staff shared a tacit understanding of the advantages of working with "good clients" with the double aim of achieving higher institutional outcomes (measured by the number of successful citizenship applications) and reducing the stress of working with survivors of violence. Immigrants who were compliant, tidy, constant, resolute, autonomous, responsible, deferent, considerate, discreet, redeemable, considerably recovered from the battering, and "good" parents (when applicable) were preferred by nonprofit staff. These informal standards discriminated against the most underprivileged immigrants who approached the organization, since they tended to either be given a low priority as clients or not be selected as clients at all, independently from their traumatic past and eligibility under VAWA or VTVPA. By incorporating ORA's institutional history and the political-economic context of nonprofit organizations in general, I analyze the logic beneath such labor practices. Common processes of bureaucratization, verticalization, professionalization, co-optation, and corporatization moved the organization away from its original grassroots, radical, and holistic character and contributed to the development of selective mechanisms and political passivity among ORA staff. These reduced the power that advocates and community organizations have in challenging an inequitable status quo (in this case, by incorporating marginalized immigrants into American society and/or by pushing for more inclusive policies) and complicated (or even prevented) immigrant survivors' quest for citizenship. By accepting that such processes are likely to happen, institutional strategies can be focused on how to resist or counter their negative effects in order to keep a critical and creative spirit alive. The recognition that nonprofits are not immune to inequality regimes typical to all kinds of organizations is also helpful because it allows advocates to be attentive to how systems of gender, sexual, racial, ethnic, and class inequality have influenced their workplace and relationships with their public. The question remains as of how to motivate advocates into having such a critical and proactive attitude in an institutional and social context that awards the opposite.

Chapter 5 brings a confident view, since it focuses on the ways in which all these structural constraints have been and can be negotiated by immigrant survivors and advocates. By bringing back the stories of the battered immigrants, as well as the thoughts of ORA staff, Cathy, Jenna, Courtney, Maggie, Valerie, Sophia, and other advocates, I look into individual and collective expressions of agency. Agency, that is, the power to negotiate formal and informal constraints, must be understood with its nuances: agency does not occur in a vacuum, is relative to others' agency, can be expressed as resistance as well as compliance, and can be either the result of strategic planning or unintended. When one looks at it through these lenses, one is able to understand expressions of agency that may initially seem contradictory (such as survivors returning to their abusers, or advocates selecting which survivors to help in their quest for citizenship) and propose alternative actions for change from a more realistic basis (i.e., by acknowledging the frames, relations of power, limitations, and possibilities of individual, interactional, and collective action). Based on my experiences at ORA and networks of battered immigrants' advocates, I share propositions with the aim of countering the exclusionary rules and practices that have left the most disadvantaged battered immigrants unprotected. By insisting on the need to believe that change is possible, and by emphasizing the necessity of acting upon this belief, I stress that advocates must first defy a set of ideas that counter the possibilities of change (such as the myth that nothing can be done against the powers that be, or that service provision and politics cannot go together). Then, I offer practical suggestions (from organizational readjustments and information for immigrants, to policy recommendations), with the caveat that the best routes of action will come from within the groups that are willing to put them into practice. While one may wonder whether moderate or radical measures are more or less conducive to long-lasting change, the ideas presented in this chapter contribute to an understanding of how the struggle to end violence against immigrant women has been and can be forged.

As a whole, this book contributes to the literature about intimate partner violence against Latina immigrants by exposing the complexities and vulnerabilities they encounter in their lives of migration and abuse, as well as the obstacles they find in their quest for nonviolence, autonomy, and citizenship in the United States. My work expands the call for culturally sensitive services, typical of intimate partner violence scholarship and represented by the work of Hazen and Soriano,[1] by redefining the meaning of cultural sensitivity. I argue that in understanding culture, one must go beyond simplistic interpretations of ethnic customs, language, and religion (because culture is a complex and dynamic entity), get rid of cultural determinism (because culture partially influences, but does not fully determine, behavior), and develop a more complete cultural picture by including the culture of the receiving country (because it is within this context that violence occurs and survivors try to break free). Accordingly, culturally sensitive services should acknowledge both the cultural background of immigrant survivors and the cultural context in which they may be seeking support. Both influence how violence is perpetrated and endured, whether survivors believe in the option of leaving their abusers, and the conception that survivors have of themselves in relation to the broader society. While culturally, the United States has condemned intimate partner violence in the last thirty to forty years, Latin American countries began this process later—a difference that may influence Latina immigrants' ability to understand violent relationships as unfair and unacceptable. Immigrants' self-worth is affected by their culture of origin, their family history, and their abusive relationship. But survivors' self-worth is also affected by the context in which they currently live in the United States. As presented in this book, this context may open opportunities for battered immigrants, but it may also be ruthless, as Latina (particularly Mexican and poor) immigrants are usually discriminated against (as an exploitable labor force, as foreigners unworthy of immigration documents, as immigrants who are coming to take advantage of other minorities). Therefore, when one claims the need for culturally sensitive services, the sensitivity should be broadened to include U.S. culture and its pervasive social inequalities, since they influence the lives of immigrant survivors and their willingness and ability to seek formal and informal support to break free from violence. In this regard, my work complements Brabeck and Guzmán's research on how Mexican-origin survivors search for support to survive abuse,[2] adding to their efforts to counter stereotypes that portray battered immigrants as passive or ignorant (as well as to Salcido and Adelman's efforts to defy views of immigrant survivors who stay in violent or dependent relationship as pathological or irrational).[3] The stories of all the immigrants presented here prove the contrary by focusing on their nuanced agency, specifically, by sharing and valuing all the ways in which survivors keep their struggle to *"salir adelante,"* despite all kinds of obstacles. My analysis also picks up on Salcido and Adelman's call to put intimate partner violence research in dialogue with immigration studies, particularly as I build on other literature that explores the links between gender violence, citizenship, and social inequality. This book follows Crenshaw's intersectional analysis of violence against women of color and also emphasizes the need for building coalitions between groups with diverging agendas, since I believe that the struggle to end violence against immigrant women of color cannot be put on hold any longer or be successfully fought from an essentialist or fragmentary position. In unison with other advocates and activists from organizations like INCITE! Women of Color against Violence and Arte Sana, and feminists of color like Anzaldúa and Keating,[4] I agree that it is time to bridge differences, cross over, and take action because violence against immigrant women of color will never end as long as other social injustices (from poverty to racism) remain in place. Community organizations and grassroots networks are critical pieces in this struggle, as indicated by Abraham.[5] However, my work shows that the role of these institutions and their advocates may not always be advantageous to immigrant survivors. While these findings uphold critical analyses by Rudrappa,[6] Ong,[7] and Menon and Bhasin[8] of ethnically based and culturally sensitive community organizations, my research differs because I believe in the ability of advocates to engage in critical and creative thinking to defy the perverse effects of embedded systems of inequality. By recognizing that no one is exempt from the workings of power, particularly because of its disciplinary and capillary character, and that domination occurs in the constitution of marginal others (as theorized by Foucault),[9] I stress the importance of continuing to work *in* the community to ameliorate the treatment of immigrant survivors who are now being marginalized. My research shows how VAWA, VTVPA, and battered immigrants' advocates have not escaped the long history of the U.S. immigration system as a tool for the state to sustain a hierarchical social order along gender, sexual, racial, ethnic, and class inequalities—as demonstrated by Glenn,[10] Luibhéid,[11] Calvo,[12] Chapkis,[13] Ngai,[14] Haney López,[15] Omi and Winant,[16] Feagin,[17] Bonilla-Silva,[18] Hing,[19] and Johnson.[20] However, I am confident that once they become cognizant, battered immigrant women's advocates may continue to struggle collectively to get rid of such unwanted inheritance by modifying day-to-day unequal practices and pushing for policy changes.

The development of activist research was indispensable to realize the particular hardships that Latina battered immigrants find along the way, as well as the frames within which advocates work (thus highlighting the benefits of using such methodology). While in principle all battered immigrants are meant to be protected, praxis proves otherwise. By looking at the way in which Latina survivors go through the citizenship application process at the nonprofit level, I uncovered how the most underprivileged battered immigrants are excluded. As is regularly the case for marginalized groups, their reality is often repudiated or silenced. I hope that my research will break the apathy and denial by bringing their stories to the fore,[21] making "the invisible visible,"[22] and emphasizing the link of Latina battered immigrants' experiences with broader social conditions to which, in one way or another, we are all related. As other feminists of color have pointed out, gender violence is always an expression of dominance in its intersection with sexual, racial, ethnic, and class oppression, as well as the construction of nationhood and citizenship. As much as social hierarchies are established through laws and regulations, domination is acted and reenacted (purposely or not) at the very local level. What occurs in the margins defines the center—the lines of exclusion and inclusion may have been established at the top, but they are sustained and/or defied in practice at the very bottom. This phenomenon can be seen in the experiences of battered immigrants: who they are, how they experience abuse, what resources are available, who assists them, and whether they are able to break free from violence and become citizens, all reveal parameters of social worth that mark which individuals are considered valuable and which are considered expendable. The fact that the exclusion of certain battered immigrants was not perceived as problematic (or problematic enough) is ultimately related to the social processes by which the privileges of belonging, of being part of the norm, are (sometimes unwillingly) reaffirmed by sustaining barriers that keep *others* outside. These processes are common and powerful, but not less than the counterprocesses of individually and collectively challenging exclusionary boundaries. The arduous lives of Latina battered immigrants are testament to the need to continue with the struggle for equality and nonviolence.

Notes

NOTES TO CHAPTER 1

1. Although the term *feminists of color* may be problematic because of its "homogenizing tendencies," it has been used with the aim of indicating "common struggles" among various feminisms that opposed "the deficient and exclusionary tenets of white middle-class Western feminisms," recognized that "their particular civil rights struggles transcended U.S. borders and resonated in the human rights, socioeconomic, and political survival struggles of the rest of the hemisphere and other parts of the third world," and "fostered a national and international dialogue on the intersections of gender, [sexuality], race, and ethnicity, on the power differentials between developed and developing countries" (Acosta-Belén and Bose, 2000, pp. 1114–1115). I adopt a transformative feminist of color perspective, responding to Anzaldúa and Keating's call to "bridge," to "define who we are by what we include," to do "away with demarcations like 'ours' and 'theirs,'" to honor "people's otherness in ways that allow us to be changed by embracing that otherness rather than punishing others for having a different view, belief system, skin color, or spiritual practice. Diversity of perspectives expands and alters the dialogue, not in an add-on fashion but through a multiplicity that's transformational" (Anzaldúa, 2002, pp. 3–4).

2. Mills's (2000) distinction between private troubles and public issues, together with Blumer's (1971) and Kitsuse and Spector's (1973) collective action theories of social problems are useful tools to understand the process by which the battered women's and immigrants' movements were able to legitimize the struggle to end violence against women (Villalón, 2008).

3. Schechter, 1982; Schneider, 2000; Garfield, 2005; Richie, 2000.

4. Sokoloff and Dupont, 2006; Wing, 2003; Bograd, 2006; Crenshaw, 1995; Richie, 2000.

5. Abraham, 2000; Menjívar and Salcido, 2002; Salcido and Adelman, 2004.

6. Crenshaw, 1995; Menon and Bhasin, 1998; Coker, 2006; Almeida and Lockard, 2006; B. Smith, 2006; Miller, 2008; A. Smith, 2005; Dasgupta, 2007; Richie, 2000, 2006.

7. Chakrabarty, 2000; A. Smith, 2005, 2006; Almeida and Lockard, 2006.

8. Newland, 2006, p. 403.

9. Menon and Bhasin, 1998, p. 8.

10. Bhattacharyya, 1998.

11. Naples, 2003; Hale, 2006.

12. Bunch and Fried, 1996; Chow, 1996; National Task Force to End Sexual and Domestic Violence against Women, 2005; Roe, 2004; Barnish, 2004, Menjívar and Salcido, 2002; Abraham, 2000; Richie, 2006.

13. Durkheim, 1966; Goffman, 1961; Foucault, 1965, 1979; Sjoberg and Nett, 1997.

14. According to the official guidelines of USCIS in 2008 (accessed at http://www. uscis.gov/portal/site/uscis/menuitem.5af9bb95919f35e66f614176543f6d1a/?vgnextoid= 6a096c854523do10VgnVCM10000048f3d6a1RCRD&vgnextchannel=4f719c7755cb901 oVgnVCM10000045f3d6a1RCRD, March 2009).

15. According to data released by the Office of Immigration Statistics of the U.S. Department of Homeland Security. See, for example, the reports of 2007 at http:// www.dhs.gov/ximgtn/statistics/.

16. Calculation based on data available at the Bureau of Justice Statistics of the U.S. Department of Justice (http://www.ojp.gov/bjs/intimate/ipv.htm#contents), the Texas Council of Family Violence (http://www.tcfv.org/pdf/dvam07/Year%20 2006%20Family%20Violence%20Statistics(HHSC).pdf), and the U.S. Census Bureau (http://factfinder.census.gov/servlet/ThematicMapFramesetServlet?_bm=y&- geo_id=01000US&-tm_name=DEC_2000_SF1_U_M00092&-ds_name=DEC_2000_ SF1_U&-_MapEvent=displayBy&-_dBy=040#?306,337).

17. Menjívar and Salcido, 2002.

18. Mindry, 2001; Ong, 2003; Menon and Bhasin, 1998; Rudrappa, 2004.

19. Fox Piven and Cloward, 1977; Abel and Nelson, 1990; Perlmutter, 1994; INCITE! Women of Color against Violence, 2007.

20. Case studies have been questioned about their reliability, especially when compared with quantitative studies, which are considered the easiest to test and repeat for corroboration. Instead of statistical formulas and numerical analyses, qualitative research presents detailed in-depth observations and analyses based on field notes and interviews, which are carefully documented in journals with the purpose of sharing the sources and thinking processes beneath the case studies (Lofland and Lofland, 1995; Emerson, Fretz, and Shaw, 1995). Ultimately, the process of testing the accuracy of my research is in the hands of the audience and the academic community, especially those familiar with my research issues, who may compare my findings and analysis with their own observations and/or experiences, contributing in such manner to the construction of knowledge over time and space. I believe that my commitment to honor ethical codes and theoretical and methodological procedures and to be transparent about my thinking process and the original data is part of the process of creating reliable and valid research.

21. Esterberg, 2002.

22. Sjoberg and Nett 1997, p. 211.

23. Naples, 2003; Menon and Bhasin, 1998.

24. Hazen and Soriano, 2007.

25. Brabeck and Guzmán, 2008.

26. Hazen and Soriano, 2007, p. 579.

27. Hazen and Soriano, 2007, p. 579.

28. Brabeck and Guzmán, 2008, p. 1283.

29. Brabeck and Guzmán, 2008, p. 1283.

30. Brabeck and Guzmán, 2008, p. 1284.

31. Brabeck and Guzmán, 2008, p. 1290.

32. Salcido and Adelman, 2004, p. 162.

33. I do not intend this book to be a social work, health care, criminal justice, law, or public policy study—all fields that are beyond my area of expertise. As a sociologist, I intend to contribute to the understanding of violence against women by looking into the social processes at play in the reproduction of gender oppression (in this case, against Latina immigrants in the United States) as it intersects with the construction of citizenship in a context of severe inequalities.

34. Crenshaw, 1995, p. 359.

35. Abraham, 2000, p. 2.

36. Rudrappa, 2004, p. 21.

37. Ong 2003, p. 156.

38. Ong, 2003, p. 167.

39. Menon and Bhasin, 1998, p. 167.

40. Menon and Bhasin, 1998, p. 192.

41. Menon and Bhasin, 1998, p. 192.

42. Haney López, 1996.

43. Omi and Winant, 1986.

44. Feagin, 2001.

45. Bonilla-Silva, 2006.

46. Hing, 2004.

47. Johnson, 2007.

48. Glenn, 2002.

49. Ngai, 2004, p. 2.

50. Luibhéid, 2002.

51. Calvo, 2004.

52. Chapkis, 2003.

53. Foucault, 1980, p. 105.

54. Foucault, 1980, p. 234.

55. Foucault, 1980, p. 233.

56. Anzaldúa, 2002, p. 2.

57. CONADEP, 1984; Ciollaro, 1999; Villalón, 2004.

58. Up until the recent enactment of a law to prevent and eradicate gender violence in March 2009, Argentina did not have comprehensive legislation to protect survivors of intimate partner violence; such violence was not considered a legitimate social problem, and concomitantly, social awareness and public information were meager. While a few support centers for battered women existed before that time, their resources and accessibility were minimal and typically were devoted to survivors of physical violence as opposed to verbal, emotional, economic, and overall psychological abuse.

59. Keating, 2002, p. 20.

60. Lehrner and Allen, 2009, p. 661.

61. Naples, 2003, p. 41.

62. Naples, 2003, p. 41.

63. Naples, 2003, p. 38.

64. As defined by Hill Collins (1986, p. S14) and enhanced by Naples (2003, pp. 49–66), I was aware of my outsider within standpoint as an activist researcher at

ORA, as well as how this position was ever changing as a result of social interactions and other contextual matters that affected the subjects, including myself, in the field.

65. Naples, 2003, p. 37.

66. Naples, 2003, p. 63.

67. Throughout my research, I took into account several ethical considerations. First, in order to gain access and work in the organization as a volunteer who was both working and doing field research, I presented and explained the intentions and procedures of my research in general, and the research method of participant observation in particular, to the corresponding members of the local organiza- tion (i.e., the volunteer coordinator and the attorney in charge of the management of VAWA and VTVPA cases). I gave them the option to choose whether or not to remain anonymous or to be cited in my work. I also explained that their participa- tion in the research was not going to cost anything or bring material benefits to them or me, except for contributing to the development of my research project and the understanding of social phenomena in the long term. Moreover, I specified that the participant observation would not imply any potential physical risks, but that, in case something extraordinary happened, neither my research institution nor I would be responsible to pay for any kind of treatment for injuries. I made sure to obtain the organization's informed consent in a written version to keep in my records. Second, regarding the respondents' rights, I told the clients that I was working as a volunteer staff member in ORA and was also doing research about the process immigrants go through to get legal protections against gender violence. The clients could choose to either collaborate or not in the study and were assured confidentiality and anonymity during and after the research. If a client agreed to be part of my research, I took her experience as data. In the case of legal assistants, attorneys, and other persons whom I interviewed, I asked for their informed consent to participate as interviewees. Third, regarding my responsibilities as a researcher, I committed to follow the code of ethics and to act with my best intentions not to harm or put anyone at risk. I was conscious that I was studying sensitive and controversial issues, and consequently I made sure that confidentiality, anonymity, privacy, transparency, consent, reliability, and validity remained priority issues during and after my research. For this purpose, I made sure to maintain the anonymity of the respondents and the organization, with the aim of avoiding any possible risks for them. I understand that I did research at the margins of legality in terms of immigration and citizenship laws, which may bring ethical dilem- mas. I was cautious about and conscious of my ethical commitments, I respected the respondents' confidentiality and trust in my person, and I took into consideration ORA's procedures and regulations at all times. In short, while I was aware of the existing debates about the limitations of pure ethics when carrying out ethnographic research—like issues of impression management in front of diverse informants at diverse settings, and degrees of coverage and secrecy about the goals pursued in the research (Fine, 1993)—I believe that my research was more fruitful and suggestive if I maintained a consciously overt, transparent, and honest attitude throughout the entire process of accessing, collecting, and analyzing the data and writing my book.

68. Menon and Bhasin, 1998, p. 19.

69. Menon and Bhasin, 1998, p. 19.

70. Garfield, 2005, p. 34.

NOTES TO CHAPTER 2

1. Angela gave me her consent to share her story, in which I used pseudonyms and changed dates and locations for security and confidentiality purposes. The same applies to all the immigrants' stories that I share in this book.

2. Zhang, 2007, p. 7.

3. Zhang, 2007, p. 9.

4. Zhang, 2007, p. 13.

5. According to the official guidelines of USCIS of 2006, accessed at the U.S. Citizenship and Immigration Services (USCIS) website at http://www.uscis.gov/portal/site/uscis/menuitem.5af9bb95919f35e66f614176543f6d1a/?vgnextoid=6a096c854523do 10VgnVCM10000048f3d6a1RCRD&vgnextchannel=4f719c7755cb9010VgnVCM10000 045f3d6a1RCRD.

6. Pyke, 2008, p. 210.

7. Roy and Burton, 2008, p. 353.

8. Roy and Burton, 2008, p. 353.

9. Roy and Burton, 2008, p. 354.

10. Roy and Burton, 2008, p. 353.

11. Roy and Burton, 2008, p. 353.

12. Roy and Burton, 2008, p. 358.

13. Dasgupta, 1998, 2007; Abraham, 2000; Barnish, 2004; Menjívar and Salcido, 2002; Sokoloff and Dupont, 2006; Coker, 2006; Almeida and Lockard, 2006.

14. Abraham, 2000, p. 118.

15. Brochure prepared by the Texas Council on Family Violence, accessed at the National Domestic Violence Hotline, http://www.ndvh.org/ads/TCFV_friends_family_guide.pdf, December 2008.

16. Johnson, 2007, p. 120.

17. For a comprehensive view on intimate partner violence, see, for example, Barnish (2004) and O'Toole, Schiffman, and Edwards (2007).

18. Abraham reproduces common questions that nonvictims pose about battered women's behavior: "There are people who hear of incidents of domestic violence and respond: 'Maybe it was her fault. It can't be just his fault. What is wrong with these women? Why don't they fight back? They are not children! They could have gotten out or done something about it! Why do they go back? I don't understand these women, why do they just lie down and take this stuff? Why do they suffer in silence?' Often it is easy to blame women and assume that they passively accept abuse" (Abraham, 2000, p. 132). But, building on other studies, Abraham shows battered women's acts of resistance.

19. See, for example, Dunn's analysis of the various ways of portraying and understanding battered women, where she claims that "when battered women are depicted as staying in or returning to their violent relationships, this violates the normative expectation that people ordinarily act in their own best interest, which rests on the assumption that they are free to do so. This violation results in a discrepancy between the ideal of who people are, and the reality of who people are" (Dunn, 2005, p. 4).

20. Salcido and Adelman, 2004, p. 170. These authors' analysis of the relationship between migration, illegality, and battering questions "domestic violence research

and policy's emphasis on the termination of relationships and the pathologizing of women who refuse or fail to exit" (p. 170) by exposing that in many instances staying with or returning to the abuser, as well as not reporting the abuse to state authorities, may lead to safer life conditions than doing the opposite. In the same line, Brabeck and Guzmán (2008) show that survivors' strategies to cope with the abuse tend to include submissive attitudes that may be wrongfully disregarded as passive acceptance by outsiders. Moreover, staying with, temporarily leaving, and returning to the abuser are all acts that are better interpreted within the larger context of why the survivor could not end the relationship and, ultimately, whether or not the survivor is able to end the violent relationship in the long run. Focusing on the fact that battered women tried to leave (as opposed to focusing on their return) not only legitimizes their struggle but also allows researchers and advocates to better understand (and help with) their quest for nonviolence. In their research, Brabeck and Guzmán adopt this so-called survivor theory, which breaks "the 'staying versus leaving' dichotomy" (p. 1276) by looking into the specific ways in which immigrant battered women originally from Mexico seek "formal and informal help" and employ "personal strategies" to cope with the abuser while still living in the relationship (p. 1277).

21. Rudrappa, 2004, p. 39.

22. Johnson, 2007, p. 126.

23. As explained by Padilla, "When a victim experiences a hurt that is not healed, distress patterns emerge whereby the victim engages in harmful behavior. Internalized oppression has been described as the process in which these distress patterns reveal themselves: '[T]hese distress patterns, *created by oppression and racism from the outside*, have been played out in the only two places it has seemed "safe" to do so. First, upon members of our own group—particularly upon those over whom we have some degree of power or control. . . . Second, upon ourselves through all manner of self-invalidation, self-doubt, isolation, fear, feelings of powerlessness and despair. . . .' Thus internalized oppression commences externally; . . . and . . . [t]hose at the receiving end of the prejudicial behavior then internalize negative perceptions about themselves and other member of their own group and act accordingly. . . . Internalized racism has its roots in internalized oppression" (Padilla, 2003, p. 287–288).

24. Padilla, 2003, p. 288.

25. Padilla, 2003, p. 289.

26. Feagin, 2001, p. 211.

27. Feagin, 2001, p. 219.

28. Johnson, 2003, p. 292.

29. Padilla, 2003, p. 289.

30. This is a typical expression used in Spanish-speaking Latin American countries to express motivation to move on and move forward after a crisis. All the battered immigrants I met at ORA used this phrase to share their commitment to leave behind their abusive past.

31. To become a citizen, immigrants must first become legal permanent residents, live lawfully for five years in the United States with such status, and then apply for citizenship. Married immigrants can apply for citizenship after three years of lawful permanent residency as opposed to five. The rest of the residency applications are

made through employment (15 percent), refugee and asylee programs (13 percent), diversity lotteries (4 percent), and ad hoc exceptions (2 percent) (Jefferys and Monger, 2008).

32. Jefferys and Monger, 2008.

33. Abraham, 2000; Schneider, 2000; Roe, 2004; Bunch and Fried, 1996; Bunch, 2004; Chow, 1996; Coomaraswamy, 1997; National Task Force to End Sexual and Domestic Violence against Women, 2005; Miller and Iovanni, 2007.

34. Whereas the initial VAWA was dedicated exclusively to women survivors of gender violence, its reenactment in 2000 expanded its definition of gender violence to include men and gay, lesbian, bisexual, and transgender survivors within its provisions. VAWA retained its name with the aim of emphasizing that women have been the vast majority of victims of gender violence. In this spirit, I will mostly use female pronouns when referring to survivors and male pronouns when referring to perpetrators.

35. In certain states, like Alabama, Colorado, District of Columbia, Iowa, Kansas, Montana, Oklahoma, Rhode Island, South Carolina, Texas, and Utah, common-law unions are recognized as marriages; therefore, for VAWA applicants in those states, a common-law union may suffice. For more information on common-law marriages, refer to http://www.expertlaw.com/library/family_law/common_law.html.

36. This option has been available since the enactment of VTVPA in 2000. USCIS grants a maximum of 10,000 U visas per fiscal year. These visas are distributed among noncitizen crime victims who have suffered substantial physical or mental abuse from criminal activity (including domestic violence) and are certified by law enforcement officers in their assistance in the investigation or prosecution of such criminal activity in the United States. Once the cap of 10,000 visas is reached, victims requesting U visa applications are placed in a consecutive waiting list and are issued deferred action (victims are no longer eligible for deportation). The regulations for U visas were not enacted until 2007, which meant that instead of U visas, applicants would obtain "U visa interim relief." USCIS offered a window of 180 days after the effective date of the regulations for U visa interim relief holders to send in their petitions to obtain their U visa, which would allow them to keep their lawful status (U visa approval was retroactive to the date of initial interim relief approval. For example, if an immigrant got her U visa interim relief visa in August 2005, her U visa will be issued as of August 2005). If U visa interim relief holders failed to petition their U visa, USCIS could reevaluate and terminate their cases (information accessed at http://www.womenslaw.org/laws_state_type.php?id=10271&state_code=US, January 2009). Once a petitioner is granted a U visa, the immigrant may be able to obtain legal permanent residency as long as she has been living continuously, lawfully, and autonomously in the United States for three years. The waiting period to be granted the residency probably will depend on the applicant's nationality (ranging from less than a year to more than eight years due to the backlog USCIS has in processing applications from different countries). As explained by a CIS ombudsman in the Department of Homeland Security, "The rule that will allow adjustment of status based upon an approved I-918 is currently pending with the Office of Management and Budget," which means that there is still no certainty about the process (accessed at http://www.dhs.gov/xabout/structure/gc_1192724755499.shtm#4 January 2009; the page had been last reviewed and modified on November 24, 2008).

37. According to data presented at a meeting of the National Network to End Violence against Immigrant Women in Irvine, California, November 2005.

38. In her evaluation of VAWA's success, Garfield asks, "Are women safer? This question remains unanswered. We can only hope that this is the case, but who knows? . . . Along the way, women have gotten lost in the transition that has bureaucratized and publicly resourced the *issue* of violence against women. As a result, women and what they know to be *true* about the experiences of violence and the *problem* they face in their daily lives appears [*sic*] to be even less of a concern to those who frame, guide, and direct funding. . . . women and their experiences of violence continue to be reified within the working of the government-sponsored discourse; they have become yet another good, though a public good, in a market economy that is now the government-sponsored discourse on violence against women" (Garfield, 2005, p. 250). Similarly, in her analysis of battered women and feminist lawmaking, Schneider concludes, "The thirty-year history of feminist lawmaking on battering reveals the affirmative vision of equality, liberty, and freedom that has shaped legal strategy and decision making, and the inevitable limitations of legal reform that does not take gender into account. Until we see violence squarely linked to gender, and situate the problem of abuse within broader problems of gender subordination, thus reaffirming this historic link between violence and equality and making the promise of equality real, we will not and cannot move forward" (Schneider, 2000, p. 232). For an analysis of the current status of the battered women's movement, see Lehrner and Allen, 2009.

39. National Task Force to End Sexual and Domestic Violence against Women, 2005.

40. Haney López, 1996; Omi and Winant, 1986; Glenn, 2002; Luibhéid, 2002; Ngai, 2004.

41. Acker, 2006; Arrighi, 2007; Hing, 2004.

42. Glenn, 2000; Soysal, 1994; Yuval-Davis, 1997.

43. Weber, 1947.

44. Foucault, 1980, p. 105.

45. Ong, 2003, p. 6.

46. Johnson, 2007, p. 125.

47. Johnson, 2007, p. 126.

48. Somers 1999, p. 153.

49. Undocumented immigrants working in the United States may file income taxes, especially if they are spouses of a citizen or resident who files income taxes as married. Moreover, as Johnson claims, "The Social Security coffers gain billions of dollars from contributions made by undocumented immigrants. Because undocumented immigrants almost never access Social Security benefits, these contributions are all gain for the federal government and the baby boomers retiring in greater numbers every day" (Johnson, 2007, p. 202). However, the unlawful status of immigrants tends to correlate with unstable and off-the-books employment, which does not require immigrants to file income taxes and even deters them from doing so. Moreover, even if undocumented immigrants may obtain a taxation identification number, their fear of deportation deters them from approaching the IRS, one of the many official offices undocumented immigrants

avoid. Finally, it is important to stress that by living in the United States, particularly through daily consumption, all individuals (undocumented immigrants included) pay taxes.

50. Ong, 2003, p. 14.

NOTES TO CHAPTER 3

1. Martha is the only battered immigrant included in this book who is not Latina. Given the ethnographic character of my research, I included all the immigrants with whom I worked at ORA in the analysis. In this case, there is an added comparative value to including her case in this context: her non–Latin American country of origin provided her with a better stance in order to obtain her legal permanent residency as a married battered wife of a legal permanent resident.

2. Schechter, 1982; Rudrappa, 2004.

3. Ritter, 2006, p. 69.

4. Calvo, 2004, p. 154.

5. Calvo, 1991, p. 600.

6. Abraham, 2000, p. 51.

7. Luibhéid, 2002, p. 21.

8. Calvo, 1991, p. 595.

9. Calvo, 1991, pp. 607–608.

10. Luibhéid, 2002, p. 25.

11. Calvo, 2004, p. 155.

12. Chapkis, 2003, p. 935.

13. Kanuha, 1990, p. 143.

14. García, 1999, p. 170.

15. Kanuha, 1990, p. 150.

16. Luibhéid, 2002, p. 26.

17. National Resource Center on Domestic Violence, 2007, p. 3.

18. Information accessed at Womenslaw.org (2007), http://www.womenslaw.org/laws_state_type.php?id=10271&state_code=US&open_id=10842#content-10376.

19. ORA has filed asylum cases for LGBTQ immigrants who were escaping their countries of origin because there they had been persecuted on the basis of their sexual orientation. These immigrants had not been victims of intimate partner violence or related crimes in the United States; instead, they considered this country to be safer and more respectful than their own in regard to their sexual preferences. However, as documented by Luibhéid, LGBTQ immigrants were allowed to seek asylum only after exclusion bars for homosexuals were lifted in 1990, and since then, "those seeking asylum still [have] faced great difficulty in persuading judges" (Luibhéid, 2002, p. 152).

20. Luibhéid, 2002, p. xviii. On heteronormativity and immigration, see also the recently published work by Cantú, 2009. Because of publication schedules, I did not elaborate on the complementary nature of his analysis and mine in this book.

21. Ana applied for a U visa before the regulations were issued by USCIS, which meant that while she enjoyed U visa interim relief, she had to apply for the visa itself once possible. If USCIS approved her U visa, it would be dated back to when she

obtained her interim relief. After regulations were issued in 2007, new U visa applicants have received their visa directly.

22. As explained by a CIS ombudsman in the Department of Homeland Security, "The rule that will allow adjustment of status based upon an approved I-918 is currently pending with the Office of Management and Budget" (accessed at http://www.dhs.gov/xabout/structure/gc_1192724755499.shtm#4, January 2009; the page had been last reviewed and modified on November 24, 2008). However, one can deduce that U visa holders will have to wait in line to receive their residency depending on their own country of origin. In Ana's case, the wait will be at least five years due to the USCIS backlog in processing petitions from Mexican nationals.

23. Haney López, 1996, p. 1.

24. Hing, 2004, p. 15.

25. The Alien and Sedition Laws of 1798 included the Naturalization Act, requiring that "aliens be residents for fourteen years instead of five before they became eligible for U.S. citizenship"; the Alien Friends Act, authorizing the president to deport "dangerous" aliens; the Alien Enemies Act, allowing the "wartime arrest, imprisonment and deportation of any alien subject to an enemy power"; and the Sedition Act, defining treasonable activities "punishable by fine and imprisonment" (Hing, 2004, p. 18).

26. Hing, 2004, p. 21.

27. Hing, 2004, p. 20.

28. Haney López, 1996, p. 37.

29. Hing, 2004, p. 21.

30. Hing, 2004, p. 36.

31. Hing, 2004, p. 37.

32. Hing, 2004, p. 38.

33. Hing, 2004, p. 42.

34. Glenn, 2002, p. 26.

35. Hing, 2004, p. 43.

36. Hing, 2004, p. 51.

37. Hing, 2004, p. 68.

38. Hing, 2004, pp. 46–47.

39. Hing, 2004, p. 46.

40. Hing, 2004, p. 122.

41. Johnson, 2007, p. 124.

42. Johnson, 2007, p. 81.

43. Haney López, 1996, p. 38. For a detailed summary of the operation, see Ngai, 2004, pp. 155–158.

44. This act reopened Asian immigration but in a very limited fashion; only 2,000 visas per year were offered to the entire Asian-Pacific triangle (Hing, 2004, p. 91).

45. Hing, 2004, p. 73.

46. Johnson, 2007, p. 51.

47. Ngai, 2004, p.227.

48. Ngai, 2004, p. 261.

49. Hing, 2004, p. 161.

50. Hing, 2004, p. 157.

51. Hing, 2004, p. 183.
52. Hing, 2004, p. 167.
53. Ngai, 2004, p. 266; Hing, 2004, pp. 179–183.
54. Diversity programs were implemented to "help thirty-six countries that had been 'adversely affected' by the 1965 changes," which meant that "a country must have been issued fewer visas after 1965 than before." These countries included "Great Britain, Germany and France, but no countries from Africa, which had sent fewer immigrants prior to 1965" (Hing, 2004, p. 100).
55. Johnson, 2007, pp. 111–116; Hing, 2004, pp. 184–205; Ngai, 2004, p. 266.
56. Johnson, 2007, p. 112.
57. Hing, 2004, pp. 106–110.
58. Haney López, 1996, p. 129.
59. Hing, 2004, p. 93.
60. Hill Collins, 1998b, p. 70.
61. Haney López, 1996, p. 134.
62. As Feagin articulates in his analysis of contemporary racial attitudes and images, "Racist ways of thinking and feeling can be conscious and directly stimulative of discriminatory action, or they can be unconscious and implicit in that action. Moreover, most racial prejudice not only portrays the racial others negatively but also imbeds a learned predisposition to act in a negative way toward the others. In this manner, racist attitudes commonly link to discriminatory practices" (Feagin, 2001, p. 107).
63. Bonilla-Silva, 2006, p. 3.
64. Bonilla-Silva, 2006, p. 2.
65. Bonilla-Silva, 2006, pp. 3–4.
66. Other studies on the institutional embeddedness and social practices sustaining racism can be found in Roberts, 2002; Crenshaw et al., 1995; and Wing, 2003.
67. This is as opposed to Luisa's case, mentioned in the previous section, in which the applicant was not successful in obtaining certification from the police and consequently lost her chance to find relief with a U visa. Luisa had to apply through VTVPA instead of VAWA because even if her abusive partner was a U.S. citizen, she was separated but not divorced from her first husband, who still resided in Mexico.
68. Hing, 2004, p. 5.
69. For instance, Haney López briefly touched on the issue of social stratification in his analysis of Thind's prerequisite case by alluding to the puzzle that the claimant's caste posed in the racial equation: Did higher social class or caste whiten individuals? (Haney López, 1996, p. 87). Omi and Winant's work emphasized race over ethnicity, gender, and class and claimed that race in the United States had been a "fundamental organizing principle of social relationships" as opposed to a "manifestation or epiphenomenon of other supposedly more fundamental categories of sociopolitical identity, notably those of ethnicity, class and nation" (Omi and Winant, 1986, p. 66).
70. Hing, 2004, p. 14.
71. This is a process that Ngai documented with Filipino and Mexican laborers as examples of colonialism and imported colonialism (Ngai, 2004), and that Johnson (2007) elaborates on as he develops his explanation to endorse a comprehensive immigration reform.

72. Glenn, 2002.
73. Hing, 2004, p. 14.
74. Glenn, 2002, p. 24.
75. Hing, 2004, p. 40.
76. Luibhéid, 2002, p. 9.
77. Hing, 2004, pp. 42–43.
78. Hing, 2004, p. 60.
79. Hing, 2004, pp. 47–49; Ngai, 2004, pp. 96–126.
80. Ngai, 2004, pp. 127–166.
81. Ngai, 2004, p. 166.
82. Hing, 2004, 131.
83. Ngai, 2004, p. 166.
84. Hing, 2004, p. 96.
85. Hing, 2004, pp. 166–170.

86. A total of 130,000 were "regular" occupational visas, and 65,000 were H-1B visas, reserved for foreign workers with "distinguished merit and ability." The number of H-1B visas increased to 195,000 in 2001, 2002, and 2003 (Hing, 2004, pp. 108–110); it is currently capped at 65,000, although "not all H-1B nonimmigrants are subject to this annual cap," like those "who are employed, or who have received an offer of employment, by institutions of higher education or a related or affiliated nonprofit entity, as well as those employed, or who will be employed, by a nonprofit research organization or a governmental research organization are exempt from the cap." Moreover, "The H-1B Visa Reform Act of 2004 makes available 20,000 new H-1B visas for foreign workers with a Master's or higher level degree from a U.S. academic institution. For each fiscal year, 20,000 persons who hold such credentials are statutorily exempted from the cap" (information accessed at USCIS website, http://www.uscis.gov/portal/site/uscis/menuitem.5af9bb95919f35e66f614176543f6d1a/?vgnextoid=138b6138f898d010VgnVCM10000048f3d6a1RCRD, March 2009).

87. Hing, 2004, p. 108.

88. According to the official guidelines of USCIS in 2008 (accessed at http://www.uscis.gov/portal/site/uscis/menuitem.5af9bb95919f35e66f614176543f6d1a/?vgnextoid=6a096c854523d010VgnVCM10000048f3d6a1RCRD&vgnextchannel=4f719c7755cb9010VgnVCM10000045f3d6a1RCRD, March 2009).

89. Sjoberg, Brymer, and Farris, 1966, p. 330.
90. Crenshaw, 1995, p. 360.

NOTES TO CHAPTER 4

1. Samuel is the only battered man included in this book because he was the only one I had the opportunity to work with at ORA (during my two years at the organization, there was only one other man who sought services in the program to assist immigrant survivors of violence). Besides the fact that this is an ethnographic account, and, as such, intends to reflect what occurred in the "field" as comprehensively as possible, his case brings in a significant comparative component: his criminal background combined with his gender made him more vulnerable and eventually rejected as a client at ORA.

2. Personal interview with Sophia, central Texas, August 20, 2008.
3. Personal interview with Sophia, central Texas, August 20, 2008.
4. Hing, 2004, p. 238.
5. Hing, 2004, p. 247.
6. Hing, 2004, pp. 247–248.
7. Hing, 2004, pp. 248–251.
8. Personal interview with Sophia, central Texas, August 20, 2008.
9. Personal interview with Valerie, central Texas, July 13, 2006.
10. Example from a "call for volunteers" printed as part of a package distributed at the "Immigration Seminar: Asylum and Suspension of Deportation," a free seminar organized by ORA in 1993. Other examples can be found in ORA's newsletters, like its volunteer drive in 1995, as a response to the expiration of the Temporary Protected Status/Deferred Enforced Deportation for Salvadorans of December 1994, where ORA claimed that the organization "wants to help all the clients possible, who are eligible for asylum and/or the suspension of deportation. HOWEVER, WE WOULD NEED 250 LAWYERS, TRANLATORS, PARALEGALS AND DOCUMENTERS. Please, please help these clients! If [ORA] is unable to solicit sufficient help from the community, these people may be returned to a hostile situation, not because of INS, but because of our own apathy" (ORA newsletter, Winter–Spring 1995, p. 3); and the newsletter's regular section "*Mil Gracias*" (A Thousand Thanks), which listed the volunteers who helped ORA accomplish specifically listed tasks, noting that ORA's "work was possible due to the hundreds of volunteers and community sponsors that have supported us in diverse ways" (ORA newsletter, October 1998, p. 2).
11. I discuss this issue further in chapter 5. Fox Piven and Cloward, 1977; Abel and Nelson, 1990; Perlmutter, 1994; INCITE! Women of Color against Violence, 2007.
12. Personal interview with Carlos, central Texas, July 24, 2006.
13. Personal interview with Carlos, central Texas, July 24, 2006.
14. Personal interview with Marina, central Texas, July 26, 2006.
15. Personal interview with Jenna, central Texas, July 12, 2006.
16. Personal interview with Maggie, central Texas, May 5, 2006.
17. Personal interview with Maggie, central Texas, May 5, 2006. Maggie grew up in the United States, but always maintained her connection with Latin America.
18. Personal interview with Courtney, central Texas, July 25, 2008.
19. Personal interview with Courtney, central Texas, July 25, 2006.
20. Personal interview with Cathy, central Texas, June 30, 2006.
21. Personal interview with Cathy, central Texas, June 30, 2006.
22. Personal interview with John, central Texas, July 12, 2006.
23. Personal interview with John, central Texas, July 12, 2006.
24. For confidentiality reasons, I cannot provide the organization's website that I am citing here.
25. In this respect, the use of pseudonyms makes it difficult to reflect the tremendous difference between the original and the new name of the organization.
26. Personal interview with Cathy, central Texas, July 11, 2008.
27. Personal interview with Courtney, central Texas, July 25, 2008.
28. Personal interview with Valerie, central Texas, July 25, 2008.
29. Personal interview with Valerie, central Texas, July 13, 2006.

30. Personal interview with Kathy, central Texas, June 30, 2006.

31. A. Smith, 2007, pp. 3–8.

32. Pérez, 2007, p. 95.

33. Pérez, 2007, p. 99.

34. Pérez, 2007, p. 98.

35. Guilloud and Cordery, 2007.

36. Bierria, 2007, p. 162.

37. Participant observation at Arte Sana national conference, San Antonio, Texas, August 18–19, 2008.

38. Kivel, 2007, p. 130.

39. Personal interview with Courtney, central Texas, July 25, 2008.

40. Personal interview with Jenna, central Texas, July 12, 2006.

41. Personal interview with Courtney, central Texas, July 25, 2006.

42. Personal interview with Maggie, central Texas, May 5, 2006.

43. In chapter 5, I include ORA staff's reactions to my analysis of the pervasive formal and informal barriers to accessing citizenship.

44. As articulated by Lucy (field notes from report to all ORA staff, central Texas, July 11, 2008), and Jenna (group interview with Cathy, Jenna, and Maggie, central Texas, July 11, 2008).

45. If an immigrant has been married to the sponsoring citizen for less than two years, she obtains legal conditional residency, which after two years of marriage can be switched to legal permanent residency if the immigrant shows that the marriage has been in good faith. When the immigrant spouse is abused and has been married for less than two years, VAWA allows her to apply for removal of conditions, that is, to be granted legal permanent residency before two years of marriage pass.

46. The question remains, what did she have to do to become a "good, desirable" client? I address the issue of immigrants' agency in the following chapter.

47. As explained in chapter 3, in the section on the legacies of coverture, since 1986, immigrant spouses are issued legal permanent residency only after they have been married longer than two years with their citizen or resident spouse, who must be present at the interview with immigration officers for the conditions on the residency to be removed and thus become permanent.

48. Personal interview with Valerie, central Texas, July 13, 2006.

49. Mills, 2000, p. 8.

50. A. Smith, 2007, p. 7.

51. Fox Piven and Cloward, 1977; Naples, 1998.

52. Wilson Gilmore, 2007, p. 45.

53. Personal interview with Valerie, central Texas, July 25, 2008.

54. Wilson Gilmore, 2007, p. 46.

NOTES TO CHAPTER 5

1. A similar version of these two initial sections was included in an article of mine to be published in *Women's Studies International Forum*.

2. Comte, 1830–1842; Durkheim, 1982; Parsons, 1951; Bourdieu, 1977.

3. Mead, 1967; Homans, 1958; Berger and Luckmann, 1966; Garfinkel, 1967.

4. Giddens, 1984; Goffman, 1961.

5. Marx, [1845–1846] 1970; Foucault, 1980; Butler, 1993.

6. Spivak, 1988; Mani, 1998; Hill Collins, 1986, 1998a; Crenshaw, 1995; Mahmood, 2001; Menon and Bhasin, 1998.

7. Mahmood, 2001, p. 203.

8. Hill Collins, 1986; Crenshaw, 1995.

9. Menon and Bhasin, 1998, p. 8.

10. Bhattacharyya, 1998.

11. Mani, 1998, p. 190.

12. The nuances of agency may well be more than the ones I encountered in this research.

13. Hollander and Einwohner (2004) present a review of the various ways in which agency has been equated with resistance in sociological and other social sciences literature. They show that resistance has been defined within a wide range (from national revolutions to rebellious haircuts), and in an effort to bring some order to the conceptual chaos, they elaborate a typology of resistance. The categories are overt, covert, unwitting, target-defined, externally defined, missed, and attempted resistance, and not resistance. While one may find similarities between my proposition and Hollander and Einwohner's, two main points distinguish us. First, I do not equate agency with resistance; contrarily, I suggest looking into compliance as a type of agency different from contentious agency. Second, I build my conceptual tool from a feminist of color approach, which does not coincide with Hollander and Einwohner's perspective. Indeed, these authors ignore the literature by feminists of color in their review (e.g., they omit authors such as Spivak [1988], Mani [1998], and Chakrabarty [2000] in their discussion of the issue of recognition and agency, central to postcolonial feminist theory).

14. A comprehensive view of the types of violence that most of these women suffered can be found at http://www.endabuse.org/userfiles/file/ImmigrantWomen/Power%20and%20Control%20Tactics%20Used%20Against%20Immigrant%20Women.pdf.

15. Personal interview with Cathy, central Texas, July 1, 2008.

16. Personal interview with Cathy, central Texas, July 1, 2008.

17. Personal interview with Cathy, central Texas, July 1, 2008.

18. Personal interview with Cathy, central Texas, July 1, 2008.

19. Group interview with Cathy, Jenna, and Maggie, central Texas, July 11, 2008.

20. Personal interview with Cathy, central Texas, July 1, 2008.

21. Group interview with Cathy, Jenna, and Maggie, central Texas, July 11, 2008.

22. Group interview with Cathy, Jenna, and Maggie, central Texas, July 11, 2008.

23. Group interview with Cathy, Jenna, and Maggie, central Texas, July 11, 2008.

24. Group interview with Cathy, Jenna, and Maggie, central Texas, July 11, 2008.

25. This position reflects the change of grassroots social change organizations to nonprofit social service providers organizations. As Hawk explains when recalling her years of activism in the American Indian Movement (AIM) in the 1960s and 1970s and in Women of All Red Nations (WARN) in the late 1970s, "When we first started organizing, we were rookies. We did not know how to organize but learned as we went along. Today, when young people ask me about my days in AIM and what

they could do now, their first question is: 'Where will we get the money?' Often they are surprised by my response. But back then, we did not focus on fundraising. (Nor did we see activism as something we would get paid to do.) We organized first, and then figured out how to make it happen" (Hawk, 2007, p. 102).

26. Bales, 2004; Wright, 2006.

27. Group interview with Cathy, Jenna, and Maggie, central Texas, July 11, 2008.

28. Group interview with Cathy, Jenna, and Maggie, central Texas, July 11, 2008.

29. Group interview with Cathy, Jenna, and Maggie, central Texas, July 11, 2008.

30. Group interview with Cathy, Jenna, and Maggie, central Texas, July 11, 2008.

31. Personal interview with Courtney, central Texas, July 24, 2008.

32. Personal interview with Courtney, central Texas, July 24, 2008.

33. Personal interview with Courtney, central Texas, July 24, 2008.

34. Personal interview with Courtney, central Texas, July 24, 2008.

35. Personal interview with Courtney, central Texas, July 24, 2008.

36. Personal interview with Courtney, central Texas, July 24, 2008.

37. Personal interview with Courtney, central Texas, July 24, 2008.

38. Personal interview with Courtney, central Texas, July 24, 2008.

39. Personal interview with Courtney, central Texas, July 24, 2008.

40. Lipsky, 1983, p. xii.

41. Wolch, 1990.

42. Wilson Gilmore, 2007, p. 47.

43. Lipsky, 1983, p. xii (emphasis in the original).

44. Personal interview with Courtney, central Texas, July 24, 2008.

45. See, for example, Weber, 1947; Michaels, 1962; Acker, 2006; Ward, 2004; Naples, 1998; Perlmutter, 1994.

46. Acker, 2006, p. 443. Inequality in organizations is defined as "systematic disparities between participants in power and control over goals, resources, and outcomes; workplace decisions such as how to organization work; opportunities for promotion and interesting work; security in employment and benefits; pay and other monetary rewards; respect; and pleasures in work and work relations" (p. 443).

47. Personal interview with Courtney, central Texas, July 24, 2008.

48. Personal interview with Cathy, central Texas, July 1, 2008.

49. Personal interview with Maggie, central Texas, May 5, 2006.

50. Personal interview with Cathy, central Texas, July 1, 2008.

51. Personal exchange with Jenna before the group interview with Cathy, Jenna, and Maggie, central Texas, July 11, 2008.

52. Personal interview with Courtney, central Texas, July 24, 2008.

53. Personal interview with Cathy, central Texas, July 1, 2008.

54. Group interview with Cathy, Jenna, and Maggie, central Texas, July 11, 2008.

55. Field notes from report to all ORA staff, central Texas, July 11, 2008.

56. Field notes from report to all ORA staff, central Texas, July 11, 2008.

57. Field notes from report to all ORA staff, central Texas, July 11, 2008.

58. Field notes from report to all ORA staff, central Texas, July 11, 2008.

59. Group interview with Cathy, Jenna, and Maggie, central Texas, July 11, 2008.

60. Personal interview with Courtney, central Texas, July 24, 2008.

61. Personal interview with Valerie, central Texas, July 25, 2008.

62. Personal interview with Sophia, central Texas, August 20, 2008.

63. Personal interview with Sophia, central Texas, August 20, 2008.

64. Reviewers have criticized me because of my suggestion that these three steps were necessary to provoke institutional and structural change; I was told that I was not recognizing the value of ORA's services and that I was romantically expecting too much from the organization. However, my view of social change is backed up by major authors, such as Marx ([1845–1846] 1970; [1848] 1969; [1851] 1978); Tilly (1978); Fox Piven and Cloward (1977); and Naples (1998), to mention a few. I do value ORA's efforts, which is why I am interested in seeing the organization changing back to a more politically aware group. Last but not least, if expecting people who have devoted themselves to social services for the disfranchised to be more aware of their crucial role as challengers or reproducers of social inequality is considered romantic, I am comfortable to be such.

65. Arte Sana, 2008, p. 22.

66. Zárate, August 18, 2008, opening remarks of the Arte Sana national conference *"Nuestras Voces/*Our Voices: Collaboration and Transformation *en la Comunidad,"* San Antonio, Texas, August 18–19, 2008. Field notes.

67. Arte Sana, 2008, p. 1.

68. Lehrner and Allen, 2009, p. 669. My work complements this recently published study on the status of the battered women's movement (their research was based on interviews with "21 women employed by 16 domestic violence advocacy or service agencies across a large Midwestern state" (p. 658). With an age spread of forty-two years among respondents and a predominantly white sample, the authors recommend "openness to new strategies and approaches, better inclusion of communities of color, a rethinking of community engagement and collaboration, and attention to mentoring the next generation of advocates" (p. 669) (who they find to be unaware of the history of the movement and the significance of social change struggles). They, as well as the most seasoned advocates of the movement, believe in the relevance of connecting advocates with the "movement philosophy" (p. 674) in order to avoid co-optation as well as balancing the political and service provision sides of violence against women activist/advocate work. For the battered women's movement to survive, "systematic self-assessment" (p. 658) and repoliticization are due.

69. Sjoberg, Gill, and Cain, 2003, p. 210.

70. Johnson, 2005, p. 229.

71. Hawk, 2007, p. 105 (emphasis in the original).

72. Guilloud and Cordery, 2007.

73. Pérez, 2007.

74. Bierria, 2007.

75. Personal interview with Courtney, central Texas, July 24, 2008.

76. Field notes from Arte Sana national conference, San Antonio, Texas, August 18–19, 2008.

77. INCITE! Women of Color against Violence, 2006, 2007.

78. Hill Collins, 1986; Acker, 2006; Naples, 2003.

79. Personal interview with Courtney, central Texas, July 24, 2008.

80. McIntosh, 1988, p. 1.

81. Despite their critical analyses, most researchers recognize the genuine intentions of nonprofit workers and believe in their pivotal role as means of change. See, for example, Menjívar and Salcido, 2002; Abraham, 2000; Sokoloff and Dupont, 2006; INCITE! Women of Color against Violence, 2007.

82. Lipsky, 1983, p. xiii.

83. Or a "sociological imagination," as theorized by Mills, 2000.

84. Marx, [1845–1846] 1970; [1848] 1969; [1851] 1978.

85. Naples, 2003, p. 199.

86. Members of Arte Sana as well as other coalitions of activists and advocates of color have been trying to challenge the pervasiveness of oppression by looking into how privilege works in overt and, most important, covert ways. Nowadays, many documents, reports, and group exercises are accessible electronically at no cost and make it easier to put workshops together. Another means for ORA would be to find people at local universities who are willing to organize this kind of session on a volunteer basis.

87. Smith, Richie, Sudbury, White, and the INCITE! Anthology Co-editors, 2006, p. 4 (emphasis in the original).

88. Because I am not a legal expert, instead of suggesting how to reform immigration policy comprehensively, let me recommend the work of Hing (2006) and Johnson (2007). I believe that in order for comprehensive immigration reform to be successful, it should be aimed at getting rid of pervasive systems of gender, sexual, racial, ethnic, and class inequality.

89. Arte Sana's website at http://www.arte-sana.com, and http://www.arte-sana.com/capacitadoras_en_accion.htm.

90. Brabeck and Guzmán, 2008.

91. I have been offering free community workshops that include this information and hope to distribute these materials through online national networks, such as Alianza Latina en contra de la Agresión Sexual (ALAS) from Arte Sana (http://www.arte-sana.com/alas.htm), and community organizations to further accessibility.

92. Sharing this information in advocate networks also provides me with the chance of obtaining advocates' perspectives on how they have helped (or not) immigrants in their organizations and also what they would like from immigrants as they are obtaining services. It is important to recall that advocates and immigrants in principle are not at odds; therefore, I work on improving their relationship.

93. Berger and Luckmann, 1966.

94. Garfield (2005) entitled her book about African American women's experiences of violence and violation in such a way as to stress the value of the knowledge that these women have on their victimization and survival, as well as to motivate the readers to act against injustice (as opposed to denying it, now that they have learned [again] about it).

95. Glenn, 2002, p. 52. Members of civil society, as Alexander points out, historically have tended to "conceptualize the world into those who deserve inclusion and those who do not. . . . This distinction is not 'real.' Actors are not intrinsically either worthy or moral: they are determined to be so by being placed in certain positions on the grid of civil culture" (Alexander, 1992, p. 291). Thus the need of keeping our criti-

cal awareness alive in order to develop inclusive, more equal communities *beyond* the dualistic principles of worth pointed by Alexander.

96. On adopting this nonessentialist stance toward change, see Anzaldúa and Keating, 2002.

97. Mason, 2007, p. 309.

NOTES TO CHAPTER 6

1. Hazen and Soriano, 2007.
2. Brabeck and Guzmán, 2008.
3. Salcido and Adelman, 2004.
4. Anzaldúa and Keating, 2002.
5. Abraham, 2000.
6. Rudrappa, 2004.
7. Ong, 2003.
8. Menon and Bhasin, 1998.
9. Foucault, 1980.
10. Glenn, 2002.
11. Luibhéid, 2002.
12. Calvo, 2004.
13. Chapkis, 2003.
14. Ngai, 2004.
15. Haney López, 1996.
16. Omi and Winant, 1986.
17. Feagin, 2001.
18. Bonilla-Silva, 2006.
19. Hing, 2004.
20. Johnson, 2007.
21. By "constantly shifting the center" of analysis "to communities that face interlocking forms of oppression, we gain a more comprehensive view of the strategies needed to end all forms of violence" (Smith, Richie, Sudbury, White, and the INCITE! Anthology Co-editors, 2006, p. 4).
22. O'Toole, Schiffman, and Kiter Edwards, 2007, p. 421.

Bibliography

Abel, E., and M. Nelson. (1990). *Circles of Care: Work and Identity in Women's Lives*. Albany: State University of New York Press.

Abraham, M. (2000). *Speaking the Unspeakable: Marital Violence among South Asian Immigrants in the United States*. New Brunswick, NJ: Rutgers University Press.

Abusharaf, R. (2001). "Virtuous Cuts: Female Genital Circumcision in an African Ontology." *Differences* 12 (1): 120–140.

Acker, J. (2006). "Inequality Regimes: Gender, Class, and Race in Organizations," *Gender and Society* 20 (4): 441–464.

Acosta-Belén, E., and C. Bose. (2000). "U.S. Latina and Latin American Feminisms: Hemisphere Encounters." *Signs* 25 (4): 1113–1119.

Alexander, J. (1987). *Twenty Lectures: Sociological Theory since World War II*. New York: Columbia University Press.

Alexander, J. (1992). "Citizen and Enemy as Symbolic Classification: On the Polarizing Discourse of Civil Society." In M. Lamont and M. Fournier (Eds.), *Cultivating Differences: Symbolic Boundaries and the Making of Inequality*, pp. 289–308. Chicago: University of Chicago Press.

Almeida, R., and Lockard, J. (2006). "The Cultural Context Model: A New Paradigm for Accountability, Empowerment, and the Development of Critical Consciousness against Domestic Violence." In Natalie Sokoloff (Ed.) with Christina Pratt, *Domestic Violence at the Margins: Readings on Race, Class, Gender, and Culture*, pp. 301–320. New Brunswick, NJ: Rutgers University Press.

American Sociological Association. (1999). *Code of Ethics and Policies and Procedures of the ASA Committee on Professional Ethics*. Washington, DC: American Sociological Association.

Anzaldúa, G. (2002). "(Un)natural Bridges, (Un)safe Spaces." In G. Anzaldúa and A. Keating (Eds.), *This Bridge We Call Home*, pp. 1–5. New York: Routledge.

Anzaldúa, G., and A. Keating (Eds.). (2002). *This Bridge We Call Home*. New York: Routledge.

Apter, T., and E. Garnsey. (1994). "Enacting Inequality: Structure, Agency, and Gender." *Women's Studies International Forum* 17: 19–31.

Arrighi, B. (Ed.). (2007). *Understanding Inequality: The Intersection of Race/Ethnicity, Class, and Gender*. Lanham, MD: Rowman and Littlefield.

Arte Sana. (2008). "*Nuestras Voces/*Our Voices: Collaboration and Transformation *en la Comunidad.*" Arte Sana National Conference, San Antonio, Texas, August 18–19, 2008.

Bales, R. (2004). *Disposable People: New Slavery in the Global Economy*. Berkeley: University of California Press.

Barnish, M. (2004). *Domestic Violence: A Literature Review*. London: HM Inspectorate of Probation.

Berger, P., and T. Luckmann. (1966). *The Social Construction of Reality: A Treatise in the Sociology of Knowledge*. New York: Anchor Books.

Bhattacharyya, G. (1998). *Tales of Dark-Skinned Women: Race, Gender and Global Culture*. London: UCL Press.

Bierria, A. (2007). "Pursuing a Radical Anti-violence Agenda Inside/Outside a Non-profit Structure." In INCITE! Women of Color against Violence, *The Revolution Will Not Be Funded: Beyond the Non-profit Industrial Complex*, pp. 151–164. Cambridge, MA: South End Press.

Blumer, H. (1971). "Social Problems as Collective Behavior." *Social Problems* 18 (3): 298–306.

Bograd, M. (2006). "Strengthening Domestic Violence Theories: Intersections of Race, Class, Sexual Orientation, and Gender." In Natalie Sokoloff (Ed.) with Christina Pratt, *Domestic Violence at the Margins: Readings on Race, Class, Gender, and Culture*, pp. 25–38. New Brunswick, NJ: Rutgers University Press.

Bonilla-Silva, E. (2006). *Racism without Racists: Color-Blind Racism and the Persistence of Racial Inequality in the United States*. 2nd ed. Lanham, MD: Rowman and Littlefield.

Bourdieu, P. (1977). *Outline of a Theory of Practice*. Cambridge: Cambridge University Press.

Bourdieu, P. (1986). "The Forms of Capital." In J. G. Richardson (Ed.), *Handbook of Theory and Research for the Sociology of Education*, pp. 242–258. New York: Greenwood.

Bourdieu, P., and L. J. D. Wacquant. (1992). *An Invitation to Reflexive Sociology*. Chicago: University of Chicago Press.

Brabeck, K., and M. Guzmán. (2008). "Frequency and Perceived Effectiveness of Strategies to Survive Abuse Employed by Battered Mexican-Origin Women." *Violence against Women* 14 (1): 1274–1294.

Bunch, C. (2004). "What Are the Implications of a Rights-Based Approach for the Struggle against Violence against Women?" Interview with Charlotte Bunch by Women's Human Rights Net (February 2004). Accessed at http://www.whrnet.org/docs/interview-bunch-0402.html.

Bunch C., and S. Fried. (1996). "Beijing '95: Moving Women's Human Rights from Margin to Center." *Signs* 22 (1): 200–204.

Butler, J. (1993). *Bodies That Matter: On the Discursive Limits of Sex*. New York: Routledge.

Calvo, J. (1991). "Spouse-Based Immigration Laws: The Legacy of Coverture." *San Diego Law Review* 28: 593–644.

Calvo, J. (2004). "A Decade of Spouse-Based Immigration Laws: Coverture's Diminishment, but Not Its Demise." *Northern Illinois University Law Review* 24: 153–209.

Cantú, L., Jr. (2009). *The Sexuality of Migration: Border Crossings and Mexican Immigrant Men*. Nancy Naples and Salvador Vidal-Ortiz (Eds.). New York: NYU Press.

Chakrabarty, D. (2000). *Provincializing Europe: Postcolonial Thought and Historical Difference.* Princeton: Princeton University Press.

Chapkis, W. (2003). "Trafficking, Migration, and the Law: Protecting Innocents, Punishing Immigrants." *Gender and Society* 17 (6): 923–937.

Chow, E. (1996). "Making Waves, Moving Mountains: Reflections on Beijing '95 and Beyond." *Signs* 22 (1): 185–192.

Ciollaro, N. (1999). *Pájaros Sin Luz: Testimonios de Mujeres de Desaparecidos.* Buenos Aires: Planeta.

Coker, D. (2006). "Shifting Power for Battered Women: Law, Material Resources, and Poor Women of Color." In Natalie Sokoloff (Ed.) with Christina Pratt, *Domestic Violence at the Margins: Readings on Race, Class, Gender, and Culture*, pp. 369–388. New Brunswick, NJ: Rutgers University Press.

Comte, A. (1830–1842). *Cours de philosophie positive.* 6 vols. Paris: Bachelier.

CONADEP. (1984). *Nunca Más: Informe de la Comisión Nacional Sobre la Desaparición de Personas.* Buenos Aires: EUDEBA.

Coomaraswamy, R. 1997. "Reinventing International Law: Women's Rights as Human Rights in the International Community." Edward A. Smith Lecture, Harvard Law School. Cambridge, MA: Human Rights Program Publications.

Crenshaw, K. (1995). "Mapping the Margins: Intersectionality, Identity Politics, and Violence against Women of Color." In K. Crenshaw, N. Gotanda, G. Peller, and K. Thomas (Eds.), *Critical Race Theory: The Key Writings That Formed the Movement*, pp. 357–383. New York: New Press.

Crenshaw, K., N. Gotanda, G. Peller, and K. Thomas (Eds.). (1995). *Critical Race Theory: The Key Writings That Formed the Movement.* New York: New Press.

Dasgupta, S. (1998). "Women's Realities: Defining Violence against Women by Immigration, Race, and Class." In R. K Bergen (Ed.), *Issues of Intimate Violence*, pp. 209–219. Thousand Oaks, CA: Sage.

Dasgupta, S. (Ed.). (2007). *Body Evidence: Intimate Violence against South Asian Women in America.* New Brunswick, NJ: Rutgers University Press.

Davis, R. (2005). "VAWA 2005: Ideology and Bias Breed Injustice." The Reality Check. Accessed at http://www.therealitycheck.org/GuestColumnist/rldavis061705.htm.

Dunn, J. (2005). "'Victims' and 'Survivors': Emerging Vocabularies of Motive for 'Battered Women Who Stay.'" *Sociological Inquiry* 75 (1): 1–30.

Durkheim, E. (1966). *Suicide.* New York: Free Press.

Durkheim, E. (1982). *The Rules of Sociological Method and Selected Texts on Sociology and Its Methods.* Steven Lukes (Ed.). New York: Free Press.

Emerson, R., R. Fretz, and L. Shaw. (1995). *Writing Ethnographic Fieldnotes.* Chicago: University of Chicago Press.

End Abuse. (2005). "The Facts on Immigrant Women and Domestic Violence." Accessed at http://endabuse.org/userfiles/file/Children_and_Families/Immigrant.pdf

Esterberg, K. (2002). *Qualitative Methods in Social Research.* New York: McGraw-Hill.

Family Violence Prevention Fund. (2005). *You Have a Right to Be Free from Violence in Your Home: Questions and Answers for Immigrant and Refugee Women.* San Francisco: Family Violence Prevention Fund.

Feagin, J. (2001). *Racist America: Roots, Current Realities, and Future Reparations*. New York: Routledge.

Feagin, J., A. Orum, and G. Sjoberg. (1991). *Case for the Case Study*. Chapel Hill: University of North Carolina Press.

Fine, G. (1993). "Ten Lies of Ethnography: Moral Dilemmas of Field Research." *Journal of Contemporary Ethnography* 22 (3): 267–294.

Foucault, M. (1965). *Madness and Civilization*. New York: Random House.

Foucault, M. (1978). *The History of Sexuality*. New York: Pantheon.

Foucault, M. (1979). *Discipline and Punish: The Birth of the Prison*. New York: Random House.

Foucault, M. (1980). *Power/Knowledge: Selected Interviews and Other Writings, 1972–1977*. New York: Random House.

Fox Piven, F., and R. Cloward. (1977). *Poor People's Movements: Why They Succeed, How They Fail*. New York: Vintage Books.

Fraser, N. (1997). *Justice Interruptus: Critical Reflections on the "Postsocialist" Condition*. New York: Routledge.

Fraser, N., and L. Gordon. (1993). "Contract versus Charity: Why Is There No Social Citizenship in the United States?" *Socialist Review* 22: 45–68.

García, M. L. (1999). "A 'New Kind' of Battered Woman: Challenges for the Movement." In S. Lundy and B. Leventhal (Eds.), *Same-Sex Domestic Violence: Strategies for Change*, pp. 165–172. Thousand Oaks, CA: Sage.

Garfield, G. (2005). *Knowing What We Know: African American Women's Experiences of Violence and Violation*. New Brunswick, NJ: Rutgers University Press.

Garfinkel, H. (1967). *Studies in Ethnomethodology*. Malden, MA: Blackwell.

Giddens, A. (1984). *The Constitution of Society: Outline of the Theory of Structuration*. Berkeley: University of California Press.

Glenn, E. N. (2000). "Citizenship and Inequality: Historical and Global Perspectives." *Social Problems* 47 (1): 1–20.

Glenn, E. N. (2002). *Unequal Freedom: How Race and Gender Shaped American Citizenship and Labor*. Cambridge: Harvard University Press.

Goffman, E. (1961). *Asylums*. Garden City, NY: Doubleday, Anchor Books.

Guilloud, S., and W. Cordery. (2007). "Fundraising Is Not a Dirty Word: Community-Based Economic Strategies for the Long Haul." In INCITE! Women of Color against Violence, *The Revolution Will Not Be Funded: Beyond the Non-profit Industrial Complex*, pp. 107–112. Cambridge, MA: South End Press.

Hale, C. (2006). "Activist Research v. Cultural Critique: Indigenous Land Rights and the Contradictions of Politically Engaged Anthropology." *Cultural Anthropology* 21 (1): 96–120.

Haney López, I. (1996). *White by Law: The Legal Construction of Race*. New York: NYU Press.

Hawk, M. T. (2007). "Native Organizing Before the Non-Profit Industrial Complex." In INCITE! Women of Color against Violence, *The Revolution Will Not Be Funded: Beyond the Non-profit Industrial Complex*, pp. 101–106. Cambridge, MA: South End Press.

Hazen, A., and F. Soriano. (2007). "Experiences with Intimate Partner Violence among Latina Women." *Violence against Women* 13 (6): 562–582.

Hill Collins, P. (1986). "Learning from the Outsider Within: The Sociological Significance of Black Feminist Thought." *Social Problems* 33 (6): S14–S32.

Hill Collins, P. (1998a). *Fighting Words: Black Women and the Search for Justice.* Minneapolis: University of Minnesota Press.

Hill Collins, P. (1998b). "It's All in the Family: Intersections of Gender, Race and
Nation." *Hypatia* 13 (3): 62–82.

Hing, B. O. (2004). *Defining America through Immigration Policy.* Philadelphia:
Temple University Press.

Hing, B. O. (2006). *Deporting Our Souls: Values, Morality, and Immigration Policy.*
New York: Cambridge University Press.

Hollander, J., and R. Einwohner. (2004). "Conceptualizing Resistance." *Sociological
Forum* 19 (4): 533–554.

Homans, G. (1958). "Social Behavior as Exchange." *American Journal of Sociology* 63:
597–606.

INCITE! Women of Color against Violence. (2006). *Color of Violence: The INCITE!
Anthology.* Cambridge, MA: South End Press.

INCITE! Women of Color against Violence. (2007). *The Revolution Will Not Be
Funded: Beyond the Non-profit Industrial Complex.* Cambridge, MA: South End
Press.

Jefferys, K., and R. Monger. (2008). *U.S. Legal Permanent Residents: 2007.* Washington, DC: Office of Immigration Statistics.

Johnson, A. (2005). *The Gender Knot: Unraveling Our Patriarchal Legacy.* Philadelphia:
Temple University Press.

Johnson, K. (2003). "Immigration and Latino Identity." In K. Johnson (Ed.), *Mixed
Race America and the Law: A Reader*, pp. 290–293. New York: NYU Press.

Johnson, K. (2007). *Opening the Floodgates: Why America Needs to Rethink Its Borders
and Immigration Laws.* New York: NYU Press.

Kandel, W., and D. Massey. (2002). "The Culture of Mexican Migration: A Theoretical and Empirical Analysis." *Social Forces* 80 (3): 981–1004.

Kanuha, V. (1990). "Battering in Lesbian of Color Relationships." In L. Brown and M.
Roots (Eds.), *Diversity and Complexity in Feminist Therapy*, pp. 142–157. Bingham-
ton, NY: Haworth.

Katz, M. (1993). *The "Underclass" Debate: Views from History.* Princeton: Princeton
University Press.

Keating, A. (2002). "Charting Pathways, Marking Thresholds . . . A Warning: An
Introduction." In G. Anzaldúa and A. Keating (Eds.), *This Bridge We Call Home*,
pp. 6–20. New York: Routledge.

Kitsuse, J., and M. Spector. (1973). "Toward a Sociology of Social Problems: Social
Conditions, Value-Judgments, and Social Problems." *Social Problems* 20 (4):
407–419.

Kivel, P. (2007). "Social Service or Social Change?" In INCITE! Women of Color
against Violence, *The Revolution Will Not Be Funded: Beyond the Non-profit Industrial Complex*, pp. 129–150. Cambridge, MA: South End Press.

Lehrner, A., and N. Allen. (2009) "Still a Movement after All These Years? Current
Tensions in the Domestic Violence Movement." *Violence against Women* 15 (6):
656–677.

Lipsky, M. (1983). *Street-Level Bureaucracy: Dilemmas of the Individual in Public Services*. New York: Russell Sage Foundation.

Lofland J., and L. Lofland. (1995). *Analyzing Social Setting: A Guide to Qualitative Observation and Analysis*. Belmont, CA: Wadsworth.

Luibhéid, E. (2002). *Entry Denied: Controlling Sexuality at the Border*. Minneapolis: University of Minnesota Press.

Mahmood, S. (2001). "Feminist Theory, Embodiment, and the Docile Agent: Some Reflections on the Egyptian Islamic Revival." *Cultural Anthropology* 12: 202–236.

Mani, L. (1998). *Contentious Traditions: The Debate on Sati in Colonial India*. Berkeley: University of California Press.

Martinez, R., and A. Valenzuela (Eds.). (2006). *Immigration and Crime: Race, Ethnicity and Violence*. New York: NYU Press.

Marx, K. ([1845–1846] 1970). *The German Ideology*. New York: International Publishers.

Marx, K. ([1848] 1969). *The Communist Manifesto*. Moscow: Progress Publishers.

Marx, K. ([1851] 1978). "The Eighteenth Brumaire of Louis Bonaparte." In R. Tucker (Ed.), *The Marx-Engels Reader*, pp. 594–617. New York: Norton.

Mason, R. (2007). "Building Women's Social Citizenship: A Five-Point Framework to Conceptualise the Work of Women-Specific Services in Rural Australia." *Women's Studies International Forum* 30: 299–312.

McIntosh, P. (1988). "White Privilege and Male Privilege: A Personal Account of Coming to See Correspondences through Work in Women's Studies." Working Paper 189. Wellesley, MA: Wellesley College Center for Research on Women.

Mead, G. (1967). *Mind, Self, and Society: From the Standpoint of a Social Behaviorist*. Vol. 1. Charles W. Morris (Ed.). Chicago: University of Chicago Press.

Menjívar, C., and O. Salcido. (2002). "Immigrant Women and Domestic Violence: Common Experiences in Different Countries." *Gender and Society* 16 (6): 898–920.

Menon, R., and K. Bhasin. (1998). *Borders and Boundaries: Women in India's Partition*. New Brunswick, NJ: Rutgers University Press.

Michaels, R. (1962). *Political Parties: A Sociological Study of the Oligarchical Tendencies of Modern Democracy*. New York: Free Press.

Milkman, R. (1985). *Women, Work, and Protest: A Century of U.S. Women's Labor History*. Boston: Routledge and Kegan Paul.

Miller, J. (2008). *Getting Played: African American Girls, Urban Inequality, and Gendered Violence*. New York: NYU Press.

Miller, S., and L. Iovanni. (2007). "Domestic Violence Policy in the United States: Contemporary Issues." In L. O'Toole, J. Schiffman, and M. Kiter Edwards (Eds.), *Gender Violence: Interdisciplinary Perspectives*, pp. 287–296. New York: NYU Press.

Mills, C. W. (2000). *The Sociological Imagination*. Fortieth anniversary edition. New York: Oxford University Press.

Mindry, D. (2001). "Nongovernmental Organizations, 'Grassroots,' and the Politics of Virtue." *Signs* 26 (4): 1187–1211.

Naples, N. (1998). *Grassroots Warriors: Activist Mothers, Community Work, and the War on Poverty*. New York: Routledge.

Naples, N. (2003). *Feminism and Method: Ethnography, Discourse Analysis, and Activist Research*. New York: Routledge.

National Resource Center on Domestic Violence. (2007). *LGBT Communities and Domestic Violence: Information and Resources Overview*. Harrisburg, PA: National Resource Center on Domestic Violence.

National Task Force to End Sexual and Domestic Violence against Women. (2005). "The Violence Against Women Act: 10 Years of Progress and Moving Forward." Accessed at http://www.ncadv.org/files/OverviewFormatted1.pdf.

Network to End Violence Against Immigrant Women. (2005). Tenth National Network Conference. Conference Participant Training Manual, Irvine, California, November 9, 10, and 11.

Newland, L. (2006). "Female Circumcision: Muslim Identities and Zero Tolerance Policies in Rural West Java." *Women's Studies International Forum* 29: 394–404.

Ngai, M. (2004). *Impossible Subjects: Illegal Aliens and the Making of Modern America*. Princeton: Princeton University Press.

Novak, D. (1978). *The Wheel of Servitude: Black Forced Labor after Slavery*. Lexington: University Press of Kentucky.

Omi, M., and H. Winant. (1986). *Racial Formation in the United States: From the 1960s to the 1980s*. New York: Routledge and Kegan Paul.

Ong, A. (2003). *Buddha Is Hiding: Refugees, Citizenship, the New America*. Berkeley: University of California Press.

O'Toole, L., J. Schiffman, and M. Kiter Edwards. (2007). "Changing Our Minds: Transforming Gender Relations." In L. O'Toole, J. Schiffman, and M. Kiter Edwards (Eds.), *Gender Violence: Interdisciplinary Perspectives*, pp. 421–425. New York: NYU Press.

O'Toole, L., J. Schiffman, and M. Kiter Edwards (Eds.). (2007). *Gender Violence: Interdisciplinary Perspectives*. New York: NYU Press.

Padilla, L. (2003). "Social and Legal Repercussions of Latinos' Colonized Mentality." In K. Johnson (Ed.), *Mixed Race America and the Law: A Reader*, pp. 287–289. New York: NYU Press.

Parsons, T. (1951). *The Social System*. New York: Free Press.

Pérez, A. (2007). "Between Radical Theory and Community Praxis: Reflections on Organizing and the Non-profit Industrial Complex." In INCITE! Women of Color against Violence, *The Revolution Will Not Be Funded: Beyond the Non-profit Industrial Complex*, pp. 91–100. Cambridge, MA: South End Press.

Perlmutter, F. (1994). *Women and Social Change: Nonprofit and Social Policy*. Washington, DC: National Association of Social Workers.

Portes, A., and R. Rumbaut. (1996). *Immigrant America: A Portrait*. Berkeley: University of California Press.

Pyke, K. (2008). "Immigrant Families in the US." In S. Coontz (Ed.) with Maya Parson and Gabrielle Raley, *American Families: A Multicultural Reader*, pp. 210–221. New York: Routledge.

Richie, B. (2000). "A Black Feminist Reflection on the Antiviolence Movement." *Signs* 25 (4): 1133–1137.

Richie, B. (2006). "Foreword." In Natalie Sokoloff (Ed.) with Christina Pratt, *Domestic Violence at the Margins: Readings on Race, Class, Gender, and Culture*, pp. xv–xviii. New Brunswick, NJ: Rutgers University Press.

Ritter, G. (2006). *The Constitution as Social Design: Gender and Civic Membership in the American Constitutional Order*. Stanford, CA: Stanford University Press.

Roberts, C. (2005). "VAWA Law Polarizes the Sexes, Weakens the Family." *Men News Daily*. Accessed at http://www.mensnewsdaily.com/archive/r/roberts/2005/roberts051905.htm.

Roberts, D. (2002). *Shattered Bonds: The Color of Child Welfare*. New York: Basic Civitas Books.

Roe, K. (2004). "The Violence against Women Act and Its Impact on Sexual Violence Public Policy: Looking Back and Looking Forward." National Alliance to End Sexual Violence. Accessed at http://www.nrcdv.org/docs/Mailings/2004/NRCD-VNovVAWA.pdf.

Rose, N. (1992). "Governing the Enterprise Self." In P. Heelas and P. Morris (Eds.), *The Values of the Enterprise Culture: The Moral Debate*, pp. 141–164. London: Routledge.

Roy, K., and L. Burton. (2008). "Mothering through Recruitment: Kinscription of Nonresidential Fathers and Father Figures in Low-Income Families." In S. Coontz (Ed.) with Maya Parson and Gabrielle Raley, *American Families: A Multicultural Reader*, pp. 351–365. New York: Routledge.

Rudrappa, S. (2004). *Ethnic Routes to Becoming American: Indian Immigrants and the Cultures of Citizenship*. New Brunswick, NJ: Rutgers University Press.

Rudrappa, S., and S. Elliot. (2005). "Emotional Enactments of Citizenship: Personal Fronts in Court in the Quest for Justice." Paper presented at the University of Texas at Austin Gender Symposium of the University of Texas Department of History, April 1.

Salcido, O., and M. Adelman. (2004). "'He Has Me Tied with the Blessed and Dammed Papers': Undocumented-Immigrant Battered Women in Phoenix, Arizona." *Human Organization* 63 (2): 162–172.

Schechter, S. (1982). *Women and Male Violence: The Visions and Struggles of the Battered Women's Movement*. Cambridge, MA: South End Press.

Schneider, E. (2000). *Battered Women and Feminist Lawmaking*. New Haven: Yale University Press.

Schuett, T. (2004). "Why YOU Should Fight VAWA." *Desertlight Journal.*. Accessed at http://desertlightjournal.blog-city.com/why_you_should_fight_vawa.htm.

Schuett, T. (2005). "Betrayal of Women—VAWA 2005." *Renew America*. Accessed at http://www.renewamerica.us/columns/schuett/050612.

Shklar, J. (1991). *American Citizenship: The Quest for Inclusion*. Cambridge: Harvard University Press.

Sjoberg, G., R. Brymer, and B. Farris. (1966). "Bureaucracy and the Lower Class." *Sociology and Social Research* 50: 325–357.

Sjoberg, G., E. Gill, and L. Cain. (2003). "Countersystem Analysis and the Construction of Alternative Futures." *Sociological Theory* 21 (3): 210–233.

Sjoberg, G., and R. Nett. (1997). *A Methodology for Social Research: With a New Introductory Essay*. Prospect Heights, IL: Waveland Press.

Smith, A. (2005). *Conquest: Sexual Violence and American Indian Genocide*. Cambridge, MA: South End Press.

Smith, A. (2006). "Looking to the Future: Domestic Violence, Women of Color, the State and Social Change." In Natalie Sokoloff (Ed.) with Christina Pratt, *Domestic Violence at the Margins: Readings on Race, Class, Gender, and Culture*, pp. 416–434. New Brunswick, NJ: Rutgers University Press.

Smith, A. (2007). "Introduction: The Revolution Will Not be Funded." In INCITE! Women of Color against Violence, *The Revolution Will Not Be Funded: Beyond the Non-profit Industrial Complex*, pp. 1–20. Cambridge, MA: South End Press.

Smith, A., B. Richie, J. Sudbury, J. White, and the INCITE! Anthology Co-editors (2006). "The Color of Violence: Introduction." In INCITE! Women of Color against Violence, *Color of Violence: The INCITE! Anthology*, pp. 1–10. Cambridge, MA: South End Press.

Smith, B. (2006). "Battering, Forgiveness, and Redemption: Alternative Models for Addressing Domestic Violence in Communities of Color." In Natalie Sokoloff (Ed.) with Christina Pratt, *Domestic Violence at the Margins: Readings on Race, Class, Gender, and Culture*, pp. 321–339. New Brunswick, NJ: Rutgers University Press.

Sokoloff, N., and I. Dupont. (2006). "Domestic Violence: Examining the Intersections of Race, Class, and Gender: An Introduction." In Natalie Sokoloff (Ed.) with Christina Pratt, *Domestic Violence at the Margins: Readings on Race, Class, Gender, and Culture*, pp. 1–13. New Brunswick, NJ: Rutgers University Press.

Somers, M. (1999). "The Privatization of Citizenship: How to Unthink a Knowledge Culture." In V. Bonnell and L. Hunt (Eds.), *Beyond the Cultural Turn*, pp. 121–161. Berkeley: University of California Press.

Sowel, T. (1981). *Ethnic America: A History*. New York: Basic Books.

Soysal, Y. (1994). *Limits of Citizenship: Migrants and Postnational Membership in Europe*. Chicago: University of Chicago Press.

Spivak, G. (1988). "Can the Subaltern Speak?" In C. Nelson and L. Grossberg (Eds.), *Marxism and the Interpretation of Culture*, pp. 271–313. Urbana: University of Illinois Press.

Taylor, C. (1994). "The Politics of Recognition." In C. Taylor and A. Gutmann (Eds.), *Multiculturalism: Examining the Politics of Recognition*, pp. 25–74. Princeton: Princeton University Press.

Tilly, C. (1978). *From Mobilization to Revolution*. New York: Random House.

Tocqueville, Alexis de. ([1853] 1969). *Democracy in America*. J. P. Mayer (Ed.). Garden City, NY: Doubleday.

Vaughan, T. R., G. Sjoberg, and L. T. Reynolds. (1993). *A Critique of Contemporary American Sociology*. New York: General Hall.

Villalón, R. (2004). "Necropolitics and Women in Argentina's Dirty War." Paper presented at the ninety-ninth annual meeting of the American Sociological Association, San Francisco, California, August 14–17.

Villalón, R. (2008). "Battered Immigrants, Immigration Laws, and Gatekeeping: The Subtleties of Selection." Paper presented at the fifty-eighth annual meeting of the Society for the Study of Social Problems, Boston, July 31–August 2.

Villalón, R. (Forthcoming). "Latina Battered Immigrants' Acts of Passage: The Nuances of Agency." *Women's Studies International Forum*.

Volpp, L. (1994). "(Mis)Identifying Culture: Asian Women and the 'Cultural Defense.'" *Harvard Women's Law Journal* 57: 57–101.

Ward, J. (2004). "'Not All Differences Are Created Equal': Multiple Jeopardy in a Gendered Organization." *Gender and Society* 18 (1): 82–102.

Weber, M. (1947). *The Theory of Social and Economic Organization*. New York: Free Press.

Weissman, D. (2000). "Addressing Domestic Violence in Immigrant Communities." *Popular Government* 65 (3): 13–18.

Wilson Gilmore, R. (2007). "In the Shadow of the Shadow State." In INCITE! Women of Color against Violence, *The Revolution Will Not Be Funded: Beyond the Non-profit Industrial Complex*, pp. 41–52. Cambridge, MA: South End Press.

Wing, A. (Ed.). (2003). *Critical Race Feminism: A Reader*. New York: NYU Press.

Wolch, J. (1990). *The Shadow State: Government and the Voluntary Sector in Transition*. New York: Foundation Center.

Wright, M. (2006). *Disposable Women and Other Myths of Global Capitalism*. New York: Routledge.

Yuval-Davis, N. (1997). "Women, Citizenship, and Difference." *Feminist Review* 57: 4–27.

Zaher, C. (2002). "When a Woman's Marital Status Determined Her Legal Status: A Research Guide on the Common Law Doctrine of Coverture." *Law Library Journal* 94: 459–486.

Zhang, S. (2007). *Smuggling and Trafficking in Human Beings: All Roads Lead to America*. Santa Barbara, CA: Greenwood Publishing Group.

Index

Abusers: abuse and/or neglect of children, 57, 60, 63, abusers' family, 29–30, 50, 54, 60; addictions, 22, 25, 26, 30, 62, 100–101, 164; apologies, 22, 25, 27, 28–29, 30, 31, 60, 177n18; citizen abusers, 69, 71; control of immigration papers, 29–30, 44, 93; control/threats against survivors' jobs, 22, 31, 72; deportation, 62, 63; infidelity, 21, 58, 63; jail, 20–21, 27–28, 100–101, 106, 112; jealousy, 26, 30, 33; legal permanent resident abusers, 69, 71; lies, 22, 58; power and control, 22; pregnancy/birth control, 56, 63, 64; promises, 27; rape, 58, 63, 64; stalking, 60, 64; threats regarding deportation, 22, 25, 31, 32, 43, 44, 50, 59, 62, 76–77, 93, 101, 106; threats regarding separation/divorce, 21, 45; threats regarding tenancy of children, 43, 64, 106; undocumented abusers, 70–71

Affidavit (sworn statement), 18–19, 91, 92, 103, 106–107, 108, 109, 113, 115, 117

Agency, 121–123, 146; and collective action, 146, 147–148; immigrants' agency, 128–132; nuances of agency, 122–123, 158–159, 187nn12, 13; ORA staff's agency, 132–133, 146

Alien and Sedition Laws (1798), 65

Alien Land Law (1913), 66, 74, 182n25

American Baptist Churches v. Thornburgh, 81, 82

Arte Sana, 88–89, 145, 147–148, 150, 159

Battered women's movement, 1–2, 148, 156, 189n68

Border Patrol operations, 68

Bracero program, 67, 74

Central American asylees, 80–83

Chastisement doctrine, 51–52

Chinese Exclusion Act (1882), 66, 74

Citizenship: acquisition through birth and naturalization, 34; acquisition through VAWA, 34–35, 36, 179nn34, 35; acquisition through VTVPA, 35, 36, 179n36; broker of citizenship (gatekeeper), 79, 89–90, 117–119, 167; and disciplinary mechanisms, 9, 37, 41; economic membership, 37–38, 180n49; and employment authorizations, 74–75, 184n86; and gender barriers, 41, 47, 51–52, 53–54; liberalism, 37–38; and nation building (nationhood), 36–38; and race and ethnicity, 65–71; and social class, 71–78; and social order, 37; and social worth, 190n95

Class action suits, 81, 82, 135

Coverture doctrine, 51–52, 53–54; and chastisement doctrine, 51–52

Deportation operations, 67, 74

Diversity programs, 68, 183n54

Essentialism, 160–161, 191n96

Federal immigration law (1864), 65–66

About the Author

Roberta Villalón is assistant professor of sociology at Saint John's University, New York City, where she is affiliated with the Committee for Latin American and Caribbean Studies and the Women's and Gender Studies Program.